Luther and the False Brethren

But because of certain false brethren, interlopers who stole in to spy upon the liberty we have in Christ Jesus, that they might bring us into bondage—not for a moment did we yield submission to them, that the truth of the gospel might be maintained for you.

—*Galatians* 2: 4–5

𝕷uther
and the False Brethren

MARK U. EDWARDS JR.

Stanford University Press

STANFORD, CALIFORNIA

1975

Stanford University Press
Stanford, California
© 1975 by the Board of Trustees of the
Leland Stanford Junior University
Printed in the United States of America
ISBN 0-8047-0883-5
LC 75-181

Published with the assistance of
The Andrew W. Mellon Foundation

To
Elizabeth Spilman Rosenfield
and
Linda Johnson Edwards

Preface

In *A Tramp Abroad* Samuel Clemens, better known as Mark Twain, wrote:

> I have a prejudice against people who print things in a foreign language and add no translation. When I am the reader, and the author considers me able to do the translating myself, he pays me quite a nice compliment, —but if he would do the translating for me I would try to get along without the compliment.

I heartily concur, and so all my quotations are in English. Where there was an English translation available, I used it, sometimes with modification, and noted the source of the translation in parentheses following the citation of the original source. In this regard I wish to thank Fortress Press and Concordia Publishing House for their kind permission to quote from *Luther's Works. American Edition*, edited by Jaroslav Pelikan and Helmut T. Lehmann (St. Louis and Philadelphia, 1955–), 55 volumes. Where no English source is cited, the translation is mine.

This study would not have been possible but for the three years I spent as a Junior Fellow of the University of Michigan Society of Fellows. Next to discussions with my wife, I profited most from discussions with Fellows Don Hall, Roland Davis, Lynn Hunt, and Bernard Frischer. I owe these friends and the Society of Fellows my sincere thanks. I also owe sincere thanks to the Danforth Foundation for a summer support grant and funds to cover the cost of typing the manuscript, and to Wellesley College for a grant to cover the final preparation of the manuscript.

Professors Lewis Spitz, Paul Seaver, Wilhelm Pauck, and William

Clebsch, all of Stanford University, and Professor Edward Gulick of Wellesley College read and commented extensively on this study, and I benefited greatly from their suggestions. Professor Spitz has had an especially profound influence on my thought and my life, since it was his lectures on the reformation that won me over to the study of history.

I have dedicated this study to Elizabeth Spilman Rosenfield and Linda Johnson Edwards. Mrs. Rosenfield took me and Linda into her home in 1968 when I entered graduate school. During the three years we lived with her and in the years since, I have learned more from her about the English language than from all previous teachers. She has read this entire study, and by her incisive questions and her quarrels with the words I chose to use, has forced me to rethink and clarify many of my arguments. In dedicating this book to her and Linda, I wish in some small way to thank them both for the encouragement and assistance that made it possible.

M.U.E.

Contents

Introduction   1

1. The Wittenberg Movement   6

2. The Rebellious Spirit   34

3. The Peasants' War   60

4. Against the Fanatics   82

5. The Mature Paradigm   112

6. The Wittenberg Concord   127

7. Against the Antinomians   156

8. The Last Testament   180

Conclusion   197

Notes   209   Index   235

Luther and the False Brethren

Introduction

Few men have had a greater or more lasting effect on Western thought than Martin Luther. He initiated a successful revolution against a system that had endured for centuries. His reformation of the Christian message profoundly changed men's minds, providing them with a new understanding of their religion and consequently a new understanding of themselves and their society.

As happens with most revolutions, the initial attack was directed wholly at the old order. But as also happens with most revolutions, when the new order became established and the danger of an immediate and overwhelming counterattack receded, internal differences began to appear. Members of the new order disagreed on subsidiary issues, and Luther soon found himself engaged with the Roman Catholics on one flank and with fellow evangelicals on the other. Luther called the Roman Catholics "papists," and his evangelical opponents "fanatics" and "false brethren," and despite the wide disparity in their views, he saw them as having much in common. Both groups were wrong, both were hypocritical, and both were lying minions of Satan who were wantonly violating their consciences. And so, with a considerable sense of righteousness, he condemned and attacked them both.

One's first impression of Luther's polemics against evangelical opponents is that they are very similar to his polemics against Catholics, but a closer look reveals some striking differences. For example, in formulating his doctrinal position and polemicizing against Rome, Luther pointed to the different assumptions and authorities on which he and the Catholics based their doctrinal positions. They argued from Scripture and tradition as interpreted by the church and Christ's vicar, he argued from Scripture as interpreted by the Word acting within the faithful.[1] He made no special claim about himself. On the contrary, he tried to separate his name from the beliefs he espoused; he strenuously combated the attempt by Catholic opponents to link the reformation movement to his name; and he chastised all those who believed something because Luther or anyone else had advocated it. But when confronted with evangelical opponents, Luther occasionally bolstered his theological arguments with claims about himself. He pointed to the fact that he was the first to preach the purified gospel and that God had accomplished a great deal with him as His instrument, and he frequently used himself as an example of the conduct proper to an evangelical minister in order to show the shortcomings of his evangelical opponents.

Other differences become apparent. Luther was incredibly abusive to all his opponents, and saw Satan behind them all. His Catholic opponents returned the abuse with interest and lodged a similar charge of satanic motivation. In striking contrast, Luther's evangelical opponents, with a few notable exceptions, never repaid in the same coin the unqualified condemnation he meted out to them.[2] Although Luther accused them of being the devil's false apostles and of not believing any tenet of Christianity sincerely, most of his major evangelical opponents—men like Zwingli, Oecolampadius, Bucer, Agricola, Bullinger, and Schwenckfeld—acknowledged publicly that Luther was a fellow Christian whom God had used to accomplish great things. They attacked his arguments, complained bitterly about his polemical style, and accused him of violating the requirements of Christian charity, modesty, and decorum, but they still said that they wished only to correct him where he had erred, not to reject his teaching entirely, or to condemn his person outright.

Catholic and evangelical opponents discussed the issue of Luther's authority in very different terms. Catholic opponents attempted to discredit his authority, portraying him as one insolent individual claiming on his own authority to correct Christ's body, the church, and His vicar on earth, the pope. Most evangelical opponents said only that he could err and that people should test his arguments against Scripture. They were willing to pay honor to Luther and his accomplishments, while warning their readers and congregations not to accept everything he said solely on the strength of his name.

In this essay, which traces these internecine disputes from 1522 to Luther's death, I attempt to develop a coherent explanation for Luther's claims about himself, for his often brutal personal attacks on his evangelical opponents, and for the reluctance of these opponents to respond in kind. At issue is more than rhetorical excesses. For one thing, Luther seems to have sincerely believed his claims about himself and his characterizations of his evangelical opponents. For another, Luther's followers never seriously disputed either Luther's claims about himself or his judgment of other evangelicals. There is evidence, moreover, that these claims and attacks were telling weapons in Luther's fight to preserve his version of the gospel message. According to his major evangelical opponents, many people were sufficiently captivated by his claims and moved by his attacks that they unquestioningly accepted his theological arguments and came to hate his evangelical opponents. Finally, the seemingly peculiar response of his evangelical opponents to Luther's attacks may reveal some fundamental differences between Luther's position in the reformation movement and the positions of these opponents.

In 1956 the great Luther scholar Heinrich Bornkamm counseled historians to devote their efforts to the older Luther:

Biographical research in the future must expend its main effort on the *old Luther*. The life span from 1532 to his death is almost as long as that from 1517 to 1532, yet the literature dedicated to this period is only a small fraction of that which has been written on the young Luther and on the period of conflict to about 1530 and the Diet of Augsburg. If we did not have the solid work on the last decade and a half [of Luther's life] by Köstlin and Kawerau, we would have practically no guidance for this period. And the shorter general accounts do not, for the most part, go beyond 1525, or at the latest, 1530. Likewise, monographs, of a biographical as well as of a theological nature, are also lacking. As a result, this long and significant period of [Luther's] life lies generally under the shadow of truly murky conceptions about the old Luther, about his theological rigidity and human callousness.[8]

This essay responds in part to Bornkamm's counsel. Chapter 1 begins with Luther's return to Wittenberg in 1522 to deal with his first false brethren: Karlstadt and Zwilling. Chapter 2 continues the study of the relations between Karlstadt and Luther through 1524, and discusses also Luther's clash with the "Satan at Allstedt," Thomas Müntzer. Chapter 3 deals briefly with Luther's part in the Peasants' War, with his reaction to Müntzer's death, and with the problem of his responsibility for Karlstadt, Müntzer, and the war itself. Chapter 4 traces the controversy over the Lord's Supper that began in 1525 and ended in a temporary truce at the Colloquy of Marburg in 1529, highlighting the issue of Luther's authority among his evangelical opponents. With Chapter 5 we begin consideration of the *old Luther*. This chapter is the only one dedicated solely to the study of a text, Luther's 1531 lectures on St. Paul's letter to the Galatians. It gives a detailed exposition of Luther's mature view of himself and of his evangelical opponents. Chapter 6 sketches the negotiations that led to the Wittenberg Concord in 1536 and the return of the Upper German evangelicals to the Lutheran fold. Chapter 7 is devoted to reconstructing the controversy between Luther and his one-time friend John Agricola over the proper use of the law. Finally, Chapter 8 examines Luther's conflicts with false brethren in the last years of his life.[4]

Needless to say this essay deals with only a fraction of Luther's activities during these years. He did not spend all his time and energy from 1522 to his death combating false brethren. Among other things he translated the Bible into German, lectured extensively on several books of the Bible, carried on an extensive correspondence, advised rulers and commoners, followed the politics of his day, performed a multitude of university duties, preached regularly, and enjoyed a rich personal life with family and friends. It should also be mentioned that his pen was very active combating "papists," Turks, and Jews as well as false brethren.

The controversies between Luther and other evangelicals were over issues of theology, and if this essay concentrates on the men rather than on theology it is not because the theology is unimportant and the differences simply those of conflicting personalities. On the contrary, the theological issues were profoundly important and, as a result, have been well studied.[5] What we must remember, however, is that Luther and his evangelical opponents did not restrict their arguments solely to matters of theology. From the beginning, debate aimed at strictly theological questions was greatly complicated by bitter disputes over both the motives and the authority of those taking part. We run the risk of oversimplifying the clash of ideas and misunderstanding the history of the controversies if we disregard an issue of such great importance to the adversaries themselves.[6]

❧ [1] ❧

The Wittenberg Movement

In 1522 Luther was called home from the Wartburg by members of his Wittenberg congregation to meet the challenge of his first evangelical opponents. His year on the Wartburg was an interlude between what may be called the first and the second acts of the reformation. In the first act Luther had broken with the old church, uncovered the "papal Antichrist," rallied a major portion of Germany, and faced the leaders of the Empire at Worms—and had survived. His Elector, Frederick the Wise, then had him spirited away to the Wartburg castle overlooking Eisenach to keep him off the public stage and safe from the Catholic authorities. When he returned to Wittenberg a year later, there began the second act in which evangelicals, though united in their opposition to the Roman Church, began to fight among themselves.

A half-century ago an acrimonious debate raged over whether the reasons for Luther's return to Wittenberg were religious or political.[1] The issue was made difficult of resolution by apparent contradictions in the facts. The Wittenberg movement had Luther's strong support through January 1522, and all the Wittenberg leaders defended the reforms undertaken and codified by the Ordinance of 24 January 1522 when they met with electoral representatives in mid-February. Yet only a few days later Luther claimed that Satan had entered his fold, that Judases were at work, and that his colleague on the theological faculty Andreas Bodenstein von Karlstadt and his fellow Augustinian Gabriel Zwilling had "authored" a monstrosity in Wittenberg. He professed that he would willingly have given his life to avert this calamity.

What caused this dramatic change is of importance to our study of Luther because it is at this crucial point that he seems first to have felt threatened by what he determined were false brethren. It is at this point, too, that we begin to see the first tentative changes in Luther's claims about himself, and to see how he identified and characterized his evangelical opponents. Despite vast amounts of scholarly work, much is still unclear. For instance: What precisely did Luther mean by the "monstrosity"? Why did he single out Karlstadt and Zwilling as its perpetrators? Why did he find the reforms as embodied in the Wittenberg Ordinance suddenly unacceptable? The best we can do with questions such as these is to consider what is known of the events immediately preceding and following Luther's return to Wittenberg, and to try to arrive at plausible answers.[2]

The Wittenberg movement can probably be said to have begun on 29 September 1521 when the young humanist Philipp Melanchthon and several of his students reportedly communed in both kinds.[3] A few days later the Augustinian Gabriel Zwilling, who was being hailed by some as a prophet and "another Martin," preached an impassioned sermon against the mass that quickly brought out a delegation from the University to discuss the matter and prompted the Elector to appoint an investigating commission.[4] Zwilling was uncowed, however, and on 13 October the Augustinians under his leadership ceased celebrating the mass.[5] Four days later Karlstadt raised questions about the mass in a disputation over which he was presiding. During the debate Melanchthon advocated reform without regard for objections raised by the weak in conscience. In contrast, Karlstadt recommended that the magistrates and the full congregation should first be consulted before reforms were undertaken.[6]

On 20 October the investigating commission sent the Elector its report defending the reforms undertaken by the Augustinians and advocating further action.[7] The Catholic canons at All Saints (Castle) church sent in a minority report that painted a dark picture of events and laid the major blame for excesses on Gabriel Zwilling, although they also criticized their provost, Justus Jonas.[8]

As November wore on, the Wittenberg Augustinians began to leave the cloister. By January it was reported that there were scarcely five or six monks left.[9] Meanwhile, the Augustinian prior, who had opposed the reforms, felt unsafe on the street.[10]

He was not the only adherent to the old faith who had reason to feel threatened. On 3 December a mob occupied the Parish church and interrupted the mass. The next day the Franciscan church had a manifesto nailed to its door and there were threats that it would be occupied by the crowd.[11] The town watch was reinforced, and the Elector demanded that the guilty parties be apprehended and that a full investigation be made.[12]

On the day the crowd threatened to storm the Franciscan church, Luther arrived in Wittenberg for a short visit.[13] In a letter to his friend George Spalatin, the court chaplain and librarian, he announced that he would issue a public exhortation to counter rumors, which he had heard on his journey to Wittenberg, of improper conduct by the Wittenbergers. Nonetheless, he made defiantly clear his approval of the events of the previous months. "Everything else that I hear and see," he wrote, "pleases me very much."[14]

Luther remained only a few days in Wittenberg, and was soon back on the Wartburg. His promised treatise, *A Sincere Admonition by Martin Luther to All Christians to Guard Against Insurrection and Rebellion*, was finished and shipped off to Spalatin by mid-December and was printed and in the hands of the public perhaps as early as January.[15]

Even as Luther was writing his treatise and it was being set in the press, pressure for actual reforms was building in Wittenberg. On 12 December the reform-minded members of the investigating commission, including Karlstadt, Melanchthon, Amsdorf, and the jurist Jerome Schurf, submitted a majority report strongly advocating reforms in the mass.[16] About the same time citizenry in Wittenberg petitioned the City Council to free those who had been imprisoned following the disturbances of early December.[17] They also submitted six articles to the Council, calling for free preaching, the abolition of various practices concerning the mass, communion in both kinds, and the abolition of taverns and whorehouses.[18]

On 22 December Karlstadt announced to the public that he would celebrate communion in both kinds with a simplified liturgy on New Year's Day, the next date when he was responsible as archdeacon for services at All Saints.[19] The Elector moved to forestall Karlstadt's plans.[20] On Christmas Eve bands of students and townspeople roamed the streets, causing mischief for adherents to the old church who were attempting to perform their Christmas Eve services.[21] On Christmas day Karlstadt entered All Saints without vestments, preached a sermon urging the congregation to commune even if they had not made confession, and then celebrated communion in both kinds, omitting all references to sacrifice, speaking the words of institution in German, and eliminating the elevation of the consecrated host.[22]

Karlstadt now preached twice every Friday, and drew large crowds, many of whom, it was said, had rarely attended a sermon in previous years.[23] The day after Christmas he and a group of university and town notables, including Melanchthon and Jonas, made a trip to the neighboring village of Sagrena, where Karlstadt was betrothed to Anna von Mochau, a young daughter of a poor nobleman.[24] The marriage took place in mid-January and was a fancy affair, complete with formal invitations and a written justification to the Elector.[25]

Meanwhile, another incident was brewing. Late in December three men, who came to be called the "Zwickau prophets," had arrived in Wittenberg from Zwickau, a textile and silver-mining center at the foot of the Erzgeberge about forty miles up the Mulde River from Leipzig. These men—Nicholas Storch and Thomas Drechsel, both weavers, and Marcus Stübner, a former Wittenberg student and acquaintance of Melanchthon's—claimed that they had been called by God and that their teachings came from the Spirit rather than from the Bible.[26] Their apocalyptic warnings and criticism of infant baptism caused a brief stir. Melanchthon wrote worried letters to Luther and the Elector;[27] and, although Luther dismissed these prophets as unimportant,[28] the Elector was sufficiently disturbed to have Melanchthon and Nicholas von Amsdorf of the theological faculty meet with George Spalatin and Haugold von Einsiedel, an electoral councillor. It was decided, however, that there should simply be no further dealings with the prophets, and they were soon forgotten in the press of other events.[29]

During January the reforms spread through the surrounding towns and villages; "evangelical masses" were celebrated and priests married.[30] Zwilling was in the forefront of the movement, agitating from the pulpit against the practices of the old faith.[31] The General Chapter of the German Augustinians met in Wittenberg under the leadership of Luther's friend and supporter Wenzel Link, and issued two documents supporting and justifying the exodus of their Wittenberg brethren from the cloister.[32] Then on 10 or 11 January the Augustinians under Zwilling's leadership tore down all the altars in the cloister except one and ripped the pictures from the walls and burned them.[33]

The movement reached its climax on 24 January when the reforms of the previous months were codified in the Wittenberg Ordinance.[34] Modifications in the mass were specified: communion in both kinds was to be allowed, the elements could be taken directly by the communicants, the words of institution were to be said in the vernacular, and the elevation of the host and passages in the canon referring to sacrifice were to be eliminated. Images in the churches were gradually to be removed, beggars were no longer to be tolerated, a community chest for the care of the poor was to be instituted, and brotherhoods and various forms of the private mass were to be done away with. Christian Beyer, who had been recently elected mayor of Wittenberg, announced to the Elector that the University and the City Council were united on these decisions.[35]

There can be no doubt that Luther had encouraged and supported many of the reforms set out in the Wittenberg Ordinance. In public treatises and private letters he had inspired and endorsed clerical marriage,[36] the exodus of religious from convents and monasteries,[37] and changes in the practice of the mass.[38] In early December, after his short, secret visit to Wittenberg, he had announced to Spalatin his approval of events taking place there[39]—this despite the fact that students and townspeople had recently occupied the Parish church and disrupted the mass and threatened to do the same to the Franciscan church.[40]

True, Luther had disapproved of the accompanying tumults. He had reprehended the student riots in Erfurt against the clergy there, ascribing these disturbances to the influence of Satan, who wished by such means to bring the evangelical movement into disgrace,[41] and he had censured the harassment of a St. Anthony brother by Wittenberg students and townspeople. But he seemed more annoyed about having to apologize to his Catholic critics for every little fault of the evangelicals than by the incidents themselves.[42] His disapproval may have been tempered by a belief at this time that such incidents were either typical student excesses or partially justified anticlericalism.[43] And although it was after his December visit to Wittenberg that he wrote *A Sincere Admonition ... to Guard Against Insurrection and Rebellion*,[44] and some of the incidents in Wittenberg may have prompted the treatise, his letter to Spalatin suggests that his admonition was directed more at people outside Wittenberg than at the Wittenbergers themselves.[45]

Luther's friends in Wittenberg, who were certainly his primary source of information on events there, were in apparent agreement on the reforms through mid-February despite some disturbances accompanying their implementation. Both the City Council and the University supported the Wittenberg Ordinance.* In the first week of February some townspeople, unwilling to await official enforcement of the Ordinance, destroyed images in the Parish church.† About the same time Karlstadt and Zwilling were singled out by the Electoral Councillor Einsiedel as being responsible for rabble-rousing, and Melanchthon reported discussing the need for moderation with both men.[46] It is not clear, however, if Melanchthon disapproved of their activities.[47] Einsiedel claimed in mid-February that Karlstadt was unable to deny that his sermons were to some extent responsible for the disturbances. But at the 13 February meeting with electoral representatives Karlstadt reportedly agreed to refrain from sermonizing if not altogether at least on inflammatory issues.[48] And, most important, while they decried the excesses and promised appropriate punishment for infractions of the public peace, the Wittenberg representatives at this meeting—Eisermann, Jonas, Karlstadt, Melanchthon, and Amsdorf—stood together in support of

---

* Nikolaus Müller, *Die Wittenberg Bewegung 1521 und 1522* (Leipzig, 1911), no. 75. Mayor Beyer argued for the retention of the crucifix but was overruled.

† The Elector stated that the Council, by setting a date for the removal of the images, excited the populace into taking matters into its own hands. *Ibid.*, no. 92.

the Ordinance.[49] Many of the reforms were retained in a compromise that apparently was satisfactory to them and to the electoral representatives, if not to the Elector himself.[50]

At least through January of 1522, Luther thought fairly well of Karlstadt. He had earlier disagreed with some of Karlstadt's scriptural arguments about clerical marriage and monastic vows, but he saw the defects in Karlstadt's arguments as due more to Karlstadt's ineptness than to any sinister motive.[51] As late as January he voiced unqualified approval of Karlstadt's marriage,[52] and his own treatises on the mass advocated many of the reforms that Karlstadt actually initiated.[53] And, finally, though it was known that the Elector objected to much that was going on in Wittenberg, Luther certainly did not object to defiance of the Elector's wishes when these wishes ran counter to what he saw as the requirements of the gospel. On several occasions he lectured his prince on his unwarranted interference in religious matters,[54] and he upbraided Spalatin for his "prudence" and for the faintheartedness and political calculation of the electoral court—there was, he said, too much talk and not enough action.[55] He insisted that his own politically inflammatory treatises on monastic vows and private masses be published, and acceded only grudgingly to the withholding of his treatise against the Archbishop of Mainz.[56] When he finally returned to Wittenberg, it was against the Elector's wish.[57]

Perhaps the first hints of disquiet on Luther's part appear in his letter to Spalatin of 17 January, in which he reports hearing rumors about more significant goings-on in Wittenberg than those that prompted his short visit in December.* He informed Spalatin that

---

* *D. Martin Luthers Werke. Briefwechsel* (Weimar, 1930–), 2: 443 (hereafter cited as WABr); translated in *Luther's Works. American Edition* (Philadelphia and St. Louis, 1955–), 48: 380–81 (hereafter cited as LW). Preus concludes that by the time Luther wrote this letter he "had probably already identified Carlstadt in his mind as the main culprit at Wittenberg, and was no doubt aware how much his colleague had become the main problem for the electoral court, but it was a situation that could only be handled personally. That may account for Luther's failure to mention Carlstadt by name at this stage." (See James S. Preus, *Carlstadt's "Ordinaciones" and Luther's Liberty* [Cambridge, Mass., 1974], p. 59.) Such a conclusion is possible but it is by no means certain. I am inclined to accept K. Müller's argument that the distress and intensity manifested in Luther's late February letter to the Elector suggest

he was considering another visit, although not because of the lay preachers, the so-called Zwickau prophets, who were also active in the Wittenberg vicinity. These laymen he dismissed at this time as unimportant. Earlier he had announced his intention of returning to the vicinity of Wittenberg by Eastertime to consult with his colleagues about the translation of the Bible.[58] Perhaps the rumors—unfortunately, we do not know what they were[59]—reinforced his resolve to be nearer to the action in Wittenberg.

We have no clear word from Luther between 17 January and about 22 February 1522, when he wrote the Elector an ironic letter from the Wartburg, congratulating his prince, an avid relic collector, on the acquisition of a "new relic." "Stretch out your arms confidently," Luther advised him, "and let the nails go deep." Disturbances always accompany God's Word, he explained, and Satan attacks from without, but also from within. "Not only must Annas and Caiaphas rage, but Judas must be among the apostles and Satan among the children of God." Luther cautioned the Elector to be wise (a play on Frederick's epithet?) and not to judge according to reason or appearances. Satan was at work but had not yet won the fight. The Elector should have confidence in Luther, who was familiar with the wiles of Satan. "God willing," Luther concluded, "I shall soon be there."[60] Apparently in the week or so between the 13 February meeting of the university representatives with the electoral officials, and this hurried letter in late February, Luther had received information that drastically changed his evaluation of the Wittenberg movement.

The Elector responded immediately to Luther's letter, writing out an Instruction for John Oswald, one of his officials in Eisenach, to convey to Luther. Stung by Luther's advice that he be wise and not judge these events according to reason, the Elector pointed out that so far he had not judged anything and had in fact done less than was appropriate for such a serious situation. He called attention to the absence of any unity of opinion in Wittenberg, either in the Uni-

that Luther had just received news from Wittenberg that convinced him he had to return immediately. See Karl Müller, *Luther und Karlstadt. Stücke aus ihrem Gegenseit* (Tübingen, 1907), pp. 90ff.

versity or in the Chapter, noting that ceremonial practices varied from priest to priest in Wittenberg and in the surrounding towns; furthermore, students were dropping out of the University and the sons of nobility were being summoned home. The Reichsregiment had recently forbade innovations and commanded that preachers admonish the populace to remain within the old faith. The bishop of Meissen was taking this command seriously and had written the Elector for aid in carrying out a personal visitation in parts of Electoral Saxony.[61] If he were to be wise and not judge according to reason, would Luther please suggest what he should do instead? He was willing as a Christian to suffer what he must. But the situation in Wittenberg was so confused that he did not know what to do.

The Elector did, however, feel that he knew what should not be done. Twice he indicated that he thought it would be unwise for Luther to return to Wittenberg at this time, and he outlined the legal and political consequences of his doing so. He suggested that instead of returning Luther should write a formal opinion on the situation that could be presented to an impending imperial diet. But he left the final decision to Luther: "Should, however, God's will and work be hindered [by Luther's remaining on the Wartburg], this would not be agreeable to the Elector, and so he wishes to leave everything to the judgment of Luther who has had experience in these lofty matters."[62]

In the Instruction that he sent to Luther the Elector had explained some of the political pressures to which he was being subjected—the order of the Reichsregiment and proposed visitation by the bishop of Meissen—but he did not mention the steps he had already taken directly and indirectly to reverse the course of reform in Wittenberg. The 24 January 1522 Ordinance of the City of Wittenberg had confirmed modifications in the celebration of the mass. Communion in both kinds and the taking of the elements by hand were to be permitted, and the elevation of the host and all references to sacrifice eliminated. The Elector had opposed all these innovations, and through the agency of one of his councillors, Haugold von Einsiedel, had attempted to silence Karlstadt and Zwilling. These two men were by no means the only leaders in the movement, but they were the most conspicuous, having forcefully advocated the reforms from their pulpits.[63]

In the negotiations between the city officials and the electoral representatives, Karlstadt and Zwilling were twice cited by name as the primary troublemakers.[64] Finally, in mid-February there was a meeting between representatives of the Wittenberg University and Chapter and several electoral councillors. Throughout the controversy it had been the Elector's position that until the Wittenbergers could agree among themselves and until they were joined by other universities, it was permissible to dispute, write, and preach about innovations but not to introduce them into practice.[65] In his Instructions to his representatives at this meeting, the Elector told them to remind the Wittenbergers of his position and to point out that the Wittenbergers' lack of unity was causing offense as were the innovations they had introduced despite the disagreements among them. He criticized the manner in which images had been removed, laying the blame for past and future scandals in this regard on Karlstadt and Zwilling, and requested that Karlstadt be more moderate or keep silent. He suggested that the Wittenbergers discuss further the issue of images, beggars, and brotherhoods, and explain to him why brotherhoods and begging by monks should not be permitted and why they undertook changes in the mass and how those changes they deemed Christian and good would be dealt with.[66] He also ordered, among other things, that the elements in the mass be treated with respect and no longer be taken by hand, that useful aspects of the mass be retained, and that images in church be preserved pending further deliberations.*

In the ensuing negotiations the Wittenberg representatives said that they realized the Elector had forbade innovations, but since Karlstadt had celebrated a new form of the mass and confusion had resulted about what the proper form of the mass should be, they had, after consultations, established a uniform practice. They denied responsibility for the iconoclasm that had occurred, defended the re-

---

* N. Müller, no. 92. Preus rightly points out (p. 43) that there is no direct challenge to the Wittenberg Ordinance in the Elector's Instructions. He may have been attempting to postpone its implementation, however, by calling for further discussion and by stressing the need for unity of opinion as the prerequisite for action. In any case, his letter of 17 February shows that he had not expected the meeting to take the decisive action it did. See N. Müller, no. 99.

forms concerning beggars and brotherhoods, blamed the disturbances on those who resisted the reforms, and explained and justified the changes they had made in the mass.[67] After some discussion a compromise was reached, whereby some of the innovations were to remain while others would be either modified or eliminated with appropriate explanations to the congregation.[68]

The Elector found the compromise totally unacceptable. Apparently fearing the political repercussions if it appeared that he sanctioned the proposed changes in ecclesiastical practice, he wrote an angry letter to Einsiedel in which he reiterated his instructions that there were to be no innovations, and ordered Einsiedel to contact the University and Chapter and make sure there was no appearance of electoral approval for the compromise articles.[69]

The Elector's refusal to accept the compromise presented the Wittenbergers with a dilemma: they must either undo the reforms or defy the Elector. Subsequent events indicate that the majority were unwilling to take the latter course, but Karlstadt may have been an exception. He may have agreed to this compromise but balked at any further compromise, since, as several of his later treatises indicate, he believed that it was sinful to neglect many of the reforms, and believed also that lenience toward the weak in conscience frequently disguised a sinful unwillingness to institute reforms demanded by the gospel.[70] Furthermore, he was so publicly committed to the reforms through his many sermons that it may have been extremely difficult psychologically for him to change his position.*

If his colleagues, including Melanchthon, were willing to back down further or were frightened into doing so, and if Karlstadt was not, he would have found himself alone and without support. There is some evidence that a split between Karlstadt and the other Wittenberg representatives may have been well under way before this mid-February meeting. At the meeting the Wittenbergers blamed Karlstadt for the need to institute a new uniform practice for the celebration of the mass, even though they too had called for such reforms in earlier reports to the Elector and had taken an active and, to all appearances, willing part in the framing of the Wittenberg Ordinance.[71] Karlstadt

---

* On the other hand, Zwilling was also publicly committed to the reforms, but this did not prevent him from recanting after Luther's return.

himself later complained that others had advocated a position on the removal of church images similar to his, but that he had been left "with his head in the noose" when the others drew back.[72] If he in fact took a stand in support of the Ordinance, this complaint would be accounted for.

Defiance of the Elector's order that there were to be no innovations could well have precipitated electoral intervention, and presumably Melanchthon and the others would have wished to avoid this. They had been unable to control Karlstadt and Zwilling in the past, however,[73] and they may well have found it impossible to do so now. Whatever the exact situation, they apparently turned to Luther for assistance, begging him to return to Wittenberg,[74] and Luther judged his presence there was necessary despite the Elector's objections.

While on his way to Wittenberg, he wrote the Elector one of his most famous letters. He explained that he had written his previous letter to reassure the Elector for the sake of the "untoward movement introduced by our friends in Wittenberg to the great detriment of the gospel," for he feared that this movement would be a great burden to the Elector. Moreover, he was so overwhelmed by this "calamity" that he would willingly have averted the trouble at the cost of his life if that had been possible. Although he was not responsible for what had happened, it was blamed on him and, what was worse, on the gospel.[75] The Elector should know that Luther had received the gospel not from men but from heaven alone, through Christ, so that he could boast and call himself a minister and evangelist. He had appeared at Worms out of "excess humility," in order to persuade others. But this humility abased the gospel and the devil took advantage of it. Now Luther felt that he must act differently. He had remained in hiding for a year on the Elector's wish. Now he must return, he said:

I have written this so Your Electoral Grace might know that I am going to Wittenberg under a far higher protection than the Elector's. I have no intention of asking Your Electoral Grace for protection. Indeed I think I shall protect Your Electoral Grace more than you are able to protect me.[76]

Luther condemned any interference by the secular arm in affairs of religion: "God alone must do it." And he thought that the Elector had already done too much. If the imperial agents wished to take action against him, Luther advised the Elector not to interfere, "for no one should overthrow or resist authority save Him who ordained it."[77] Luther arrived in Wittenberg on the sixth of March. To defuse as much as possible the explosive implications of Luther's public return, the Elector instructed the jurist Jerome Schurf to obtain a letter from Luther setting forth the reasons for his return and explaining that he was returning without the Elector's permission. Luther was also to express his willingness to exercise self-restraint and to state that he had no desire to cause difficulties for anyone. The Elector intended to send this letter from Luther to his representatives in Nuremberg, who could use it to counter Catholic objections.[78]

Luther complied with the Elector's request, although the effort required two drafts before the language was mild enough to suit the Elector (and thereby so "cosmetic" that Luther was annoyed).[79] Luther set forth three major reasons for his return: first, the Wittenberg congregation had called him, and "since no one can deny that the commotion has its origin" in Luther and since Luther was the minister of the congregation, he could not deny their call without also denying his Christian responsibility; second, on account of Luther's absence, Satan had intruded into his fold at Wittenberg, and Luther could no longer heal this injury with letters; third, Luther feared that real rebellion was brewing in Germany, and he and his friends hoped that by acting now they could turn away or defer God's punishment.[80]

In a postscript to the first draft of this letter, Luther offered to revise whatever was not satisfactory to the Elector. And he added a revealing remark about his earlier letter to him:

... I am not afraid of having my last letter to Your Electoral Grace get out into the public. From now on I do not want to undertake anything of which I would be ashamed should others see me doing it during the day. I was not afraid of rebellion; thus far I have taken it quite lightly, thinking it was directed only against the clergy. Now I am worried, however, that it might also surge against the authorities and, like an epidemic, draw in the clergy as well.[81]

In his *Admonition Against Insurrection and Rebellion,* written in December 1521, Luther had expressed his convictions very explicitly. He warned that mob action and rebellion never brought about the needed improvement and thus "no insurrection is ever right, no matter how right the cause it seeks to promote."[82] He unequivocally stated his position toward any and all rebellion:

I am and always will be on the side of those against whom insurrection is directed, no matter how unjust their cause; I am opposed to those who rise in insurrection, no matter how just their cause, because there can be no insurrection without hurting the innocent and shedding their blood.[83]

He argued repeatedly that Satan was "at work trying to stir up an insurrection through those who glory in the gospel, hoping thereby to revile our teaching as if it came from the devil and not from God."[84] Finally, Luther withdrew in advance the support of his name to any insurrection, denying totally any responsibility for any rebellion, and begged all the adherents of the gospel not to give occasion to the papists to find fault with them or with the gospel.[85]

We should also remember that Luther felt strongly that reforms in ecclesiastical practice should never be made matters of conscience or carried through precipitously without due regard for the sensibilities of those sincere Christians who were slow to understand and accept the changes. He had not freed consciences from rules and regulations of the papacy to see them reenslaved by rules for "evangelical ceremonies." He might favor the changes and work hard to see them instituted, but he would never argue that their nonobservance was a sin. Furthermore, he was willing to move slowly in accomplishing these reforms, giving his congregation time to realize that Christ had freed them from all works-righteousness, including the ceremonial practices of the papal church. Christian charity demanded as much.[86]

Taking these convictions of Luther's together with the events in Wittenberg, it seems reasonable to believe that the "monstrosity" was the confrontation between the Elector and the Wittenbergers caused on one side by the Elector's fears that the Ordinance would lead him into conflict with the imperial government, and on the other side by the insistence of some Wittenbergers that certain ecclesiastical reforms *were* matters of conscience and must be carried through immediately, whatever the consequences. For Luther, defiance of the Elector on these issues was theologically unwarranted. To make matters worse, such defiance lent credence to the charge that the reformation movement led inexorably to rebellion and violence. Possibly Luther believed that the movement was about to be discredited, and much of what had been accomplished undone because of "matters of conscience" with which he had no sympathy.*

In Luther's late February letter to the Elector quoted earlier, Annas and Caiaphas obviously stand for the Catholic opponents of the reformation. And by Judas, Luther may mean false brethren generally or Karlstadt or Zwilling specifically.[87] However that may be, a few days later Luther named Karlstadt and Zwilling as the authors of the "monstrosity."[88] He now also held Karlstadt responsible for the Wittenberg Ordinance despite the fact that the City Council and the University had apparently agreed upon the reforms in January and the representatives of the University, including Melanchthon, Jonas, and Amsdorf, had defended them stoutly in mid-February.[89] Perhaps he was subscribing to the explanation given the electoral representatives at the mid-February meeting: that Karlstadt's celebration of the mass in both kinds had created the need for an ordinance establishing a uniform practice.[90] Or he may simply have identified the Ordinance with Karlstadt's insistence that certain ceremonial matters should bind Christian consciences.

There may be an additional reason why Luther held Karlstadt and Zwilling responsible for the Wittenberg Ordinance and the "monstrosity" in general. Karlstadt and Zwilling were definitely associated by most onlookers with Luther and the reformation movement. They

---

* Preus argues thus: "As far as the older debate goes—about the extent to which Luther's return was politically motivated, i.e., to relieve the Elector of pressure from the central government by cooperating in suppression of the Wittenberg reforms—the best explanation is that although there is a remarkable convergence of interest between Frederick and Luther in a couple of key issues (but not on all!), Luther's return was primarily out of concern for the religious movement at Wittenberg. Within the sphere of that concern, however, his motivation was 'political'—in the sense of religious policy, structures, pace, and, above all, leadership." (See Preus, pp. 51–52.) I would add that Luther's motivation was also "political" in a larger sphere. In the Wittenberg "monstrosity" Luther saw a threat not only to his own reputation but also, and more seriously, to the reputation of the gospel and the reformation movement. Melanchthon's failure to handle the situation convinced Luther that he had to reassert his leadership in order to regain control of the local movement and protect his and the movement's reputation in the larger world.

claimed to be advocating more or less the same teachings as Luther, and although they actually held theological positions significantly different from his, to the public at large this was not apparent. At the same time, they were believed by the Elector and others to be the principal troublemakers, and, whether or not they were actually in defiance of the constituted authorities, they were linked in the minds of the Elector and others with civil unrest and disobedience.

Certainly they had been the most public advocates of reform: Zwilling had attacked the mass, had led his brethren out of the Augustinian cloister, and had figured prominently in the destruction of altars and images; Karlstadt had defied the Elector's command by celebrating an "evangelical mass" on Christmas day, 1521, had married, and had preached and written against images in church. When the City Council named a date for the removal of images, the populace had put Karlstadt's message into tumultuous practice, breaking and burning the "idols."[91] Both men had featured as the major villains in the hostile report of the Catholic canons of All Saints.[92]

Because Karlstadt and Zwilling were associated in the public mind with Luther and his reformation, Catholics and even evangelicals might hold Luther and his movement responsible for the deeds, and especially the misdeeds, of these men. Luther told the Elector that he was highly distressed about just such a possibility:

Whatever I have suffered hitherto for this cause has been nothing compared with this. I should willingly have averted the trouble at the cost of my life if that had been possible. We can answer neither to God nor to the world for what has been done. And yet it is blamed on me and, what is even worse, on the gospel.[93]

As a practical matter, therefore, the more Luther could distinguish his position from Karlstadt's and Zwilling's, even if he had to distort —knowingly or unwittingly—their position to do so, and the more he could impugn their personal character and motives, the more he could argue with seeming justice that he and his movement were not responsible for these men. Believing that his reputation and the reputation of the reformation movement were at stake, Luther may have felt it necessary to make the issue of responsibility clear-cut and then to disavow those allegedly responsible as unequivocally and convincingly as possible.

The disavowal took the form of an *ad hominem* attack. The grounds on which he made the attack seemed theologically sound and credible not only to Luther himself but to his followers and contemporaries as well. Drawing on accounts in the Bible and on the history of heresy, he charged that Satan had once again sent his false prophets to mislead the true church. Although they appeared to adhere to the gospel, they were in fact "Judases," and Luther laid all responsibility for their excesses on the satanic spirit which he claimed motivated each of them.

In order that the false prophet could be recognized for what he was, Luther had defined the salient characteristics of the true prophet and apostle in a letter to Melanchthon in early January 1522. Relying on Scripture for his authority, he told Melanchthon that a true prophet must be called through men or at least attested to by signs, and must have experienced spiritual distress and the divine birth, death, and hell. Prophets were not to be accepted "if they state that they were called by mere revelation, since God did not even wish to speak to Samuel except through the authority and knowledge of Eli."[94] He further advised Melanchthon to look for the "certain differentiator between the spirits," the sign of the Son of Man: "If you should hear that all [their experiences] are pleasant, quiet, devout (as they say), and spiritual, then don't approve of them, even if they should say that they were caught up to the third heaven." When God speaks directly to man, man cannot bear it. So God normally speaks indirectly through other men.[95] "Therefore test them," Luther admonished Melanchthon, "and do not listen even to the glorified Jesus, unless you have first seen him crucified."[96]

At the time he wrote this, Luther intended the tests to be applied to the Zwickau prophets. But the test could as well be applied to Karlstadt and Zwilling since, as far as Luther was concerned, they, too, confessed to no spiritual distress, temptations, and doubts such as those that the true prophets and apostles and even he himself had experienced. Moreover, they all lacked the proper calling. True, Karlstadt had been called to preach in the Castle church, but he had done most of his inflammatory preaching in Luther's pulpit in the Parish church where he did not belong.* Zwilling had not been called to public preaching in Wittenberg or elsewhere. The Zwickau prophets had the least justification for their preaching of any, for they were laymen who claimed their authority solely from a divine call yet were unable to produce any signs, Luther pointed out, other than those Satan himself could produce, namely, violence and unrest.[97] The failure of Karlstadt, Zwilling, and the Zwickau prophets to meet these tests identified them to Luther's satisfaction as false prophets and Satan's minions.

Further evidence of the satanic motivation of these men, Luther believed, was their insistence that people were guilty of a sin if certain Old Testament commandments and New Testament examples were not followed to the letter. Such insistence imposed the secular kingdom upon the spiritual and reshackled consciences with laws and regulations, while Christ freed them.

Karlstadt had clearly insisted on the enforcement of, for example, the Old Testament commandment against the worship of idols, and had applied it to images in church.[98] He had also argued that the example of the first institution of the Lord's Supper made it mandatory that communion in both kinds be taken by the communicants, preferably in their own hands and without prior confession and absolution.[99] The Wittenberg Ordinance had provided for the removal of images and the establishment of a communion service along the lines of Karlstadt's practice, but when Luther returned to Wittenberg, he reestablished many of the ceremonial practices found in the Catholic church. Soon afterward he wrote to the prior of the Eisleben Augustinians, Kaspar Güttel, that Karlstadt was offended because, although Luther had not condemned his teachings, he had "annulled" his Ordinance.[100]

Luther criticized Karlstadt for expending all his efforts on ceremonies and external matters while neglecting true Christian doctrine, namely, faith and love. In all this Luther saw Satan attempting to

---

* This accusation was made prior to Luther's return; see N. Müller, nos. 81, 83, 89. Karlstadt later defended himself by pointing out that there was an overlap between his Castle church congregation and that of the Parish church. See *D. Martin Luthers Werke. Kritische Gesamtausgabe* (Weimar, 1883–), 15: 336 (hereafter cited as WA).

ruin the gospel by making nonessential issues a burden to consciences. He also alleged that Karlstadt wished to become the community's teacher and to set up his ordinances among the people on his own authority.[101] If Luther still harbored any doubts that Karlstadt believed that ceremonies were a matter of conscience, they were removed when he read Karlstadt's latest manuscript, which was turned over to the printers in April 1522. This treatise was ostensibly directed against the Catholic theologian Ochsenfart, but in its more heady passages it could have applied equally well to Luther. For example, Karlstadt wrote that if a pastor who was celebrating the Lord's Supper failed to turn toward the congregation and speak the words of institution to them, he made the people commit a deadly sin, and that it was a greater sin to have images on the altar than to commit adultery and robbery since the worship of images was against the first commandment.[102] Both these practices, which in Karlstadt's eyes were deadly sins, could be found in the Catholic church, but they could still be found in Wittenberg's churches, thanks largely to Luther's nullification of the Ordinance. Although Karlstadt assured Luther "most innocently" that he was not the target of the treatise, Luther urged him not to publish it, and said that if it were published he would feel constrained to reply.[103] The university censorship committee decided to forbid its publication and thus forestalled a clash between the two men.[104] It seems that Luther did not urge this suppression.[105]

Karlstadt and the Zwickau prophets demonstrated another important characteristic of the false prophet: they stubbornly resisted a fraternal admonition, and wished to have their teaching and claims accepted without question.[106] Karlstadt would not admit that he had erred despite several conversations with Luther,[107] and the Zwickau prophets were even more obdurate in the face of a "fraternal admonition."

It had happened that all three of the Zwickau prophets were absent from Wittenberg when Luther first returned, but one of the trio, Marcus Stübner, came back to the city early in April and, with Martin Cellarius, a theological student at the University and a recent convert of Stübner's, immediately sought a private meeting with Luther.[108] Luther later told Spalatin that in this meeting he had uncovered

Satan, who was indeed motivating these men. Their spirit was extremely proud and impatient, unable to accept a friendly admonition but rather wanting its claims to be accepted as true without discussion or opposition. When challenged by Luther to prove their unscriptural doctrine by a miracle, they had declined with a warning that Luther would soon be forced to believe them. During much of the discussion Martin Cellarius "foamed and growled and raged ... so that I could not get a word in edgewise."[109] Luther remarked to the Erfurt Augustinian John Lang that he had never seen a more furious man than Cellarius.[110]

A decade later some of Luther's table companions copied down Luther's recollections of this meeting. It seems that Stübner professed the ability to pick out those of the elect and to read people's minds. He and Luther exchanged words on these claims and on Stübner's mystical terminology. Luther then asked Stübner how anyone could understand his terminology, and Stübner replied that he taught only prepared students who had the "talent." Asked what "talent" Luther had, Stübner responded that he was presently in the stage of "activity" (*Beweglichkeit*) but would soon reach the stage of "passivity" (*Unbeweglichkeit*) which Stübner presently occupied. Luther finally demanded a miracle as a sign of the validity of Stübner's extrascriptural teaching, and Stübner promised that a sign would be forthcoming within the next seven years.[111] During this discussion Cellarius apparently attempted to flatter Luther by saying that Luther's calling was greater than the apostles'. When Luther rejected the comparison as invalid, Cellarius insulted him in the same exaggerated fashion in which he had praised him.[112]

Luther had equally bad run-ins with Nicholas Storch, who concentrated his attack on infant baptism, and with Thomas Drechsel, who appeared one day on Luther's doorstep to bring him a message from God which had come to him by way of a small fiery cloud and a dream that ended when a mug of beer was emptied over Drechsel's head—the import of the message being that God was angry with the world. Luther was not impressed and Drechsel departed in a huff, muttering sarcastically that whoever failed to agree with Luther must be a fool.[113]

Gabriel Zwilling was the only one of Luther's colleagues who acknowledged that he had erred and had pressed the matter too far.[114] Soon after Luther returned to Wittenberg he reported to Link that Zwilling had come to his senses and had been changed into another man.[115] Luther then wrote letters to Spalatin and to the Elector attempting to return Zwilling to their good graces, and after some difficulties at the outset he succeeded in finding Zwilling a position as pastor.[116]

All these men demonstrated to Luther's satisfaction the traditional view that false prophets and heretics were vain men who sought the applause of the mob. Karlstadt had, indeed, an unfortunate history of self-seeking and vanity that went back many years before the Wittenberg movement, and during the months immediately preceding Luther's return he had created a sensation by preaching frequently to large crowds in Wittenberg.[117] From this, Luther concluded that Karlstadt had been playing to the mob. As for the Zwickau prophets, with their arrogant claims to direct discourse with God and their "raging and foaming and growling," the conservative, professorial Luther could easily conclude that since their real appeal, where it existed, was among the artisan classes,[118] they must be more interested in rabble-rousing than in God's Word.

On 9 March 1522 Luther, tonsured and garbed once again as an Augustinian, mounted the pulpit of the Wittenberg Parish church to begin the famous Invocavit sermons which reestablished his control over the progress of the reformation in Wittenberg. In the initial sermon of the series Luther clearly invoked his own authority:

Therefore, dear brethren, follow me: I have never been a destroyer. And I was also the very first whom God called to this work. I cannot run away, but will remain as long as God allows. I was also the one to whom God first revealed that His Word should be preached to you. I am also sure that you have the pure Word of God.[119]

A few days later, writing the "explanatory letter" requested by the Elector, Luther said: "It cannot be denied that I began this matter, and I must confess myself the humble servant of the Wittenberg congregation to which God sent me."[120] To be sure, these claims were embedded in a lucid exposition of Luther's theological argument, and they were definitely in the context of Luther's belief that the Word was the sole power responsible for the successes of the gospel. Drawing a sharp contrast between his own behavior and what he saw as that of his false brethren, Luther told his hearers:

I did nothing; the Word did everything. Had I desired to foment trouble, I could have brought great bloodshed upon Germany; indeed, I could have started such a game that even the emperor would not have been safe. But what would it have been? Mere fool's play. I did nothing; I let the Word do its work.[121]

Nevertheless, he was now willing to claim that he had been the first whom God had called. He acknowledged his responsibility for initiating the renewed preaching of the gospel, while at the same time he hotly denied, as we have seen, any responsibility for the disturbances and the false brethren who had now appeared.

These claims are the first indication that Luther was reevaluating his personal role in the reformation movement. There have been a number of studies of what Luther thought of himself, especially for the early years of the reformation.[122] Several scholars have argued that Luther thought of himself as a prophet even in these early years.[123] But other studies have shown that this was not the case.[124] Luther dealt with the question himself when his Catholic opponents accused him of being one man alone defying an institution with hundreds of years of tradition and history behind it. The jurist Ulrich Zasius, for example, wrote Luther in 1520 that "to shake the authority of so many generations that speak for the power of the bishop of Rome and of so many saintly and pious men is imprudent and dangerous."[125] Luther was sensitive to this charge and responded to it directly. "I do not claim to be a prophet," he wrote, but he added a caution to his detractors: "...the more they scorn me and the higher they regard themselves, the more reason they have to fear that I may be a prophet."

But if Luther did not claim to be a prophet, he did not hesitate to draw parallels between himself and the true prophets. He pointed out that they were "lowly and despised persons" raised up by God "to preach against and chide those in high places." With only one exception, namely King David, "God never made prophets out of the high priests or others of lofty station." And a true prophet was always alone, one man facing a hierarchy backed by history and tradition.

Luther claimed, too, that the arguments used against him were the same arguments that had been used against the biblical prophets. The ploy of the Old Testament authorities was to say, "we are the authorities and you must obey us and not those lowly and despised prophets." "Today they act the same way," Luther wrote. "Everything that does not please the pope, the bishops, and the scholars is supposed to be wrong. We are supposed to listen to them, no matter what they say." The ancient prophets also had been reproved for proposing new ideas. "It is not to be expected that everybody else should have been so long in error," the argument ran, as it did in Luther's day. These parallels were a comfort to Luther. "Even if I am not a prophet," he wrote,

as far as I am concerned I am sure that the Word of God is with me and not with them, for I have the Scriptures on my side and they have only their own doctrine. This gives me courage, so that the more they despise and persecute me, the less I fear them.

As Luther was fond of pointing out, God even spoke once through an ass; and although there were many asses at the time, God spoke only through Balaam's ass.[126]

Despite these suggestions that Luther saw parallels between his experiences and those of the apostles and prophets, the evidence is overwhelming that in the early years he thought of himself primarily as a doctor of theology.[127] In all of his later accounts, he dated the reformation as beginning with the 95 Theses.[128] Whether or not he actually nailed the theses to the church door, the bulletin board of the University,[129] he did send copies to members of the hierarchy, and in his covering letter to Cardinal Archbishop Albrecht of Mainz, drew attention to the capacity in which he was acting by signing himself "Martin Luther Augustinian, called Doctor of Sacred Theology."[130] The reformation began, in short, as an academic exercise of a doctor of sacred theology.

Three years later this self-concept was still dominant, when Luther wrote to the Elector: "all that I have written or taught was for the sake of my conscience and my oath and obligation as a humble teacher of Holy Scripture, to the praise of God, for the welfare and salvation of all Christians, and for the good of the whole German nation."[131] Although some of these references to his "oath and obligation as a humble teacher of Holy Scripture" may have been a legal maneuver designed to reinforce his contention that the charges of heresy against him were an attack on his right of disputation, it does not follow that he was being disingenuous in his claims.[132]

Luther saw himself during this period as a theologian working together with other theologians and academics for a "purification" of Christian theology. The whole theological faculty of Wittenberg, indeed the great majority of the University, supported his position.[133] That he thought of himself as one of a team is clearly shown in his attempts, a short time later, to promote Melanchthon as his successor.

Underlying these disclaimers of his own special importance and his promotion of Melanchthon was Luther's conviction that all the successes of the gospel are due to the Word and not to the actions of men. Accordingly, although he believed that he had been personally involved in extraordinary affairs, he was unwilling to take any personal credit for the successes of the gospel. "I simply taught, preached, and wrote God's Word," he told his Wittenberg congregation:

otherwise I did nothing. And while I slept, or drank Wittenberg beer with my friends Philipp and Amsdorf, the Word so greatly weakened the papacy that no prince or emperor ever inflicted such losses upon it. I did nothing; the Word did everything.[134]

Throughout his life, even after he became convinced that he was occupying a special role in his times, Luther still insisted that the Word was the agent and that he was no more than its instrument. During this early period Luther's belief in the agency of the Word and his conviction that Melanchthon was a superior theologian and leader and would soon replace him may have kept Luther from making any special claims about himself.

One reason, therefore, for Luther's gradual reevaluation of his importance to the reformation movement may lie in the weaknesses and failures of his chosen successor: Philipp Melanchthon. From the moment of his arrival in Wittenberg in 1518 the twenty-one-year-old Melanchthon had impressed Luther favorably, although ironically he was not Luther's first choice for the Greek chair at the University.[135] Luther's admiration increased when Melanchthon advanced to the degree of Bachelor of Theology in 1519. His promotion theses were so daring that Luther wrote to John von Staupitz that Melanchthon was a marvel and that, "Christ willing, he shall replace many Martins as a most powerful enemy of the devil and scholastic theology."[136] Luther's admiration reached its zenith with Melanchthon's *Loci Communes*, first published in 1521 while Luther was on the Wartburg. Next to the Bible, Luther gave the place of honor to this book, and throughout his lifetime he maintained that it was superior to all his own work.[137] "Even though I should perish," Luther wrote to Melanchthon from the Wartburg, "the gospel will not lose anything. You surpass me now and succeed me as Elisha followed Elijah with a double portion of the Spirit."[138] On another occasion he reproached Melanchthon for extolling him too much: "You err tremendously in ascribing such great importance to me. . . . You are already replacing me; because of the gifts you have from God you have attained greater authority and popularity than I had."[139] This was not idle praise. To Spalatin he wrote:

Were I present, I would by all means work on the city council and the people so that they would ask Philipp to lecture to them privately in German on the gospels as he has begun to lecture in Latin, so that little by little he would become a German[-speaking] bishop, as he has already become a Latin[-speaking] bishop. . . . Since he is incomparably rich in the Word, you can see that it is our duty to call him and not let the Word be cheated of its fruit. . . . May Christ compensate for my absence and silence with Melanchthon's preaching and voice, to the confusion of Satan and his apostles.[140]

Luther, guessing rightly that Melanchthon would resist such a course, suggested ways to force him to accept what Luther saw as his proper responsibilities.[141]

Despite Luther's high expectations for him, Melanchthon had been quite unable to handle Karlstadt, Zwilling, or the Zwickau prophets in Luther's absence. On the very day the Zwickau prophets arrived in Wittenberg in late December 1521, Melanchthon wrote to the Elector urging that he allow Luther to return to Wittenberg, for "no one can easily judge them except Martin."[142] To Spalatin he wrote, "Great things are occurring which will result in Lord knows what if Martin does not intercede."[143] He also wrote directly to Luther and received a reproach in reply: "I do not approve of your timidity,"

Luther wrote, "since you are stronger in spirit and learning than I," and he added a brief lecture on how to test the prophets' spirit.[144] A month later, charged with the responsibility of curbing Zwilling's and Karlstadt's activities, Melanchthon wrote that he had had frequent discussions with the two men, but that he could not stem the tide. "If we have a reformation here," he said, "may God grant that it be to His honor."[145] It is likely that he added his voice to those begging Luther to return in late February.[146]

Once Luther was back in Wittenberg, Melanchthon sought to abandon theology and return to his humanistic studies.[147] His efforts in this direction vexed Luther, who wanted Melanchthon to give up his "Greek lessons for schoolboys" to devote his energies to theological lectures.[148] Melanchthon even attempted to prevent publication of the theological lectures he did give, and Luther finally had to resort to "theft," sending the manuscripts to out-of-town publishers.[149] Melanchthon never agreed to preach to the common people in German, as Luther had wished, and he refused to accept any degree beyond his bachelor in theology.[150] In the years ahead, Melanchthon's timidity was to be a recurring complaint of Luther's, and though Luther continued to bestow high praise and friendship on him throughout his lifetime, he stopped mentioning him as his immediate successor.[151]

There may be another reason why Luther first advanced these special claims about himself when combating evangelical opponents: he may not have been able to sway enough people with theological arguments alone. Unlike controversies between Catholics and evangelicals, where there was little if any confusion about the major differences in assumptions and authorities separating the two parties, in this controversy among evangelicals there was likely to be, at least for a time, considerable confusion and uncertainty that conventional arguments could not immediately dispel. After all, both parties taught the same central doctrines such as justification by faith alone, and they all based their arguments solely on Scripture. Nevertheless, while apparently arguing from the same principles and authority, one side reached a very different conclusion from the other's about the removal of images and the establishment of evangelical ceremonies. Luther may

have felt it necessary, therefore, to supplement his theological arguments with an appeal to those who were confused or uncertain simply
to trust him for the time being. Until they were able to understand
the force of his theological arguments, they should accept what he
said *because it was he who said it.* As he told his congregation:

Therefore, dear brethren, follow me: I have never been a destroyer. And
I was also the very first whom God called to this work. . . . I was also the
one to whom God first revealed that His Word should be preached to you.
I am also sure that you have the pure Word of God.[152]

We shall see in later chapters how, as the reformation spread through
Germany, Luther moved from these first, tentative claims about himself to a firm conviction that he was occupying a unique role in his
time.

The Invocavit sermons and Luther's success in regaining control
of the Wittenberg movement had tremendous effect not only on Luther himself but also on his listeners and followers. On the day of
the first sermon, Jerome Schurf in a letter to the Elector called Luther
a "veritable apostle and evangelist of Christ to this age" and prayed
that God grant Luther grace and mercy so that through his sermons
the unspiritual disturbances in Wittenberg might be halted.[153] Several
days later, on 15 March 1522, Schurf had an even more glowing evaluation of Luther. He informed the Elector that there was great rejoic-
ing among the learned and unlearned alike about Luther's return
and the sermons that he was delivering. Schurf ventured the opinion
that Luther had divine aid and was returning the Wittenbergers to
the way of truth from which they had been diverted by the interlop-
ing preachers. It was clear to Schurf from all this that "the spirit of
God is in him and is working through him, and I [Schurf] do not
doubt that he came to Wittenberg at this time through the special
providence of the Almighty."[154]

Albert Burer, a student at Wittenberg, described in a letter to the
humanist Beatus Rhenanus the impression made on him and others
by Luther's return and his powerful sermons. Even allowing for the
exaggeration common in humanist descriptions, the picture he drew
of Luther is remarkable:

As far as one can tell from his face the man is kind, gentle, and cheerful. His voice is sweet and sonorous, so that I wonder at the sweet speaking of the man. Whatever he does, teaches, and says is most pious, even though his impious enemies say the opposite. Everyone, even though not Saxon, who hears him once, desires to hear him again and again, such tenacious hooks does he fix in the minds of his listeners. In short, there is nothing lacking in that man which makes for the most perfect Christian piety, even though all mortals and the gates of hell may say the contrary.

Burer also related how Wolfgang Capito, still in the employ of the Archbishop of Mainz, had been present at two of Luther's sermons and how he had been favorably influenced by them.[155] In fact, Capito soon left the services of the Archbishop and moved to Strasbourg, where he became one of the leaders of the reform.[156]

Within weeks of his return Luther had regained complete control of the Wittenberg reformation. He had easily overcome his first evangelical opponents and in so doing had set the pattern he was to follow in the decades ahead. He saw Satan's spirit at work in these opponents attempting to accomplish through guile that which it had been unable to accomplish through force, and he had identified many of this spirit's distinguishing characteristics. To meet this spirit's challenge he had for the first time clearly invoked his own authority as the first whom God had called to preach the renewed gospel. And the events surrounding his return—his own successes and the failures and weaknesses of his co-workers—forced him to the realization that his responsibility for the reformation movement had not ended and that God might still have a major role for him to play.

❧ 2 ❧

The Rebellious Spirit

In the summer of 1523 Karlstadt, isolated and in disrepute at the University, finally quit Wittenberg for the Thuringian countryside and settled down in the vicarage at Orlamünde, much to the satisfaction of the Orlamünde City Council and congregation.[1] This living was part of Karlstadt's archdeaconry at Wittenberg and was normally filled by an appointed substitute, but Karlstadt had the idea of becoming his own vicar. Duke John, the Elector Frederick's brother and coruler, apparently gave his permission for this move, but it was fateful for later developments that the University and the Castle church, which had the legal right of nomination, were not consulted. Still, no immediate objections were raised, and Karlstadt settled down to the life of a country parson.

He had not, however, given up all interest in the wider world, and continued to turn out tracts on various theological subjects.[2] Unable to get any of his more controversial works past the censors at Wittenberg, he turned to the presses in Strasbourg and later in Jena, eleven miles down the Saale River from Orlamünde, where his followers managed to establish a press for him. Early in 1524 Luther tried to put a stop to these publishing activities, or at least to bring them under some kind of control. He argued that there was no excuse for Karlstadt's being the only member of the Wittenberg faculty who did not submit his works to the censors and that this exception could create a scandal for the Saxon princes and the Wittenberg University.[3]

To add to Luther's distrust of Karlstadt, rumors began reaching Wittenberg about the removal of images from the Orlamünde church, about changes in the celebration of the Lord's Supper, and even about the abolition of infant baptism.[4] By March 1524 Luther was characterizing these reforms as "monstrosities,"[5] and both Luther and the University felt it necessary to take steps against Karlstadt because of his activities. Luther told Spalatin that the University intended to recall Karlstadt from Orlamünde, "to which he was not called," to Wittenberg, where he had the responsibility to teach and preach. If Karlstadt failed to return, they would press charges against him with the Elector, and Luther even considered writing him an admonitory letter. He was certain that Satan was behind Karlstadt's undertaking.[6] He wrote Zwickau's pastor Nicholas Hausmann that Karlstadt was persecuting the Wittenbergers more horribly than did the papists and, according to Spalatin, had instituted various monstrosities. "Your Claus [Nicholas] Storch is ruling in these men," Luther wrote. "After he was driven out of Zwickau, he found himself a hiding place there."[7]

Karlstadt wisely heeded the university summons and returned to Wittenberg in early April. After some negotiations, he agreed to turn over the Orlamünde vicarage to a replacement designated by the University and Chapter, and to return to his academic duties in Wittenberg. This agreement having been reached, Luther entertained hopes that the situation in Orlamünde would be straightened out.[8]

Upon his return to Orlamünde to pack up, however, Karlstadt apparently began to have second thoughts. Moreover, his Orlamünde congregation were greatly upset at the prospect of losing their pastor. Karlstadt made various excuses to the Elector about the economic hardships that a sudden departure would entail, and requested on this account and for the good of his congregation that he might remain in Orlamünde through the summer. The Orlamünde Council appealed to Duke John, the University, and the Elector not to take from them their chosen pastor. They were assured that a proper pastor would be appointed for them—but this pastor would not be Karlstadt. Finally, a formal summons was issued for Karlstadt's return. This he ignored.[9]

In March of the same year, the followers of Thomas Müntzer burned a chapel dedicated to the Virgin at Mallerbach, located just outside the gates of Allstedt.[10] Müntzer had been a pastor in Zwickau from 1519 to 1521, having been recommended for the position by Luther. His beliefs had, however, gradually diverged from those of Luther, and his increasingly radical preaching and his association with the Zwickau prophets had involved him in such controversy in Zwickau that in April 1521 he had been forced to leave. After a largely unsuccessful visit to Prague, where he had attempted to rally support for his spiritualistic and chiliastic vision of the gospel, he had taken up residence in the Thuringian town of Allstedt, which was in the Harz Mountains near Saxony and under the jurisdiction of the Elector of Saxony. From Allstedt he had appealed to Luther to acknowledge his gift of the spirit. In the same letter he had lamely excused his previous conduct in Zwickau and had attempted to dissociate himself from Storch and Stübner.[11] Luther had not been satisfied with Müntzer's spirit or his excuses, and probably had not even bothered to answer the letter.[12]

After the burning of the Mallerbach chapel, Duke John insisted that the culprits be punished, but the Allstedt Council and Müntzer successfully resisted the implementation of this order. On 18 June 1524 when Luther reported to Duke John's son, Duke John Frederick, the agreement that had been reached between Karlstadt and the University, he also vented his displeasure with Müntzer, whom he labeled the "Satan at Allstedt." He suggested that the young Duke should arrange for Müntzer to come to Wittenberg to give account of his teachings "since he censors and condemns ours." Or, since Müntzer was such a fearless hero, Luther suggested that he should prove his spirit in the Catholic territory of Duke George. "It is just not right," Luther complained,

that he uses against us our protection, our victory, and all our benefits, which we won without any help from him. They sit on our manure pile and bark at us. It is an evil spirit. He should go once as I did and dare [to present his case] outside of this principality before other princes, and then we will see where his spirit is.[13]

Luther saw the unwillingness to risk persecution as a sure sign of a false prophet, and his complaint that the false brethren used the freedom and safety secured through the triumph of the gospel to spread their poison is a recurring theme in Luther's polemics.

Unable to get the fanatics to come to Luther, Duke John Frederick undertook to persuade Luther to go to the fanatics. Accordingly, on 24 June he wrote Luther asking him to visit the cities in the principality to see ("as St. Paul had done") what sort of preachers the city faithful were provided with. With the help of the authorities Luther could dismiss unfit preachers. "I do not think that you could do a more Christian service for us in Thuringia."[14]

In addition, Duke John Frederick and his father, Duke John, took the bold step of visiting Allstedt to examine the situation for themselves, and on 1 July Müntzer preached his extraordinary "Princes' Sermon" to the two Saxon princes. In it he urged the princes to place their swords at the disposal of a militant, spiritualized Christianity, threatened dire consequences if they failed to do so, and openly attacked Luther. He based his arguments less on Scripture than on his dreams and visions.[15] The princes left Allstedt with much to think about.

Additional and more palatable food for thought was given them by Luther. Sometime in July he published a warning letter to the princes concerning the "rebellious spirit." He began his letter with the explanation that Satan always opposed the gospel first with force and then, when that failed, attacked it with false brethren and false teachings:

So he did in the beginning, when the gospel first came into the world, attacking it violently through the Jews and Gentiles, shedding much blood and creating many martyrs in Christendom. When this method of attack failed, he thrust forth false prophets and erring spirits, filling the world with heretics and sects right down to the time of the pope, who (as befits the last and greatest Antichrist) has overthrown Christendom with nought but sects and heresy.[16]

Satan was following the same strategy in Luther's time. The Catholic authorities had used force to attack the gospel; now the false spirits were attempting to subvert it from within. "Thus, after Satan has been driven out and for several years has wandered around in waterless places, seeking rest but finding none, he has settled down in your Grace's principality and made himself a nest at Allstedt, thinking he can fight against us while enjoying our peace, protection, and security."[17] The Bible meant nothing to these false spirits—they were only interested in their boasts of direct discourse with God. Yet the satanic spirit intended to go further and resort to violence to support its undertaking:

I have already heard earlier from the spirit himself here in Wittenberg [a reference to the Zwickau prophets?] that he thinks it necessary to use the sword to carry out his undertaking. At that time I had a hunch that they would go so far as to overthrow civil authority and make themselves lords of the world.[18]

Luther admonished the princes that for these reasons it was their duty to anticipate the intentions of these spirits and forestall the incipient rebellion.

The refusal of Müntzer and his followers to submit to an examination before two or three theologians caused Luther great irritation. He contrasted this refusal with his own willingness to appear at Leipzig, Augsburg, and Worms. "I, poor miserable man, did not initiate my undertaking with such self-confidence, but with much trembling and fear (as St. Paul confessed even of himself in I Corinthians, though he too could have boasted somewhat of a heavenly voice)."[19] The fact that Müntzer boasted mightily from his "hiding place" was a sure sign that he was frightened and suffering under a bad conscience.

Luther advised the princes that for the moment they allow the Allstedt spirit to preach as confidently and as boldly as it was able. Were it genuine, then it would prevail. If, however, Luther's spirit was genuine, then it would prevail and the Allstedters would go to ruin. "If meanwhile some are led astray, all right, such is war!"[20] Should they turn to violence, however, then the princes ought to use force to banish these men from their country.* Luther closed his letter with a discussion of the proper removal of images and the impropriety of emulating the deeds rather than the faith of the Old and New Testament saints. Only through the Word of God which changes men's hearts could offense be truly removed.

* Luther made an unfavorable comparison between Müntzer's activities and his own successes, which were accomplished solely through the preaching of the Word: "Some would say that without force I have done more damage to the pope than a mighty king could do. But these prophets want badly to do something bigger and better." WA 15: 219 (LW 40: 58).

On 1 August Müntzer and a number of the Allstedt officials were ordered to appear in Weimar.[21] There Müntzer had a hearing apart from the others and was apparently ordered to quit the electoral territories. Back in Allstedt he discovered that the Allstedt officials had surrendered to all the princes' demands and abandoned him. It was obvious that he was in trouble, and on the eve of the seventh he fled the town. A few days later he was comfortably ensconced in the nearby imperial city of Mühlhausen, where his radical convictions were better appreciated.

It was while in Weimar on the visitation suggested by Duke John Frederick that Luther learned of Müntzer's flight.[22] He immediately sent off a warning letter to the mayor, council, and community of Mühlhausen, admonishing them to guard themselves against "this false spirit and prophet, a rapacious wolf who goes around in sheep's clothing." He clearly wished to absolve himself from all responsibility for Müntzer:

For I can boast in Christ that I have never harmed or wanted to harm anyone with my teaching and advice, as this spirit intends. Rather I have been consoling and helpful to everyone, so that you simply do not have cause to disdain my advice. If you disdain it, however, accept the prophet, and misfortune comes of it for you, I am innocent of your injury, for I have warned you in a Christian and friendly fashion.[23]

On 22 August 1524 Luther preached in Jena, and among his listeners sat Karlstadt, a felt hat pulled low on his face so that he might avoid recognition. Luther's sermon was on the Allstedt spirit, "a devilish spirit," whose fruits, Luther contended, were rebellion and murder, the destruction of images, and the elimination and negation of baptism and the Lord's Supper. After the service Karlstadt wrote Luther a sharp letter in which he requested an opportunity for a face-to-face discussion, complained about Luther's having lumped him together with the Allstedters, and disputed Luther's comments on the Lord's Supper. Luther agreed to see him, and they decided on a meeting at the Black Bear Inn.

The account of this meeting, and also of the subsequent encounter in Orlamünde, came from the pen of Martin Reinhard, the Jena preacher and a Karlstadt sympathizer. Luther claimed later that it contained a mixture of truth and falsehood intended to increase Karlstadt's fame and to diminish Luther's reputation.[24] According to Reinhard's report, the substance of Karlstadt's complaint at the Black Bear meeting was that Luther unfairly classed Karlstadt and his position on the Lord's Supper with the murderous and rebellious spirit at Allstedt. Karlstadt denied that he and the Allstedters stood together on any issue except matters of truth. Where the Allstedters were wrong, they stood not with Karlstadt but with the devil. He maintained further that Luther was wrong in his teachings on the Lord's Supper and could be proved wrong from the Scriptures and from the books he himself had written.[25]

Luther retorted that he had not named Karlstadt or his congregation in his sermon, that he had read the Orlamünders' letter to Müntzer in which they condemned rebellion,[26] and that there was no need for Karlstadt to be so exercised since the sermon was not directed at him but at the Allstedters.[27] But if Karlstadt felt injured by Luther's remarks, then he had no one to blame but himself—if the shoe fit, he would have to wear it. Luther had preached against the "spirits" and would preach against them in the future. He challenged Karlstadt to write against him publicly if he had erred in his teaching of the gospel, and he gave him a gulden as a token of this challenge. Karlstadt accepted the coin and announced that he would correct Luther's misunderstanding of the Lord's Supper.[28]

In the course of the dispute, the two men also exchanged accusations about each other's vanity and wrangled over which of them had insisted on going first at the Leipzig debate.[29] Luther brought up Karlstadt's improper occupation of the Parish church pulpit while Luther was on the Wartburg, and Karlstadt countered by pointing to his calling at All Saints and the overlap of congregations between the two churches. Karlstadt also asked why Luther had not admonished him about his error in a Christian and brotherly fashion instead of attacking him as he had.[30] Why, Luther asked, if Karlstadt's teaching was right and godly in spirit, had it not manifested itself when Karlstadt destroyed the images in Wittenberg? Instead of answering directly, Karlstadt said that he had not acted alone, that three city councillors and several of Luther's friends had also agreed to the removal of the images, but they had then pulled their heads out of the noose and left Karlstadt standing by himself.[31] The two men also bickered about whether or not Karlstadt had ever been confronted with a list of his errors, Karlstadt complaining that he had been tied "hand and foot," forbidden to preach or write, while Luther had been free to attack him as he willed.[32] All in all, this acrimonious confrontation did little more than air standing grievances.

A day or two after this scene in the Black Bear Inn, Luther's practice of attributing a common spirit to all his evangelical opponents led to another controversy, this time with Karlstadt's Orlamünde congregation. On 16 August they sent Luther a letter, the tone and substance of which could hardly have been better calculated to raise Luther's blood pressure and, more important, to confirm the very judgment that the letter protested. The Orlamünders omitted all of Luther's academic titles and employed the familiar "Du" in addressing him. They informed Luther that their pastor and minister, Karlstadt, had brought them the report from his recent visit in Wittenberg that Luther had shamelessly proclaimed from the pulpit that they were heretics and erring and fanatical spirits, and this without testing their spirits. If Luther tried to deny this report, they would refer him to his letter against the rebellious spirits in which he scorned all those who did away with the dumb idols and pagan images as they had been commanded to do by God. That Luther had condemned and slandered them, members of the body of Christ, without a hearing and without proving them to be in error, indicated that Luther was no member of the true body of Christ. They rejected in advance excuses Luther might make for his conduct, and then requested him, since he harbored such suspicions, to visit them in the near future.[33]

Luther decided to oblige them with a short visit. He and his party arrived in Orlamünde on 24 August 1524 in the afternoon, and the mayor, the council members, and the congregation, who had expected him the night before, had to be called in from the fields where they were harvesting.* From Reinhard's account, Luther appears to

* WA 15: 341. The previous day Luther preached in Kahla, a little town not far from Orlamünde. When he entered the chancel, he found pieces of a broken crucifix, an unsubtle message from a member of the audience. See Hermann Barge, *Andreas Bodenstein von Karlstadt*, 2d ed. (Nieuwkoop, 1968), 2: 130.

have come not to discuss the issues fraternally but only to confront the Orlamünders with their error. The following is Reinhard's report of the meeting. When welcomed by the mayor, Luther did not remove the red barret he was wearing and, cutting the mayor short, he announced that he could not stay long. When the mayor asked that he preach a sermon for them, Luther declined, saying that he was there not for sermonizing but for a discussion of the letter they had sent him.

A house was settled upon and the meeting began. Luther started by asking if the letter had really been written by them. "You seem like simple people to me," he explained, "and I find it hard to believe that you wrote this. I do not hold this letter against you, but I am concerned lest Karlstadt wrote this letter and then sealed it with the city seal."[34] The Orlamünders hotly denied that was so, and Luther then began reading the letter aloud and discussing it point by point.

First he asked how they could refer to Karlstadt as their pastor and minister when, in the opinion of their prince and the University of Wittenberg, he was not. A council member retorted that if Karlstadt was not their chosen pastor then both Paul and Luther himself had written improperly on the right of a congregation to choose its pastor. Luther next brought up their comments on the destruction of "dumb idols and pagan images." At this point Karlstadt entered the house and attempted to join the conversation. Luther, much offended, insisted that since Karlstadt was his enemy and had been given a gulden in token of this, his presence at this meeting was not to be tolerated. When Karlstadt refused to go, Wolfgang Stein, the court chaplain, said to him: "Herr Doctor, you reached your agreement in Jena so you really should leave."[35] Karlstadt's retort to this was: "You are not my prince to give me orders! If someone has a princely mandate, however, he should present it."[36] Not until Luther himself threatened to leave was Karlstadt persuaded to depart. Luther later claimed that Karlstadt's response to Stein, who "was there as a representative of the prince," showed his contempt for authority.[37]

After Karlstadt had left, Reinhard's report goes on to say, Luther resumed the discussion and explained that he had not had the Orlamünders in mind when writing and preaching. The city secretary objected that in Luther's letter to the Saxon princes he had in effect lumped the Orlamünders with the Allstedters, since they both had done away with images. To this Luther responded that he had spoken generally and that if they felt injured, how could he help it?

Luther next took issue with their letter to him, pointing out that they had omitted all his titles (something even his enemies among the princes did not do) and that they had condemned him as being outside the true body of Christ, from which he concluded that the letter was the letter of an enemy. There followed a heated exchange on this point, which ended by Luther's saying, "If I had not already known that you were fanatics, I would know now, for you burn before my eyes like fire. Will you not gobble me up?"[38]

Changing the subject, Luther then asked on what scriptural grounds were images to be removed. First someone pointed to the Mosaic command against graven images, but Luther countered that the commandments referred to the *worship* of images; as long as images were not worshiped, they could do no harm. A cobbler then argued that he had always previously removed his cap to images and that was idolatry, and Luther ventured that if they were going to remove images because of their misuse, they would also have to rid themselves of women and wine because of their misuse. The bystanders rejected this argument on the grounds that images were created by man while women and wine were created by God for man's proper use. Luther insisted, however, that the issue was the idolatry of images, not the images themselves, and neither side would budge.

Then the cobbler cited what he claimed was a scriptural passage: "I wish my bride to be naked and do not wish for her to be wearing her gown." Several members of the congregation interpreted this passage to mean that souls must be naked before God, that no one must lust after any creature, and that therefore no images should be made or allowed. At this explanation Luther put his face in his hands in (mock?) despair: "Ah listen to this! That means that images should be done away with. Oh, what an unusual German!"[39]

According to Luther's later account of this exchange, the cobbler first insisted on using the familiar "Du" in addressing Luther, then accused Luther of "shoving the gospel under the bench," and finally brought forth this argument about the bride and her gown. Luther held Karlstadt responsible both for the Orlamünders' behavior and for their ridiculous arguments. "But so it goes," Luther observed, when one brings the disorderly masses into the picture. Due to great fulness of the spirit they forget civil discipline and manners, and no longer fear and respect anyone but themselves alone. This appeals to Dr. Karlstadt. These are all pretty preliminaries to riot and rebellion, so that one fears neither order nor authority.[40]

In Reinhard's account, this exchange continued for some time, and then Luther repeated his charge that they had condemned him. The cobbler replied that if Luther wished to be condemned, he would continue to consider Luther condemned as long as he spoke or lectured against God and God's truth. Luther finally had enough of the discussion, and, after one or two exchanges with the city treasurer, he and his party departed. Luther was later to report that he was grateful not to have been driven from the city with stones and dung and that some persons called after him as he left, "Get out in the name of a thousand devils, and break your neck before you are out of the city!"[41]

Luther and Reinhard agree reasonably well on the incidents that Luther later pointed to as demonstrating both Karlstadt's and his congregation's contempt for authority. Each side seems to have provoked actions on the part of the other that confirmed its prejudgment. Deciding that Luther had condemned them without a hearing, the Orlamünders sent him an impolite, censorious letter. In return, they received a visit from an angry, offended man who was unwilling to hear their side. It is evident that Luther, convinced that the Orlamünders were violent fanatics, went to them for the purpose of confronting them with their error and had no intention of seriously discussing the issues. Not surprisingly, his demeanor prompted hot "fanatical" replies and curses, born, perhaps, of frustrated attempts at communication.

Back in Wittenberg, Luther shared his unfavorable impressions of Karlstadt with the young Duke John Frederick.[42] He probably repeated the charge that Karlstadt had occupied the position at Orlamünde illegally, and he may well have accused Karlstadt of encouraging, or at any rate not seriously discouraging, the "murderous spirit."[43] He may even have suggested at this time that Karlstadt be removed from his Orlamünde position and ordered out of the Saale Valley area,[44] though there is no indication that he was bent on Karlstadt's complete banishment from the Saxon lands.

Luther continued to keep in touch with developments concerning Karlstadt, and he offered advice and comment as events progressed. On 10 September he wrote Wolfgang Stein in Weimar asking for news,[45] and three days later he wrote to Spalatin that he believed Karlstadt had been so given over to his reprobate opinions that the possibility of his recovery was doubtful. He attributed Karlstadt's behavior to his "insane desire for fame and glory." "He is more hostile to me, or rather to us, than any enemy to date," he wrote, "so that I do not think that that miserable man is possessed by merely one devil."[46]

Sometime in mid-September, a copy of a letter written by Karlstadt to Duke John Frederick on 11 September was sent to Luther with a request that he comment on it.[47] In this letter Karlstadt complained about Luther's sermonizing in Thuringia and what he saw as Luther's unfair characterization of his teachings and person and his attack on them:

... Dr. Luther has appeared in many places and localities where my Christian, godly, provable, and established teaching has been planted. He says that he was dispatched with your Grace's command to proclaim such teachings of mine destructive, erroneous, and seditious and publicly to refute [them] and to warn the populace against them as if they had sprung from a fanatic spirit. He has also mendaciously lumped me with the rebellion at Allstedt and has raised suspicions about me among the populace, as much as he could, and perhaps also with your Grace.[48]

Karlstadt explained how he had challenged the "groundless, conceited impetuosity" of Luther's sermon in Jena, how he had requested a Christian and brotherly instruction for his alleged errors, and how he had volunteered to meet Luther in disputation in Wittenberg or Erfurt. Luther, he reported, had rejected all this and had challenged him to write against him and had given him a gulden as token of this challenge. But to demonstrate his moderation and to refute Luther's charge that he was a quarrelsome fanatic, Karlstadt would not answer Luther's challenge immediately, but requested a hearing instead. The prince should allow him to defend his teachings rather than accept everything Luther and his followers claimed. If this were burdensome to the prince, then he should at least allow Karlstadt to publish a defense of his teachings without his having to overcome obstacles such as the University had put in his way previously, or such as had resulted from the secret intervention of Luther and his followers.[49]

Luther was of the opinion that Karlstadt's letter should be answered with a firm and uncompromising reply. Karlstadt should be told that it was he who had started the controversy, had accepted the gulden from Luther, and had only then requested the prince's permission (*Gnad oder Gunst*). The prince should ask Karlstadt: "Why do you now, at long last, ask us for grace or favor when you have always done as you were pleased? If you handle the matter well the outcome will be satisfactory." As for Karlstadt's request for a disputation, the prince should say that his request astonished him, since Karlstadt had been so often commanded to return to Wittenberg to participate in disputations, to lecture, and to preach as his office obligated him to do, and yet no one could even drag him there. The prince should say that all his talk about disputations, as if people had hindered him from debating, was so much shadowboxing, that Karlstadt knew this, and that he should desist and act responsibly. Having made these suggestions, Luther gave Stein his estimation of the matter. If Karlstadt's actions were actually inspired by God, Luther asked, why did he put things off, why did he consult men? "Here you realize how certain that wicked spirit is about his being driven by God in what he is doing."[50]

A few days later, Luther wrote to Duke John Frederick on behalf of Kaspar Glatz, the man recently elected to replace Karlstadt in Orlamünde. Glatz felt that he did not have a chance of dealing successfully with the situation in Orlamünde as long as Karlstadt was on the scene. He had been advised therefore to request that the Duke banish Karlstadt from the Saale Valley area. Luther wrote to urge the granting of this request:

Now I told your Grace when I was with you and have also indicated to the Chancellor why Karlstadt has truly earned such treatment: because he barged in and took over the parish without your Grace's knowledge and consent and because, in addition, he has not expressed himself on or acted against the murderous spirit as he reasonably should if there were a good spark in him. Hence it is to be feared that this same spirit, if it were given room and opportunity, would institute little good.[51]

It is possible that Luther was repeating in this letter the advice that he gave the Duke earlier when they met face to face.

By the time the letter was written, however, the Duke and his father had already taken more drastic steps than Luther had suggested. On 18 September they ordered Karlstadt to vacate Orlamünde and all the lands of Electoral Saxony as well. They wrote him that he would not be hindered in his desire to publish against Luther, but he would have to do so outside of Electoral Saxony. Also he would not be allowed to preach during the interval before the arrival of his replacement. Requests by the Orlamünde Council that Karlstadt's financial plight and the welfare of his pregnant wife and young child be considered were to no avail.[52] By the end of September Karlstadt had quit Electoral Saxony, taking with him drafts of the promised attack on Luther and on Luther's doctrine.*

Karlstadt claimed later that Luther had driven him out of Orlamünde.[53] As the quoted correspondence shows, Luther did much to discredit Karlstadt with Duke John Frederick. The extent of Luther's specific recommendation was that Karlstadt be banished from the Saale Valley, but he had painted such a threatening picture of Karlstadt's spirit that it is small wonder the Saxon princes decided there was no room for such a spirit within their lands. And the correspon-

---

* Several weeks into his exile, Karlstadt sent two letters to his former Orlamünde congregation, both signed "Andreas Bodenstein, unheard and unconvicted, driven out by Martin Luther" (Barge, 2: 141). Luther commented on this designation with bitter sarcasm: "Look at this! I, who should have become a martyr, have come to the point where I make martyrs myself." Luther was resigned to his fate: "for after all there do have to be fanatics" (WABr 3: 361; cf. WABr 3: 365, 366). To Hausmann in Zwickau, Luther confided that he was putting off his reply to Karlstadt's attack on the Lord's Supper until Karlstadt had spread abroad his "poison," as Karlstadt had promised to do, and he added the fateful observation that Zwingli and Jud among the Swiss now held the same opinion as Karlstadt. See WABr 3: 373 (LW 49: 88–90); cf. WABr 3: 329–31, especially the postscript. This will be discussed further in Chapter 3.

dence shows, too, that Karlstadt did little to counteract this impression. The conflict between Luther and Karlstadt became public knowledge beyond the borders of Electoral Saxony in the autumn of 1524, following Karlstadt's expulsion from Saxony and the publication of several of his attacks on Luther. Especially noted were his attacks on Luther's belief in the real presence in the Lord's Supper. This break in the evangelical ranks and the questions raised by Karlstadt's treatises led the preachers of Strasbourg, where Karlstadt had made a visit in October, to write Ulrich Zwingli, the leader of the reform in Zurich, and Luther for their opinions.[54] In the letter to Luther, though criticizing Karlstadt on various points and deploring his personal attack on Luther, they submitted that he had raised some legitimate questions, especially about the Lord's Supper. They listed their questions and requested Luther's opinion on each of them.[55] They then summarized the ceremonial practices at Strasbourg (many of which were closer to the reforms advocated by Karlstadt than to those advocated by Luther) and the reasons for each of them. They closed their lengthy letter with an appeal that Luther reply swiftly, carefully, and with moderation, even though Karlstadt himself had not shown moderation:

We have written this to you out of a heart desiring one thing: that Christ's kingdom come forth and be brought to light. . . . You certainly know how much, as the Lord wills it, depends on you [and] how many thousands of souls hang on [the words] from your mouth because they are persuaded that it is the mouth of the Lord.[56]

At the same time they reminded Luther that, as a result of his own ministry, people could no longer be satisfied with any argument not solidly grounded in the Scriptures. And they prayed that Luther, who had often strengthened many other people in the Word, would have regard for them as well.

Accompanying this letter were five of Karlstadt's treatises, Erasmus' *Diatribe on Free Will,* and a letter from Nicholas Gerbel, a Strasbourg jurist and consistent advocate of Luther's position.[57] Addressing Luther as "apostle to an afflicted Germany," Gerbel gave an account of Karlstadt's visit to Strasbourg. He wrote that Karlstadt had entered Strasbourg secretly and, rather than seeking out the teachers of the gospel, had babbled forth his charges against Luther in corners. He told how Karlstadt's treatises were causing confusion and uproar among both papists and evangelicals "since they previously believed that you both professed the same doctrine."[58] This could not but confirm Luther's judgment of Karlstadt and his fears of Karlstadt's pernicious influence. Gerbel begged Luther to take the opportunity to repair the damage by writing a detailed exposition on the matter to the Strasbourgers. It is worth noting that throughout Gerbel's letter is the almost explicit assumption that the devil was responsible for all of Karlstadt's actions.[59] Luther would, of course, see reason to agree.

Luther replied promptly to both letters. He admonished Gerbel not to be surprised at the things done under the auspices of the prince of the world, namely Satan, for it was for this reason that only a small remnant of the church survived. "Karlstadt, therefore, is doing right," he wrote; "he was long since given over to Satan, and now, at last, he is revealing the mysteries of his god." He contended that Karlstadt had been driven to these actions because of his unconquerable lust for vainglory. But true Christians should not fear, for their cause was God's cause and they fought on God's side.[60]

Luther's letter to the Strasbourgers began with a warning that the true gospel was always attacked, persecuted, and tested "from both sides": "Christ finds not only Caiaphas among his enemies, but also Judas among his friends."[61] In this case it was clear that the Judas was Dr. Karlstadt. Having put Karlstadt in his proper place, Luther prefaced his discussion of Karlstadt's contentions with a caveat and an appeal to his personal authority:

Now my very dear friends, I am not your pastor. No one has to believe me. Each one is responsible for himself. I can warn everyone, I can thwart no one. I hope, too, that you have hitherto learned to know me through my writings so that you would admit that in regard to the gospel, the grace of Christ, the law, faith, love, the cross, human ordinances, our stand toward the papacy, monasticism, and the mass, and the articles of faith which a Christian should know, I have written with such clarity and certainty that I am blameless. Nor, I hope, would you deny that, though I am an unworthy instrument of God, he has helped many through me.[62]

He advised the Strasbourgers to hold to the single question: what made a person a Christian? All else was of minor importance, concerned with mere external matters. Those who were unable to take this advice should go slowly and wait for what Luther or others would have to say. "I have hitherto treated fairly and fully of the chief articles of faith," he contended, adding that anyone who claimed otherwise could not be a good spirit. "I hope," he said, "that I do no one harm even in the external matters on which these prophets harp so much."[63]

Luther confessed that Karlstadt, or anyone else who could have convinced him five years earlier that only bread and wine were present in the Lord's Supper, would have done him a great service, for he had suffered great doubts over the issue and had known that such a position would be a powerful weapon against the papacy. But the text, "this is my body," was too definitive to stand distortion from its proper meaning. Furthermore, Luther said that the bitter spirit in Karlstadt's attacks on him (a spirit, however, that he also detected in himself) and the ridiculous nature of Karlstadt's arguments strengthened his certainty that his own understanding of the Supper was right. Whatever he might be able to tolerate about Karlstadt, Luther added, he could not tolerate his insistence that external ceremonies and actions made a Christian.[64]

While denying any responsibility for Karlstadt's banishment, Luther did say that he was happy Karlstadt was no longer in Electoral Saxony and wished he were not in Strasbourg. "Beware of the false prophet," he warned them, "for no good will come from him." Karlstadt had nearly convinced him at Jena not to confuse his spirit with the rebellious and murderous spirit at Allstedt. "But when, on the order of the prince, I visited his Christians at Orlamünde, I soon found what kind of seed he had sown."[65]

But all this trading of accusations, Luther maintained, was the devil's trick, diverting men from the proper study of the gospel:

Ask your evangelists, my dear sirs and brothers, to turn away from Luther and Karlstadt and direct you always to Christ, but not, as Karlstadt does, only to the work of Christ wherein Christ is held up as an example, which is the least important aspect of Christ, and which makes him comparable to other saints. But turn to Christ as to a gift of God or, as Paul says, the power of God, and God's wisdom, righteousness, redemption, and sanctification, given to us.

Luther closed his letter to the Strasbourgers with a harsh judgment on his opponents. He knew with certainty, he said, that they had never prayed to God the Father or sought Him when initiating their movement, nor did they have a sufficiently good conscience to dare to implore Him for a blessed completion.[66] This charge would recur frequently in the polemics to come.

Having sent off his letters to Gerbel and the Strasbourg preachers, Luther immediately threw himself into a long response to Karlstadt's treatises. In little more than two weeks, the first part of his *Against the Heavenly Prophets* had been written and published. In it he dealt with Karlstadt's arguments on iconoclasm, on his banishment from Electoral Saxony, on the term "mass," and on the elevation of the host. In the second part, which followed on the heels of the first, he dealt exclusively with Karlstadt's arguments about the presence of the body and blood of Christ in the elements of the Lord's Supper.[67]

In the treatise Luther took deadly aim at Karlstadt and his opinions on images and the sacraments. It is apparent from the outset, however, that he had more than Karlstadt in his sights. Standing behind Karlstadt, manipulating him like a puppet on strings, he saw the prince of the world, Satan.[68] As Luther fired at Karlstadt, he intended to wound Karlstadt's master as well, and to defeat his cunning plans for the overthrow of the gospel. "Doctor Andreas Karlstadt has deserted us, and on top of that has become our worst enemy," Luther wrote in his opening lines, quickly adding, "May Christ grant that we be not alarmed, and give us his mind and courage, that we may not err and despair before the Satan who here pretends to vindicate the Sacrament, but has much else in mind." He was able to summarize Satan's goal concisely: "For since he has not thus far been able to suppress with violence the whole doctrine of the gospel, he seeks to destroy it with cunning interpretation of Scripture."[69] This metaphysical dimension of the struggle between Luther and Karlstadt influences all of Luther's arguments and characterizations and allows him to paint the controversy solely in blacks and whites.

The treatise was directed, moreover, at all the fanatics and false prophets, not just Karlstadt. Although much of the treatise deals directly with Karlstadt, it is actually Karlstadt's *spirit* (which, Luther maintained, was the same spirit driving Müntzer, the Zwickau prophets, and the other "heavenly prophets") that bears the brunt of Luther's attack. And Karlstadt is faulted not only for what he had allegedly done but also for what his spirit was allegedly capable of doing, given the opportunity. This "tactic" entailed among other things Luther's charge that Karlstadt was impelled by the "Allstedt spirit," that is, by the same "rebellious, murderous, seditious" spirit that drove Thomas Müntzer. This charge had led to the meeting between Karlstadt and Luther in Jena, the confrontation in Orlamünde, Karlstadt's complaint to Duke John Frederick, and, very likely, Karlstadt's eventual banishment from Electoral Saxony. Now Luther went to some lengths to explain and justify the accusation.

In discussing the destruction of images, Luther contended that Karlstadt was insisting that the Mosaic law be applied to the contemporary situation, and that it be enforced by the populace rather than by the constituted authorities. Luther saw a frightful consequence flowing from this insistence:

Where one permits the masses without authority to break images, one must also permit anyone to proceed to kill adulterers, murderers, the disobedient, etc. For God commanded the people of Israel to kill these just as much as to put away images.

From this consequence Luther justified his characterization of Karlstadt's spirit and motivation:

Therefore, though I have not said that Dr. Karlstadt is a murderous prophet, yet he has a rebellious, murderous, seditious spirit in him, which, if given an opportunity, would assert itself.[70]

This conclusion allowed Luther to discount evidence to the contrary:

But, you say, Dr. Karlstadt does not want to kill. That one can see from the letters which those of Orlamünde wrote to the Allstedters. Answer: I also believed it! But I believe it no longer. I no longer ask what Dr. Karlstadt says or does. He has not hit the truth for the first time. Of the spirit which they have and which impels them, I say that it is not good and is bent on murder and rebellion. Although he bows and scrapes because he sees that he is in a tight spot, I shall clearly show that what I have said is so. God forbid, but suppose Dr. Karlstadt won a large following, which he thought he could assemble on the Saale, and the German Bible alone was read, and Mr. Everybody began to hold this commandment [about killing the wicked] under his own nose, in what direction would Dr. Karlstadt go? How would he control the situation? Even if he had never intended to consent to something like that, he would have to follow through.

As long as Karlstadt persisted in image breaking and in gathering together and exciting common people, Luther could not trust him. Karlstadt's "false interpretation and understanding of the law of Moses" was a murderous weapon, and as long as Karlstadt did not put it aside, Luther feared him; Karlstadt might only be waiting for the right time and place to strike and stab.[71] Luther's argument here is cogent and shows psychological insight, but it does attribute responsibility to Karlstadt for acts of violence that he himself had publicly disavowed.

Fanatics and false prophets, according to Luther, busied themselves solely with externals and good works, ignoring faith, love, and a good conscience before God. But true Christians must hold fast to five articles. First, the law of God must be preached so that sin is revealed and recognized. Next, after the conscience is alarmed by the law, it should be comforted by the preaching of the gospel and the forgiveness of sins. Third, the old man must be disciplined and put to death by works set for men by God, not works chosen by men on their own. Fourth, works of love toward one's neighbors should flow forth naturally. Fifth, the law and its works should be proclaimed to the rough masses, not to reveal sin, but to compel them to be outwardly pious; such is the task of temporal authorities.

Luther charged the false prophets with perverting or ignoring all of these articles. He could find no evidence that any of them, including Karlstadt, preached the first two articles.[72] As for the third article, he contended that the false prophets chose works of their own devising rather than those set by God: they "wear gray garb, would be peasants, and carry on with similar foolish nonsense."* Luther saw this as the devil's plan, so to emphasize minor matters that the truly important matters would be neglected: "From this each one should recognize how false and evil the spirit of Dr. Karlstadt is, who, not

---

* WA 18: 65 (LW 40: 83). The description fits Karlstadt, who affected a gray, peasant's garb.

content to ignore and be silent concerning the great and significant articles, so inflates the least significant ones as if the salvation of the world depended more on them than on Christ himself."[73]

In refutation of Karlstadt's teaching, Luther argued that the Mosaic law was the Jews' civil code, bound to its time and circumstances. Only to the degree that the Mosaic law overlapped the natural law was it applicable to all men at all times. This qualification applied even to the Ten Commandments, which were no more than an explicit statement of certain natural laws.[74]

In several of his treatises Karlstadt had claimed that he was unjustly expelled from Electoral Saxony and that Luther was in no small part to blame. Determined to answer both charges, Luther compiled an impressive list of Karlstadt's alleged misdeeds:

Now, however, Dr. Karlstadt forsakes his duties at Wittenberg behind the prince's back, robs the university of his preaching and lectures and what he is obligated to do by reason of the prince's endowment, and retains nevertheless the salary or revenue for himself, and puts no one else in his place. At Orlamünde he also takes the pastorate belonging to the University, drives out him whom he had not appointed, nor had the power to appoint, much less to dismiss. Dear friends, why all this? Some suppose in order that he might draw that much more income, and because he believed the Elector would be lenient and not quick to punish. But I believe that a secondary reason was that the prophets sought a hide-out on the Saale, where they could spread their spirit and poison, creeping around in the darkness like mice—something they would not be able to do for long in Wittenberg.[75]

Luther held the Zwickau prophets responsible for turning Karlstadt's head.[76] He also rejected the argument that Karlstadt had left Wittenberg to escape the heresy there, and he clearly implied that Karlstadt was influenced by a desire for money.[77] Luther labeled irrelevant the belated "call" that the Orlamünders had made when it seemed that they were about to lose Karlstadt.[78] He maintained that the Saxon princes had tolerated more than enough when Karlstadt finally reneged on his agreement to surrender the Orlamünde parsonage and return to Wittenberg, and when he aroused the people of Orlamünde to write an arrogant letter to the University.[79] As for his own responsibility in Karlstadt's banishment, Luther pointed out that he had had no direct dealings with the Elector concerning Karlstadt. He had communicated with the Elector through Spalatin and had insisted that the Allstedt spirit be suppressed. He admitted that after his meeting with Karlstadt in Jena and his encounter with his followers in Orlamünde, he had spoken with Duke John Frederick about his experiences and had urged him not to put up with Karlstadt and the Orlamünders, since their actions belied their words.[80] Frankly, Luther said, under the circumstances, he was happy that Karlstadt was no longer in Electoral Saxony,[81] but if Karlstadt would desist from his fanaticism and separate himself from the "heavenly prophets," he, for his part, would be willing to forget the past and do whatever he could for him. "I will gladly have him as friend if he will," Luther wrote. "If he will not, then I must leave it in God's hands."[82]

Luther branded as "pure falsehood" Karlstadt's statement that he had offered to be instructed, and cited a number of instances when Karlstadt had, on the contrary, refused to be instructed. While Luther was on the Wartburg, Karlstadt had refused to listen to Melanchthon; when Luther returned to Wittenberg, Karlstadt had refused to listen to him, too, and had not heeded the efforts of mediation by Justus Jonas and Dietrich of Bila. At Jena, Karlstadt had dismissed Luther as being nothing to him, and at Orlamünde he had answered Wolfgang Stein, who was court preacher and acting as a representative of the prince, as if he, Karlstadt, were prince in the land.[83] Moreover, Karlstadt had been sufficiently instructed by Luther's wrtings against the Allstedt spirit and by Luther's judgment that the spirit of these prophets was the spirit of the devil. This, too, he had not heeded.[84] Luther concluded that Karlstadt's offers to be instructed were merely a "smokescreen for his obdurate mind."[85]

Luther's final judgment on Karlstadt was particularly harsh:

There is no earnestness nor truth in what this spirit proposes. They do not even themselves believe what they say, nor keep what they promise, except this, that the devil seeks only to cause trouble in the world.

Luther even interpreted Karlstadt's vacillation under pressure as a sure sign of his insincerity:

For when Dr. Karlstadt was last in Wittenberg he willingly agreed to leave the pastorate, since he saw that nothing else would do, and promised then that he would return to Wittenberg. Had he then been certain that he had been called to be pastor, he should not have given it up, but rather have given up his life, as until then he had struggled and defended himself.[86]

Finally, Luther turned to Karlstadt's attack on the term "mass" and on the practice of the elevation of the host. Using sarcasm, ridicule, and *reductio ad absurdum* to devastating effect, Luther destroyed Karlstadt's argument that "mass" meant sacrifice and that the elevation of the sacrament meant that they were offering it as a sacrifice. Luther charged that Karlstadt was once more making an external matter into an article of faith.[87] To spite Karlstadt, Luther was willing to call the mass a sacrifice, and he in fact retained the elevation of the sacrament until 1542, the year after Karlstadt died.[88]

In Part II of *Against the Heavenly Prophets*, Luther dealt at length with Karlstadt's treatises on the Lord's Supper, at the same time repeating many of the characterizations of Karlstadt and Karlstadt's motivation that are found in Part I. He began by rehearsing his contention that the heavenly prophets made external matters more important than internal matters, and thereby bound men's consciences to what was superficial while ignoring what was essential, such as faith and love. Karlstadt's attack on the term "sacrament" was dismissed as another word game typical of Karlstadt, and then Luther enunciated a principle that he was to follow throughout his career:

Therefore, my brother, listen to me. You know that for the sake of every article of the Christian faith including that of Christian freedom we ought to be willing to risk body and soul. Therefore do what is prohibited and allow what is commanded by those opposing freedom.[89]

It was the Christian's duty, in a word, to defy the devil.

The concluding pages of the second part are filled as much with *ad hominem* ridicule as they are with refutation of Karlstadt's arguments on the Lord's Supper. And it must be admitted that in a number of his arguments, Karlstadt earned the ridicule he received. In his refutation, Luther was operating explicitly on this principle of exegesis: "Where Holy Scripture is the ground of faith we are not to deviate from the words as they stand nor from the order in which they stand, unless an express article of faith compels a different interpretation or order."[90] He charged Karlstadt with violating this principle and bringing his own ideas and the arguments of "whore reason" to Scripture.

There was, for example, Karlstadt's assertion that the words "This is my body" were independent of the words "take, eat" that follow. Luther rejected with open contempt Karlstadt's argument, which was based upon the punctuation and capitalization in the verse.[91] Similarly, he dismissed as ridiculous Karlstadt's exegesis of the word *touto* ("this" in "This is my body"), which Karlstadt said referred to Christ's body rather than to the bread, and rejected Karlstadt's advocacy of a "spiritual eating," that is, a remembrance of the body of Christ.[92] Finally, he attacked five reasons derived from Frau Hulda (a personification of natural reason called by Luther the devil's whore) that Karlstadt allegedly adduced against the real presence.[93]

In the course of this refutation, Luther had much to say about Karlstadt's person and motivation. Repeatedly he insisted that the devil was "riding" Karlstadt, motivating and directing his behavior.[94] Karlstadt was lying against his own conscience, driven to such hypocrisy by the devil,[95] who wished to discredit Luther by lumping him with the papists so he could destroy everything God had accomplished through Luther. He became particularly incensed by what he perceived to be Karlstadt's willful distortions of Luther's position.[96]

The concluding pages contain the strongest judgment about Karlstadt of any in the whole treatise: "All right, I will take an oath. If Dr. Karlstadt believes there is any God in heaven or on earth, may Christ my Lord never more be merciful and gracious to me." Luther had reached this conclusion, he said, because of Karlstadt's attacks on the "whispering and breathing over the bread" (that is, the words of institution):

Tell me, if someone certainly knows that it is a Word of God and yet dares consciously to noise abroad with disdain and ridicule that it is a human whispering and breathing, thus perverting the poor mob by such lies and poison, and does this without any fear or trembling and shows no contrition for it, but rather feels joy and glee in such wickedness, as if God would give him a crown for such blasphemy and perversion of souls and dub him a knight of grace, how can such a one believe or think that there can be any God?[97]

For Luther the question, like the reply, was merely rhetorical, but Karlstadt and those sympathetic to his position were certain to take offense.

By the close of 1524 Luther had concluded that Müntzer and Karlstadt shared a "devilish spirit," whose fruits were rebellion and murder, the destruction of images, and contempt for the sacraments. Out of conviction and out of concern for his and the gospel's reputation, he tried to make clear that he and his teachings were in complete opposition to this spirit. With respect to Karlstadt this was especially difficult and at the same time of crucial importance. The problem was forcefully stated by the Strasbourg jurist Nicholas Gerbel:

The papists are seizing on this as an opportunity for all sorts of contumely. No Faber, Eck, or Emser has done more damage to your venture than this one Karlstadt, since the popular opinion prevailed among everyone to this point that you two appeared united on all matters, on all judgments, in short, on all your activities. Meanwhile, however, those who began to prosper in Christ cling to the middle, vacillate, and waver about whom they ought to follow, you or him, since they previously believed that you both professed the same doctrine.[98]

People did not know whom to follow, and could be misled by Karlstadt, believing erroneously that he advocated the same position as did Luther. Karlstadt could even trade on this confusion, using it to promote and further his own cause.

To distinguish himself unequivocally from the false brethren and to disclaim responsibility for them, Luther supplemented his theological arguments with claims about himself and what he had accomplished, using himself as an example of the proper preaching of the gospel. But he also attacked the motives and behavior of his opponents, impugning their doctrine by maligning its advocates.

Dominating his *ad hominem* attacks was the conviction that these opponents were motivated by a common satanic spirit. This belief had fateful consequences for Luther's polemics and for the course of his disputes with evangelical opponents throughout his life, and found its most telling expression in his practice of attacking this spirit rather than the opponents themselves, leading him to impute similar characteristics to all his evangelical opponents and to hold any one of them responsible for the views and misdeeds of all. Although Luther attempted to meet and refute the specific arguments advanced by certain opponents, his conviction that they all shared the satanic spirit freed him for the most part from ever having to take their arguments seriously. The deficiencies in the arguments of his less competent opponents offset the strengths in the arguments of his more competent opponents and made it easier for him to dismiss all the arguments of all his opponents.

Supporting the conviction that his evangelical opponents were motivated by a common satanic spirit was Luther's belief that he was involved in a metaphysical struggle. He stated the paradigm succinctly: Satan always first attacked the gospel with force, and when that failed, he attacked it with false brethren and false teachings. So it was in the beginning and in Luther's age as well.[99] Believing that his mortal opponents were but puppets of the devil, Luther felt free and even obligated to attack with the full force of his polemic ability and personality.

⸭ 3 ⸭

The Peasants' War

In the spring of 1525 the unrest known as the Peasants' War spread from southern Germany northward into Thuringia. Thomas Müntzer, after a tour of southern Germany, had settled down once again in Mühlhausen, where he was playing an active role in its radical politics. In southern Germany there appeared the most famous peasant document, the *Twelve Articles*.[1] The first and twelfth articles show the influence of the reformation movement: the first requested that the entire community have the power and authority to choose and appoint a pastor, and the twelfth offered to withdraw any of the previous eleven articles that was shown to be contrary to Scripture. Sandwiched between these two articles, however, were ten articles dealing with such things as tithing, serfdom, fishing and game laws, woodcutting, feudal services, rents, new laws, communal fields, and the death tax. Other treatises also appeared, some mentioning Luther by name.[2]

When Luther received a copy of the *Twelve Articles*, he felt it his duty to publish a reply, and this he did with two purposes in mind. One purpose, of course, was to correct those who misunderstood the gospel. But because of the appeal made by the treatises to Luther and the gospel, Catholics were laying responsibility for the uprisings and disorders directly at Luther's door, charging that his teachings led inexorably to sectarian unrest, violence, and insurrection and accusing him of aiding and encouraging rebellion.[3] Luther's replies show clearly that another purpose of the replies was to dissociate himself from the peasants, especially those who appealed to him or to the gospel, and to disclaim responsibility for any of their misdeeds.

The *Admonition to Peace* was Luther's direct reply to the *Twelve Articles* and to some second document, probably the so-called *Memmingen Agreement* adopted by the Swabian peasants in early March, in which Luther was appealed to by name.[4] The *Admonition* is divided into three sections. The first section addresses the princes and lords, the second the peasants and their *Twelve Articles,* the third both lords and peasants. In his introduction Luther explained that he was writing because the peasants in their twelfth article expressed willingness to accept instruction on the basis of Scripture. "I do this in a friendly and Christian spirit, as a duty of brotherly love, so that if any misfortune or disaster comes out of this matter, it may not be attributed to me, nor will I be blamed before God and men because of my silence."[5] Luther saw the rebellion as a very serious matter involving both the kingdom of God and the kingdom of the world, and he feared the permanent destruction of all Germany. "For the many terrible signs that are seen both in heaven and on earth point to a great disaster and a mighty change in Germany."[6]

In the first section, addressed to the princes and rulers, Luther blamed the unfortunate state of affairs on their persecution of the gospel and their treatment of their subjects. God was expressing his wrath by sending many false teachers and prophets among them; and if they would not yield voluntarily to God's Word, then they would be compelled by force and destruction to do so. Luther vehemently denied any responsibility for the revolt:

You, and everyone else, must bear witness that I have taught with all quietness, have striven earnestly against rebellion, and have energetically encouraged and exhorted people to obey and respect even you wild and dictatorial tyrants. This rebellion cannot be coming from me. Rather the murder-prophets, who hate me as they hate you, have come among these people and have gone about among them for more than three years, and no one has resisted and fought against them except me.[7]

Luther advised them to give way. Some of the twelve articles were eminently just. The princes should show kindness and thereby secure peace.

In the second section, addressed to the peasants, Luther admitted that many of their demands were just, but the justice of their demands did not justify their recourse to the sword. Rebellion and the taking of justice into one's own hands was contrary "not only to Christian law and the gospel, but also to natural law and all equity."[8] Moreover, they were blaspheming the name of Christ by quoting the gospel to justify their demands when in fact the gospel taught submission to the authorities and the endurance of suffering, injustice, and evil. He warned that false prophets and prophets of murder had been sent among them by the devil to lead them astray.[9]

Luther rebuked the peasants and pointed to himself as an example of proper Christian conduct:

Now what have I done that the more pope and emperor raged, the more my gospel spread? I have never drawn a sword or desired revenge. I began neither conspiracy nor rebellion, but so far as I was able, I have helped the worldly rulers—even those who persecuted the gospel and me—to preserve their power and honor. I stopped with committing the matter to God and relying confidently at all times upon His hand. This is why God has not only preserved my life in spite of the pope and all the tyrants—and this many consider a really great miracle, as I myself must also confess— but He has made my gospel grow and spread.[10]

The peasants should leave the name Christian out of their demands, or else Luther would oppose them as enemies who, under the name of the gospel, acted contrary to it and wished to suppress it.[11] The reason was clear:

For I see well that the devil, who has not been able to destroy me through the pope, now seeks to exterminate me and swallow me up by means of the bloodthirsty prophets of murder and spirits of rebellion that are among you. Well, let him swallow me! I will give him a bellyful, I know. And even if you win, you will hardly enjoy it!

Luther was certain that his cause was just and right, for he fought in behalf of the name Christian, and he warned the peasants therefore to take care lest he be forced to pray against them, for God would certainly hear and act on his prayer. He was equally certain that the peasants' cause was unjust and that they could not be praying for its success:

You cannot have such confidence and assurance in prayer because your conscience and the Scriptures testify that your enterprise is heathenish, and not Christian, and, under the name of the gospel, works against the gospel and brings contempt upon the name Christian. I know that none of you has ever once prayed to God or called upon him in behalf of this cause.[12]

They ought to trust in God, not in the sword, but since they did not, their appeal to the gospel was a sham and nothing more than an attempt to give their unevangelical and un-Christian enterprise an evangelical appearance.

Finally, Luther admonished both the rulers and the peasants that there was nothing Christian on either side: "For both of you are wrong, and both of you want to avenge and defend yourselves, both of you will destroy yourselves and God will use one rascal to flog another."[13] The rulers were tyrants, the peasants rebels; both stood condemned in the Scriptures.[14] Luther advised them to arbitrate their dispute and settle it amicably. The rulers should "give these poor people room in which to live and air to breathe."[15]

If rulers and peasants would not follow his advice, Luther had to let them come to blows. But he refused to take any responsibility for the results. He had warned them. He wrote that he would pray for reconciliation, but the "terrible signs and wonders that have come to pass in these times" gave him a heavy heart and made him fear that God's wrath had grown too great. "Would to God that you might fear His wrath and amend your ways that this disaster might be delayed and postponed a while!" Luther concluded. "In any case, my conscience assures me that I have faithfully given you my Christian and fraternal advice. God grant that it helps!"[16]

The so-called Weingarten Treaty made between the Swabian League and the Lake Constance Association was published on 22 April. A copy soon reached Luther, who found it a salutary example "in this desolate, horrible time which the devil has served up through his fanatics and murderous prophets."[17] He immediately had it reprinted with his own foreword and afterword in the hope that the local peasants would follow its example and reach agreement with the authorities before God Himself punished their "horrible raging undertaken against both divine and human law." Luther's sympathies obviously had shifted toward the authorities. "No one can deny," Luther wrote in his afterword, that our peasantry has no just cause, rather they laden themselves with enormous, grievous sins and arouse God's terrible and unbearable wrath over them, for they are breaking their trust, obedience, oath, and responsibility that they made and swore to their authorities and are falling into disobedience, setting themselves wantonly against the power ordained and commanded by God, revenging themselves, and taking the sword on the basis of their own wickedness and presumption.[18]

But it was not enough for the peasants to rage against God's order; they also plundered, robbed, and took as they wished like public highwaymen and murderers. And worst of all, they committed such misdeeds under the name Christian and under the cloak of the gospel. Woe to the damned false prophets who lead astray the poor simple people to such detriment of their souls and perhaps also to the loss of their lives and goods! Luther urged the peasants to cease their crimes, for in the long run they would have to lose both body and soul. Instead they should make peace and reach an agreement, even if it meant material losses, so that the sins and the destruction of souls might cease.[19]

Presumably Luther had finished these two treatises, or at least the *Admonition*, before he began making various excursions from Eisleben (where he had gone to dedicate a new school) into the surrounding territory to preach against the insurrection and to warn against the influence of false prophets.[20] Peasant unrest had spread into the Thuringian area, and Luther's audiences were unruly, heckling him and interrupting his sermons. Luther was later to remark that he had been lucky to escape injury and even death, so hostile had his hearers been.[21] Upon his return to Wittenberg on 6 May and with these experiences still fresh in his mind, he wrote out his short and uncompromising *Against the Robbing and Murdering Hordes of Peasants*. This treatise was first published in one volume with the *Admonition to Peace* under the joint title *Admonition to Peace and Also Against the Robbing and Murdering Hordes of the Other Peasants*, Luther's intention being that the *Admonition* was directed to the "good" peasants and the *Against the Robbing* to the "bad" peasants.[22] Printers quickly split the two treatises, however, and *Against the Robbing and Murdering Hordes of Peasants*, its title no longer reflecting its relationship to *Admonition to Peace*, soon found wide circulation on its own, pleasing many of the more ruthless rulers while offending many friends as well as foes.

Since Luther had come to the conclusion that the *Twelve Articles* were nothing but lies presented in the name of the gospel and that the peasants were doing the devil's work and particularly the work of that "archdevil" Thomas Müntzer, he felt that it was his responsibility first to show the peasants wherein they sinned and then to advise the ruling authorities how they must act under these circumstances. This is the substance of *Against the Robbing and Murdering Hordes of Peasants*. The peasants had assumed the burden of three terrible sins against God and man, thereby abundantly meriting death in body and soul: they had violated their oaths of obedience to their rulers, oaths confirmed by Christ and St. Paul; they were in open rebellion, murdering, robbing, and plundering; and they cloaked their misdeeds—their service to the devil—under the name of the gospel.[23]

With these sins of the peasants in mind, Luther advised the temporal authorities how they might act with a clear conscience. First, Luther said that he would not oppose a ruler who, even though an enemy of the gospel, would smite and punish the rebellious peasants without prior judicial process. If the ruler was a Christian, however, he should first take his case to God in prayer, submitting the outcome to His will, and then "offer the mad peasants an opportunity to come to terms, even though they are not worthy of it."[24] If attempts at reconciliation failed, then such rulers should quickly take to the sword, as was their divinely imposed duty.

The rulers could act in good conscience, for they had a just cause; the peasants were acting in bad conscience, for they had an unjust cause.

Thus, anyone who is killed fighting on the side of the rulers may be a true martyr in the eyes of God, if he fights with the kind of conscience I have just described, for he acts in obedience to God's Word. On the other hand, anyone who perishes on the peasants' side is an eternal firebrand of hell, for he bears the sword against God's Word and is disobedient to Him, and is a member of the devil.[25]

Even should the peasants prevail—and this God might allow as a prelude to the Last Day, which "cannot be far off"—their victims could die with a good conscience, confident that they would be part of the everlasting kingdom. "These are strange times," Luther wrote, "when a prince can win heaven with bloodshed better than other men with prayer!"[26]

At one point in this treatise, Luther even went so far as to say that anyone, and not just the constituted authorities, should slay a rebel, so heinous was the crime of rebellion:

> For if a man is in open rebellion, everyone is both his judge and executioner; just as when a fire starts, the first man who can put it out is the best man to do the job. For rebellion is not just simple murder; it is like a great fire, which attacks and devastates a whole land. Thus rebellion brings with it a land filled with murder and bloodshed; it makes widows and orphans, and turns everything upside down, like the worst disaster.

Luther's advice was harsh indeed: "Therefore let everyone who can, smite, slay, and stab, secretly or openly, remembering that nothing can be more poisonous, hurtful, or devilish than a rebel."[27]

As a further reason for the rulers to act, Luther pointed to the fact that the peasants were compelling many good people to join their "devilish league" against their wills and thereby damning them. "Anyone who consorts with them," he wrote, "goes to the devil with them and is guilty of all the evil deeds that they commit, even though he has to do this because he is so weak in faith that he could not resist them."[28] The rulers therefore had the responsibility to rescue these poor men.

Coloring the treatise throughout was Luther's belief that the end of the world was imminent. He suspected that the devil had broken loose so violently because he felt that the Last Day was coming. Not a devil was left in hell, Luther contended; they had all gone into the peasants.[29] And to explain and, perhaps, to justify his strident tone, Luther concluded his treatise: "If anyone thinks this too harsh, let him remember that rebellion is intolerable and that destruction of the world is to be expected every hour."[30]

On 15 May Thomas Müntzer proved unable to capture the bullets in his sleeve as he had promised he could do and the peasants were routed at Frankenhausen. Müntzer was captured the same day while hiding in bed. News of his capture and of other events reached Luther quickly.[31] On 21 May John Rühel, a jurist in the service of the counts of Mansfeld and Luther's good friend, sent Luther further news telling how Müntzer, "without doubt to play the hypocrite to the godless tyrants," had recanted, had accepted the sacrament in one kind, and had become completely papistic. Rühel also commented on the miserable fate of the peasants killed and captured at Frankenhausen, and expressed fear that the princes might fulfill Luther's prophecy (in his *Admonition to Peace*) and leave a wasteland to their descendants.[32]

Luther immediately sent a reply to Rühel thanking him for the news, especially about Müntzer. "Please let me have further details about his capture and how he acted," the letter said, "for it is profitable to know how that haughty spirit behaved himself." The peasants' fate was pitiful but necessary and according to God's will, for unless people were properly frightened, Satan would do even more harm. Those who took the sword perished by the sword. It was reassuring to Luther that the spirit had been revealed "so that the peasants will know from now on how wrong they were and perhaps cease their rioting or at least reduce it."[33]

Soon after Müntzer's capture, Luther published several of Müntzer's writings with a commentary of his own. His intent was to reveal to the world Müntzer's true spirit and motivation,

to warn, to terrify, and to admonish all those who now promote rebellion and discord and to comfort and to strengthen all those who must see and suffer such affliction so that they understand and perceive how God condemns the fanatics and rebels and how He is willing to punish [them] with His wrath. For here you see how this murdering spirit boasts that God speaks and works through them and that this is His divine will. And he acts as if he had already won, and before he looks around, he is lying in the mud with some thousand others. If God had spoken through him, such a thing would not have happened, for God does not lie but rather holds to His Word. Now that Thomas Müntzer has failed, however, it is clear that under the cover of God's name he had spoken and acted through the devil.[34]

Along with a famous manifesto of Müntzer's in which he urged the brethren to hunt down and slay the godless,[35] Luther published two defiant and threatening letters from Müntzer to Counts Ernst and Albrecht of Mansfeld, and the letter from the "Christian Assembly at Frankenhausen" to Count Albrecht in which they responded favorably to the Count's suggestion for a meeting. Luther added marginalia to the manifesto and to the letter to Count Ernst, and commented in his afterword to this collection that Müntzer was responsible for blocking Count Albrecht's attempt at reconciliation.

The poor people, confident that the Holy Spirit had been speaking through Müntzer, had been misled and in consequence more than five thousand had lost their lives and souls. According to Luther, this was what the devil intended and what he was seeking with respect to all the other rebellious peasants. He was not, he said, taking pleasure in Müntzer's misfortune, but he was happy that God's judgment on Müntzer was showing Luther and his followers with certainty that Müntzer's teaching was hateful to God and condemned by Him.[36] It should be a warning to people to be more careful in the future.

In his closing words Luther asked his readers to pray that God ward off the devil and stay His wrath. The situation was so far advanced that sermons and treatises no longer helped and only prayer was efficacious. Addressing the rulers and authorities, Luther asked first that they continue to fear God even in their victories, which were granted them not because they were pious but because God wished to punish the disobedience and blasphemy of the peasants; he also asked that they show mercy to those whom they captured or who surrendered to them, lest the tide change and the peasants be allowed by God to regain the upper hand.

On 26 May Rühel sent Luther further details about Müntzer's behavior before and after his capture, recounting how Müntzer had exhorted the peasant army to rely on God's strength and had told them that help was on the way and that when they reached Count Ernst's castle at Heldrungen not one stone would remain on another and those inside would yield. When the first shot from the encircling army fell short, Müntzer had cried out: "I prophesied that no shot would do you injury!" But the subsequent shots had the range, and Müntzer and the peasant army took to their heels. Müntzer was soon found in the city. Subsequently he was questioned by Duke George and Duke Heinrich of Braunschweig, and Landgraf Philipp of Hesse debated with him for a time, Müntzer relying on the Old Testament and Philipp on the New. In his closing remarks Rühel touched on a subject that was of concern to many of Luther's followers:

Be it as it may, it seems strange to many of your supporters that you have given permission to the tyrants to strangle [the peasants] without mercy, thereby possibly making martyrs out of them. And they say publicly in Leipzig that since the Elector [Frederick the Wise] has died, you fear for your skin and play the hypocrite to Duke George by approving of what he is doing.

Rühel did not credit these accusations but he expected that Luther would eventually have to issue an apology on the subject.[37]

In his reply to Rühel's letter, Luther showed his annoyance with the critics of the book he had written against the peasants:

That the people call me a hypocrite is good; I am glad to hear it; do not let it surprise you. For some years now you have been hearing me berated for many things, but in the course of time all these things have come to nothing and worse than nothing. I should need much leather to muzzle all the mouths. It is enough that my conscience is clear before God; He will judge what I have said and written; things will go as I have said, there is no help for it.

Luther was unsympathetic to the plight of those caught up in the rebellion. God would protect the innocent; if men were executed or killed, they certainly were not innocent, but had approved of the rebellion if only by keeping silent and thereby denying Christ through fear. One reason, he explained, for the harshness of his writings was that the peasants compelled these "fearful souls" to do their will and thereby to incur God's punishment.

Luther also criticized the way in which Müntzer was interrogated. He would have asked very different questions. Müntzer's confession was nothing else than a devilish, hardened persistence in his opinion. "He says in his confession that he had done no wrong," Luther wrote. "That is terrible. I should not have thought a human heart

could be so hardened." Anyone who had seen Müntzer, Luther concluded, could say that he had seen the devil himself and at his worst.[38]
One gets the impression that Luther was disappointed that an unusual opportunity to talk directly with the devil had been poorly
handled.

In a letter to Amsdorf, Luther gave further vent to his feelings
about his ungrateful detractors in this "adulterous generation." They
called him a flatterer of princes, Luther wrote, but Satan had conferred many such honorary titles on him during the past years. His
detractors were merely displaying their bloodthirsty and seditious
spirit when they passed judgment on him. Satan was out to get him:

For what are these [know-it-alls] but the voices of Satan, by which he
tries to disgrace me and the gospel? He, who has thus far so often beaten
Satan under my feet, and has broken to pieces the lion and the dragon,
will not allow the basilisk to tread on me. So, let them roar. My [our]
conscience is certain that whatever came from my lips in this matter is
right before God.[39]

But the clamor for some explanation of his treatises went on as
before, and on Pentecost, June 4, Luther finally made a public response to the "idle ranters" who objected to his advice that one
should freely strike and kill the peasants, and to the "pious hearts"
who were in doubt because he had advocated that mercy and love be
shown to friend and enemy alike while he condoned and advocated
slaying and killing.

A part of Luther's Pentecost sermon was devoted to explaining
this apparent inconsistency. He told his congregation that a murderer was, in fact, much more pious than a rebel, since he attacked
the members of the societal body but not the head. A murderer fled
from the constituted authorities which were instituted by God, but
a rebel attacked them. And though a murderer was responsible for
one death, a rebel brought about thousands of deaths.

Each subject had a duty to protect his rulers, and therefore a duty
to defend his rulers from the attack of a rebel. And since in rebellion the danger to the rulers was immediate, subjects did not need
to wait, and should not wait, for the rulers' command to act, but
should act freely and immediately in their rulers' defense. This ad-

vice applied only to an attack on the rulers themselves, not to an attack on their property.

In conclusion, Luther said that he did not care that some accused him of being a flatterer of princes. His responsibility as a preacher was not to wield the sword and punish injustices but to teach and wield the Word, which was his sword. This he had done. He had admonished the rulers to be just to their subjects and had pointed out to them that if they did not do this and dealt unfairly and unjustly with their subjects, they would have their own Lord and judge to answer to. Luther's major responsibility now was to help consciences and to justify those who fought to defend the authorities.[40]

This sermon lacked the circulation, and perhaps the arguments, to still Luther's critics. In mid-June Luther exclaimed to some of Count Albrecht's officials:

What a hullabaloo, my dear sirs, has been caused by my pamphlet against the peasants! All is now forgotten that God has done for the world through me. Now lords, parsons, and peasants are all against me and threaten my death.*

And he wrote to Wenzel Link:

I know that my book gives great offence to the peasants and the friends of the peasants, and that is a real joy to me, for if it gave them no offence it would give me great offence. Those who condemn this book are merely showing what it is that they have hitherto sought in the gospel. But I am surprised that some of the knowing ones do not apply the whole book to themselves, for it shows very clearly who the peasants are and who the magistrates are of whom it speaks. But he that will not understand, let him not understand; he that will not know, let him be ignorant; it is enough that my conscience pleases Christ.[41]

As it turned out, Luther finally decided that he had not said enough. In late June or early July he issued a public reply to his critics in the form of an open letter to Kaspar Müller, the chancellor of Mansfeld. This reply, *An Open Letter on the Harsh Book Against the Peasants*, was as much an attack on his critics as a defense of his book.

* WABr 3: 531; translation in *Luther's Correspondence and Other Contemporary Letters*, trans. and ed. Preserved Smith and Charles M. Jacobs (Philadelphia, 1918), 2: 323 (hereafter cited as S-J). In this same letter, Luther announced that he had married Kathrine von Bora, implying that he had done so to spite his critics.

His critics, he said, had boasted that he revealed his true spirit by teaching bloodshed without mercy, and they argued that the devil was speaking through him. But, he made answer, his critics in their very criticism revealed their own spirit: "For the man who thus sympathizes with the rebels makes it perfectly clear that he has decided in his heart that he will also cause disaster if he has the opportunity." His critics and those who sympathized with the rebels were rebels themselves at heart.[42]

Luther's critics demanded mercy for them now that the peasants were defeated; but where, he asked, were their pleas for mercy when the peasants had had the upper hand? The peasants were getting their earned deserts, and his critics were attempting to obstruct justice; they wished to do away with proper punishment:

Here you see the intention of those who condemn my book as though it forbade mercy. It is certain that they are either peasants, rebels, and bloodhounds themselves, or have been misled by such people; for they would like all wickedness to go unpunished.[43]

Luther pointed out that he had always advocated that once the peasants had surrendered, they be shown mercy.[44]

The next section of his open letter was addressed to those who were misled by the "bloodhounds" or who were too weak to reconcile Luther's book with the words of Christ. In this section he discussed the differences between the two kingdoms, the kingdom of God and the kingdom of the world. God's kingdom was a kingdom of grace and mercy; the kingdom of the world was a kingdom of wrath and severity. "Now he who would confuse these two kingdoms—as our false fanatics do—" Luther wrote, "would put wrath into God's kingdom and mercy into the world's kingdom; and that is the same as putting the devil in heaven and God in hell."[45] First they wished to fight for the gospel as "Christian Brethren" and kill other people; then, once the kingdom of the world had overcome them, they wished to ask mercy of it. Furthermore, by opposing the punishment of the peasants, these people were denying mercy to those who were victims of the peasants. For if the peasants had not been constrained by the temporal sword, no honest man would have been safe from them.[46]

Repeatedly, Luther reminded his critics that he had not advocated the merciless slaying of the peasants who were conquered or captured:

I made it plain that I was speaking of those who were first approached in a friendly way, and would not respond. All my words were directed against the obdurate, hardened, blinded peasants, who would neither see nor hear, as anyone may see who reads them; and yet you say that I advocate the merciless slaughter of the poor captured peasants. If you are going to read my books this way and interpret them as you please, what book will have any chance with you?[47]

He also denied that he was responsible for the rulers' excesses. "If they are misusing their power," Luther contended, "they have not learned it from me; and they will have their reward."[48] God would punish them at the appropriate time. Moreover, his book against the peasants dealt with what the peasants deserved, not with what the lords deserved. "When I have time and occasion to do so, I shall attack the princes and lords, too," Luther said, "for in my office of teacher, a prince is the same to me as a peasant."[49] He strongly disapproved of the cruelty shown by certain "raging tyrants" to the peasants, and was certain that these "furious, raving, senseless tyrants" would reap what they had sown and that "hell-fire, trembling, and gnashing of teeth in hell" would be their reward unless they repented.[50]

Luther also rehearsed some of the arguments that he had used in his Pentecost sermon. No injustice was done in punishing those who were forced by the peasants to participate, for they had the responsibility to resist. "If that excuse were accepted," Luther argued, "then there would be no more punishment of sin or crime; for where is there a sin to which the devil, the flesh, and the world do not drive us and, as it were, force us?"[51]

There were others besides Luther who had problems during the peasants' revolt. Karlstadt had found himself harried by peasants and by princes. Finally, on the eleventh or twelfth of June, he had arrived in Frankfurt am Main, where he had expected he could find shelter with his brother-in-law and supporter, Gerhard Westerburg. Unfortunately for Karlstadt, Westerburg had fled the city several weeks earlier to escape punishment for his participation in a city uprising.

Karlstadt was once again alone and in trouble, and in desperation he turned to Luther.

It was not entirely unreasonable for Karlstadt to look to Luther for succor. Six months earlier, while hot at work on the first part of his *Against the Heavenly Prophets*, Luther had received word from Melanchthon's close friend, the humanist and Graecist Joachim Camerarius, that Karlstadt wanted to meet with Luther and that he was suffering under his exile.[52] Apparently thinking that Karlstadt might recant, Luther had written to him immediately. The letter is now lost, but from other sources we can gather that Luther either suggested or agreed to a meeting in Electoral Saxony if it could be arranged with the Elector, and elsewhere if it could not. The purpose of this meeting may have been to see whether they could reach agreement on the disputed points of doctrine; it may also have been intended as a first step toward Karlstadt's eventual return to Electoral Saxony.[53]

Probably Luther sent this letter more out of a sense of responsibility not to overlook even the remotest chance that a fallen brother might recover than out of any real hope that reconciliation was possible. There is no indication, for instance, that he softened the attack he was preparing in *Against the Heavenly Prophets*, and two weeks after writing to Karlstadt he told John Briessmann, the evangelical preacher at Königsberg who knew Karlstadt from his student days at Wittenberg, that Karlstadt had been completely given over to the devil and was sinning unto death.[54] To Amsdorf Luther confided that Karlstadt was completely possessed by more than one devil.[55]

Then a letter arrived from Kaspar Glatz, Karlstadt's replacement at Orlamünde and no friend to the exile. Glatz reported that his fanatics at Orlamünde were using Luther's *Against the Heavenly Prophets* as toilet paper and were characterizing the treatise as entirely against Christ. And when he, Glatz, preached against these views, he was accused of being a flatterer of princes and a Martinian seducer. They were also maintaining their opposition to baptism, the Lord's Supper, and secular authority.

Glatz recounted several stories he had heard from "citizens who gladly hear the pure doctrine of faith, love, and the cross." Karlstadt, he said, had gathered together his congregation and peasants from the neighboring villages soon after Luther's visit in August and had preached,

> Lamentation to God in heaven! The man (he meant you) has a great reputation throughout the world; what he says is supposed to be true. But sad to say, I have observed by the spirit of God, that he does not use as a true servant the pound and the talent that God has given him, and he puts the gospel under the bench. O dear brothers and sisters, God's citizens, do not be terrified; endure to the end, and you shall be saved. God has given him up, and he perverts the Scriptures to suit his own opinions. O shame, shame, that we here on the Saale, who are taught by the living voice of God, must see the misery that is wrought by this monk and scribe![56]

Glatz went on to relate how Karlstadt had kept a monk for chaplain who went around in disguise, throwing rocks and boards, and who Karlstadt pretended was a spirit who wished to talk to him. Karlstadt would go away to talk to this "spirit" and then return with clumsy lies such as "Luther's doctrine is not of God and, therefore, must be shunned like the plague." This same monk supposedly hid himself in the church and rang the bells at an unusual hour, and when the people came running and wished to know what the spirit wanted, Karlstadt said that the spirit would not rest until they had taken away the pictures, the altar, the pulpit, the font, and the pyx and burned them to ashes.[57] Whatever the merits of this letter as a reliable report of Karlstadt's carryings-on, it was not questioned by Luther. It seems, in fact, to have confirmed his judgment of Karlstadt.[58] He sent copies of it to Spalatin, and reported on its contents to Link and Amsdorf.[59]

Perhaps because Karlstadt was in hiding in Rothenberg ob der Tauber, Luther's letter suggesting a meeting did not reach him until 18 February. Karlstadt responded the same day. If Luther had expected to receive a contrite, conciliatory reply, he was disappointed. Karlstadt expressed the desire to patch up the differences between them on the basis of the truth. Christ would help to overcome the division and disagreement that had arisen between them and that had caused great detriment to the church and hindered the progress of the gospel more than even Karlstadt had expected. If a safe-conduct for him could be arranged with the Saxon princes, he would "fly" to the meeting. But he would not take a step without the safe-conduct, for he had heard rumors that the princes did not wish him well, and this was something for which many would hold Luther responsible. "Why should I foolishly expose myself to so many dangers," Karlstadt asked, "when you are both willing and able to request a safe-conduct letter from the princes?" Karlstadt said that he would yield before the clear word of Christ and the enlightening judgment of the Lord. In a postscript he asked Luther to comfort his relatives about his exile and, in his closing words, he recalled Luther's promise to go into exile himself to effect a meeting if they could not meet in Saxony.[60]

Karlstadt's letter reached Luther on 2 March, and Luther immediately took steps to secure the promised safe-conduct.[61] He sent Karlstadt's letter to Spalatin together with a letter of his own for the Elector, and he requested Spalatin's aid in securing a limited safe-conduct from the princes so that the two men could parley. He was not, however, optimistic about the chances of the parley leading to anything:

For although I have little hope that Karlstadt may give way, having been puffed up and hardened by the approval of the mob, still I must undertake this so that he does not seize the opportunity to slander the gospel, for which they all are always and everywhere on the lookout, and also so that God sees and the world knows that we have not omitted anything that could serve to set these people right.[62]

He concluded his letter to the Elector by saying that he had faint hope for Karlstadt "since all his treatises sound so conceited."[63]

In view of Luther's obvious lack of enthusiasm for the meeting, it is not surprising that the Elector turned down the request. After some delay,* Spalatin sent Luther a formal letter explaining that to grant a safe-conduct to Karlstadt would violate the Elector's policy (and belie his standard response to the inquiries and complaints of the Catholic princes) not to involve himself in such matters. Furthermore, some people who did not understand the reason for the safe-conduct would erroneously conclude that the Elector supported Karlstadt's position, and the Elector had noted that Luther himself was not optimistic about the success of such a meeting.[64]

* Luther had to ask once why it was taking so long. WABr 3: 454.

Luther was frankly relieved by the refusal. "I am pleased that the Prince has refused the safe-conduct for Karlstadt," Luther wrote to Spalatin in answer. "I shall accordingly send him your letter so that I shall be free of this wretched forlorn man." He referred once again to reports from Glatz about Karlstadt's behavior in Orlamünde and expressed his regret for having any dealings with Karlstadt. "When will I ever finally wise up, having exposed myself because of my naïveté to tricks, laughter, perfidy, deceit, and mockery?"[65]

So the matter rested until mid-June when Karlstadt, now in desperate straits, wrote a long letter to Luther in the hope that Luther's earlier offer of a meeting and a possible reconciliation still held. He begged Luther to forgive him for everything "in which, motivated by the old Adam, I sinned against you," and he asked Luther to take pity on his poor wife and child and to arrange for them all to be able to return to their proper home, explaining that he had nowhere else to turn in this time of confusion and insurrection. He admitted having answered Luther's *Against the Heavenly Prophets*, but confessed that had he known what he now did about the world, he would not have replied. If his response had offended Luther, he was willing to be chastised, and he announced his decision to refrain in the future from writing, preaching, or lecturing.[66] Either at his own initiative or at Luther's suggestion in a letter now lost,[67] he also wrote his *Apology of Dr. Andreas Karlstadt for the False Reputation of Insurrection Which Is Unjustly Attributed to Him* and sent it with his wife to Luther, who published it shortly thereafter with his own foreword.

Somewhat curiously, since it was Luther who arranged for the publication of the *Apology*, Karlstadt at the outset of this attempt to clear himself held Luther partly responsible for the widespread belief that he and Müntzer were in agreement:

... I fear that the reverend, honorable, and learned Dr. M. Luther is partially at fault [since] he described me in his public writings as a fanatic and agitator and called me a companion of Müntzer's. And he did all this with such powerful words and well-put language that the simple folk could not believe anything else than that I was responsible for the Müntzerite insurrection.[68]

Karlstadt then specifically disavowed any association with Müntzer, noting in his defense the various rebuffs with which he and his congregation at Orlamünde had met Müntzer's advances. He also rejected the charge that he was one of the leaders of the rebellious peasants in Rothenburg or in Franconia and related how, in fact, the peasants had mistreated and abused him and his family during his exile. He hoped that the princes and rulers would accept his explanation, but even if they did not, he would still maintain his innocence, knowing that God would hold a judgment at which princes and rulers, burghers and peasants would have to answer for that which they had earned on Karlstadt's account.[69]

Luther's foreword to the *Apology* showed generosity to the humbled Karlstadt but surrendered no principles. Luther related how Karlstadt had sent him the *Apology* and had begged him earnestly to see that it was published so that Karlstadt could clear his name of the charge of rebellion and not be judged guilty of this charge "unheard and unconvicted."* He explained that even though Karlstadt was his greatest enemy in the matter of doctrine, he wished to return the trust that Karlstadt had shown in appealing to him by coming to Karlstadt's aid in this matter. This would be no more than following Christ's command and example that all Christians should love their enemies, and his conscience would not allow him to act otherwise. Moreover, he still hoped that Karlstadt might abandon his error in the matter of the Lord's Supper and return to the truth, for one should never despair of a man while he still lived—Christ might always work a miracle with him. Then Luther emphasized to his readers that despite this favor he was doing Karlstadt, he in no way wished to support or to approve of Karlstadt's teachings. On the contrary, he maintained his previously published position, and he asked that everyone guard himself against falling into Karlstadt's error. To those who were suspicious of Karlstadt's sincerity, Luther answered that love was not suspicious and that he would accept Karlstadt's explanation and claims until they were proved false. In his concluding paragraphs

* *"Unverhort und unüberzeugt"* (WA 18: 436, 10). Luther's use of this phrase may be ironic, since Karlstadt had used the same phrase in describing his expulsion from Electoral Saxony. See p. 47n above.

he laid most of the blame for the rebellion on the princes and bishops who had refused to appoint proper and pious preachers of the gospel to instruct the common man. God had therefore allowed seditious preachers to work their influence among the common people.[70]

Soon after Karlstadt's wife arrived, perhaps as early as the end of June, Luther secretly took in Karlstadt as well. Only his famulus, Wolf Sieberger, and later his wife, Käthie, knew of Karlstadt's presence in the former cloister, now Luther's residence.

Karlstadt could not remain hidden indefinitely in Luther's house. Eventually, the Elector would have to be persuaded to allow Karlstadt to establish a residence of his own in Electoral Saxony. Getting the Elector's consent meant, it seems, that Karlstadt had to do more than clear himself from responsibility for the recent uprising. He was required also publicly to recant his divergent teachings on the Lord's Supper.[71] Karlstadt therefore prepared an *Explanation of How Karlstadt Regards and Wishes His Teaching on the Highly Revered Sacrament and Other Matters to be Regarded*, which he completed and signed on 25 July.

The *Explanation* is not in fact a recantation, or it is only a qualified one, for Karlstadt contended that he had never proclaimed the certainty of his teachings and that people erred when they accepted them as certain without checking them against Holy Scripture:

Not only in this article on the highly revered Sacrament ... but in all matters on which I have written, on the mass, on idols, and on other articles, I wish the following: no one should think that my teaching is good, right, true, godly, or wholesome, unless he is certain of this on the basis of the wholesome Word of God, for I wish my writing to be judged according to and on the basis of God's Word.[72]

Karlstadt, admitting that he was not the best scriptural exegete, maintained that it was a grievous error to accept teachings because they were advocated by this or that man, be he Karlstadt or Zwingli or someone else.[73] But though he himself rejected, and requested his readers to reject, anything in his writings that was based solely on his own opinions and ideas, he refused to recant anything in his books that was godly.[74] He explained that he had not intended his treatises on the Supper for publication but that they had been published by a friend.[75] He expressed some surprise at the report that Zwingli accepted his teaching on the Lord's Supper but rejected his particular arguments, since he had cited the passage in John ("the flesh accomplishes nothing") which Zwingli reportedly believed was the strongest support for his interpretation.[76]

Luther's role in instigating the writing of this *Explanation* is unclear. Karlstadt was living with Luther at the time he wrote the treatise, and certainly the two men discussed the issues with each other. On 19 July, six days before Karlstadt signed the treatise, Luther wrote to a friend that he had not yet despaired of Karlstadt.[77] Sometime after mid-August Luther confided to his friend John Briessmann that he was secretly harboring Karlstadt, for whom the world had become too small and so filled with persecutions that he had been forced to seek shelter with his enemy, namely, Luther. "I treated that man in as friendly a way as I could, and helped him," Luther wrote. "But, as is usual with this type of spirit, he does not abandon his opinion, even when he is convicted [of his error]." Luther warned Briessmann against Karlstadt and his teachings: "I have found out that all [his writings] are valueless, especially in this matter."[78] Apparently Luther was now less sanguine about the chances of Karlstadt's improvement. If, by the time this letter was written, Luther had Karlstadt's *Explanation* in his hands, then it would seem that the treatise was not particularly satisfactory to Luther, which is hardly surprising. Nevertheless, Luther finally did intercede with the Elector, although Karlstadt may have had to push him a bit.[79] An agreement was reached in mid-September whereby Karlstadt was allowed to take up residence in the Wittenberg neighborhood. The price for this permission was a promise to foreswear any further preaching or writing for the rest of his life, and his *Explanation* (which was seen as a recantation) was to be published with a foreword by Luther.[80]

Luther's interpretation in the foreword was that Karlstadt's concessions were not merely an admission that his teachings should not be considered as certain, but demonstrated that they were false. True instructions by the Holy Spirit produces two virtues, Luther explained: a person so instructed is certain and sure of his position, and he will confess this position "courageously, freely, and confidently" in the face of death and the devil. Since Karlstadt, Zwingli, and others of their persuasion spoke on this matter of the Lord's Supper in terms of opinions and questions, Luther concluded that they certainly did not have the Spirit and therefore spoke from human fancy, not from the Holy Spirit. Nevertheless, because of Karlstadt's admission of uncertainty Luther could still harbor hope for his eventual return to the truth, and he saw it as his duty to help him and others of his ilk. "We who are certain in this matter have the responsibility," he wrote, "to help such vacillating and questioning hearts, to offer them our hand in their danger, to listen with friendliness to their questions and inquiries, their reasons and motives, and to refute their position with the Scriptures and help them out [of their error]."[81]

Luther's judgment on the rebellious spirit thus, in the autumn of 1525, stood vindicated by events. The spirit had driven Müntzer into rebellion and earned him a violent death at the hands of the authorities. It had prompted the Peasants' War, as Luther had anticipated. It had led Karlstadt into contempt for authority and an attack on the Lord's Supper, but God had humbled Karlstadt and forced him to admit the uncertainty of his teaching. Luther's evangelical opponents had all been brought low.

Luther's sense of personal responsibility for the gospel increased as he found himself attacked from within by other evangelicals and from without by those who held him responsible for the appearance of sects and for the revolt of the peasants. He had to disavow the false brethren and the rebellious peasants lest the gospel suffer by association. And in what he believed to be the final days before Judgment,[82] Luther attacked the devil and his minions without restraint. When, to his distress, he saw other evangelicals falling into Karlstadt's error, he concluded that they were possessed by the same spirit.

⸭ 4 ⸭

Against the Fanatics

In the autumn of 1524 Luther wrote to correspondents that Ulrich Zwingli and Leo Jud of Zurich were following Karlstadt's teachings on the Lord's Supper,[1] and early in 1525 he informed another correspondent that Karlstadt had converted John Oecolampadius, Konrad Pellican, and others in Basel as well as Otto Brunfels and other Strasbourgers.[2] So from the outset of the controversy with Zwingli and Oecolampadius, Luther believed that they were simply following Karlstadt when they denied that Christ's body and blood were physically present in the Lord's Supper. This belief shaped much of the controversy that followed, for it led Luther to attribute the same satanic spirit to these new opponents that he had previously attributed to Karlstadt, Müntzer, and the Zwickau prophets. His opponents, naturally enough, did not appreciate this, and they complained of it repeatedly in the exchanges that followed.

It was not surprising for Luther to conclude that Zwingli and Oecolampadius were simply following Karlstadt, although in fact their beliefs had been reached independently of Karlstadt, and rested frequently on different reasoning.[3] The crucial test Luther used to identify Karlstadt's "error" was a denial of the real presence of Christ's body and blood in the bread and wine of the Lord's Supper. A letter from the Wertheim preacher Franz Kolb, written in late August 1524, informed Luther of Zwingli's and Jud's understanding of the Supper, namely, that "when the eating of Christ's body is spoken of, nothing else is meant than to believe the Word that His body was given over to death for us."[4] Kolb elaborated on this contention, but its import for Luther remained the same. He wrote, "Zwingli of Zurich and Leo

Jud, among the Swiss, hold the same opinion as Karlstadt, so widespread is this evil."[5] By January 1525 Luther had come to the further conclusion that Oecolampadius, Pellican, and the French knight Anémond de Coct agreed with Karlstadt:

Oecolampadius and Pellican write that they agree with his [Karlstadt's] opinions, and Anémond de Coct is so obstinate that he threatens to write against me unless I give up my opinion. Behold Satan's portents! But as far as I can gather they are none of them convinced by Karlstadt's proofs, but rather by their own way of thinking. They previously held this opinion about the matter in question, but now they venture to speak it out more freely since they have found the author and a leader of this doctrine.[6]

Even though aware of Oecolampadius' and Pellican's rejection of Karlstadt's proofs, Luther still considered them to be in complete agreement with Karlstadt, and a few weeks later even stated that Karlstadt had converted these men to his position.[7] Their denial of the real presence of Christ's body and blood made all other differences between them and Karlstadt immaterial.

Luther was sustained in his opinion by reports from Strasbourg and by some of Zwingli's own writings. In March the Strasbourger Gerbel wrote twice linking Zwingli and Oecolampadius with Karlstadt and sent a copy of a letter on the Supper that Zwingli had written to Matthew Alber in Reutlingen in November 1524.[8] Although in this letter Zwingli disagreed with Karlstadt's interpretation of the words of institution in the Supper, he did so in a very friendly and complimentary fashion. "I gladly admit that I praise the zealous effort of this man [Karlstadt]," Zwingli wrote at one point. "However, even more I congratulate him for his faith from which he learned that one could be saved in no other way than through that faith by which we believe that Christ died for us."[9] Zwingli did fault Karlstadt's exegesis and deplored his immoderate language,[10] but by concurring with Karlstadt's conclusion, he fell heir in Luther's eyes to Karlstadt's spirit. In the same month of March Zwingli published his *Commentary on True and False Religion*, and in the following month excerpts from it and another treatise on the Lord's Supper were published in a German translation.[11] Once again he treated Karlstadt kindly, praising him, despite the ineptitude of Karlstadt's exegesis, for the faith that recognized that a physical presence could not be understood from the words of institution.[12] Small wonder that in July Luther warned John Hess, an evangelical preacher in Breslau, to "beware of the prophets who now wander about everywhere and, through the instigation of Karlstadt and Zwingli, think and speak most ill of the Eucharist,"[13] and in August alerted John Briessmann to "Karlstadt's or Zwingli's poison on the Sacrament."[14]

Though Luther commented in letters in 1524 and 1525 that Zwingli and Oecolampadius adhered to Karlstadt's error, he did not single out either man for public condemnation until September 1525 when, in his foreword to Karlstadt's *Explanation*, he briefly mentioned Zwingli and the uncertainty of belief he allegedly shared with Karlstadt. Meanwhile Zwingli had published his *Commentary on True and False Religion*, his letter to Matthew Alber of Reutlingen on the Lord's Supper, his *Rearguard or Supplement Concerning the Eucharist*, and several other treatises touching directly or peripherally on the Supper.[15] Oecolampadius, for his part, had addressed his *Genuine Exposition of the Words of the Lord, "This Is My Body," According to the Most Ancient Authors* to some of the Lutheran preachers in Upper Germany.[16]

Zwingli and Oecolampadius, though they advanced slightly different arguments to support their positions, were in substantial agreement in denying Christ's physical presence in the elements of the Lord's Supper. Specifically, they denied that Christ's body and blood were or even could be literally and physically present in the elements either through the transformation of the substance (as opposed to the accidents) of the bread and wine, or by "coexistence" in and under the bread and wine. They argued that the words spoken by Christ at the Last Supper ("Take, eat; this is my body which is given for you. Do this in memory of me," etc.) must be taken tropologically, symbolically, metaphorically, or as a metonymy, the words "This is my body" meaning "This represents my body" or "This is the sign of my body." They did acknowledge a real *spiritual* presence: Christ was truly present through and in the faith of the participants in the Supper. Hence they could even speak of a spiritual eating by faith, which was faith in Christ's act of redemption. But this presence was not tied to the elements, and it depended upon and was mediated by the faith of the communicants.

Underlying this tropological interpretation, especially in Zwingli's mind, was a very different understanding from Luther's of what the biblical concept of spirit and flesh entailed. For Zwingli it sharply distinguished man's soul from his body, and Christ's divinity from His humanity. If man's soul was a spiritual entity, it must have spirit as its object of trust and love, Zwingli contended, and could only be nourished by spiritual food. While insisting that he was not unduly separating Christ's divinity from His humanity, Zwingli argued that it was only Christ's divinity that could save man's soul. "Christ is our salvation by virtue of that part of his nature by which he came down from heaven," Zwingli wrote in his *Commentary on True and False Religion*, "not of that by which he was born of an immaculate virgin, though he had to suffer and die by this part; but unless he who died had also been God he could not have been salvation for the whole world."[17] Accordingly, if there were any special nourishment for the soul in the Lord's Supper (a view Zwingli adopted only late in the debate), the only possible source it could derive from was Christ's spiritual presence. Christ's body, a physical thing, could in no way nourish the soul.

Zwingli believed that he had found sure confirmation of this in the sixth chapter of the Gospel of John where Christ announced that "the spirit alone gives life; the flesh is of no avail."* This passage proved to Zwingli's satisfaction that Christ's physical presence in the elements of the Supper would be of no avail even if it were there. It was an absurdity, he concluded, and a backsliding into the papal error of transubstantiation to maintain that there was a bodily presence. Of course, Zwingli could, and did, adduce other arguments to buttress his position, arguments concerning the nature of a physical body, the fact that Christ in His body sat at the right hand of God, Christ's statement that He would no longer be in the world, and others.[18]

Although their different understandings of the concept of spirit and flesh constitute perhaps the most profound difference between the two

* Zwingli and Oecolampadius believed this to be their most persuasive text. The concept of spirit and flesh is at issue here.

factions, they also disagreed on the nature and efficacy of the Word, the relation between the two natures of Christ, the purposes of the Sacraments, the relation between reason and revelation, and a number of other issues both major and minor.*

At first Luther let his followers and supporters answer these men.[19] John Bugenhagen published a letter against Zwingli, and John Brenz, in the name of a group of Upper German preachers, composed the *Swabian Syngramma* in reply to Oecolampadius.[20] Zwingli and Oecolampadius each replied.[21]

The Strasbourg preachers, who were inclined to the position advocated by Zwingli and Oecolampadius, were distressed by the controversy and especially by what they saw as a rupture in the Christian fellowship,[22] and an uncharitable, immoderate stance taken by the Lutherans. In the hope of effecting reconciliation, or at least of moderating the public dispute, they sent the Hebraist Gregory Casel to Wittenberg in the autumn of 1525 to confer with Luther.[23]

In Casel's letter of introduction to Luther, the Strasbourg preachers expressed their concern about the unfavorable impact the dispute was having, especially outside the borders of Germany. They had sent Casel, they said, in hope of preserving the unity of the church and preventing the growth of discord in order that there might be a united front in the battle against Catholicism:

> For our lamented adversaries are only now beginning to have some new hope, persuading themselves that we are about to destroy ourselves in empty contentions and mutual recriminations; but their hopes will be vain if we devote ourselves to preaching the pure doctrine of Christ and lay aside our logomachies about the elements of the world.[24]

That the dispute was merely a quarrel over words is a recurrent refrain in the Strasbourg litany throughout the years of controversy. So too is the expression of concern that the dispute is making a bad impression on the populace. The Strasbourgers, and the other Upper Ger-

---

* One issue that received considerable attention in the polemics of these years was Zwingli's understanding of original sin, which he declared was like a disease but not a sin: "The original contamination is a disease, not a sin, because sin implies guilt. . . . To be born a slave is a wretched condition, but it is not a fault [*culpa*] nor a crime in him who is so born." See *Corpus Reformatorum* (Halle/Salle, 1835–60; 1905–), 92: 372; cited in LW 37: 16 n. 7.

mans and Swiss, had also to contend with a strong Catholic opposition that was not above claiming Luther for their side, at least on the issue of the Supper. This controversy with the Catholics affected their controversy with the Lutherans, often adversely.[25]

To Luther, Casel's visit seemed not an attempt to mediate the two opposing positions but rather an attempt to get him to agree to the Zwinglian doctrine on the Supper.[26] This view is reflected in his discussions with Casel (for which we have Casel's report) and in his written instructions about what Casel should tell the Strasbourgers.[27] Casel reported that Luther professed himself disposed to peace and concord but did not know how they could be brought about, since he could not accept the grounds for agreement that the Strasbourgers offered. Furthermore, the Strasbourgers wanted Luther and his supporters to abstain from abuse, claiming that they did not abuse the Lutherans, yet, Luther demanded, what more atrocious abuse could be imagined than to have one's God called an edible God, and then to be accused of idolatry? They are distressed, Luther complained, if even one mild reproach is uttered against them. Are we supposed to bear much greater abuse with equanimity? He said that in his book against Karlstadt, he had attacked no one less than he had attacked the Strasbourgers, but for some reason that he could not understand, they were unable to take this book in good part. This was also the case with other of his books. God was his witness that he wished that everything could happen as much as possible for concord, but he could not suppress Christ's Word.

When Casel said that they feared a tremendous persecution if Luther resisted so vigorously, he replied that the disaster of the Peasants' War was only the beginning and prelude of the coming disturbances, which would be much greater:

For I see that it will come to a similar situation as in the century of Arius, who also wrote and wished to judge by reason just as they do. Nor can we hinder this. For we are certain of our faith, and we do not torture God's words but simply adhere to them. Therefore we were not able not to disagree with them and not to censor their errors by speaking or writing.

Casel also reported that Luther rejected the figurative interpretation of the words of institution, the scriptural arguments advanced in its support, and any suggestion that the matter of the real presence was indifferent to salvation. One of the two opposing positions had to be of the devil.

Luther challenged the Strasbourgers to prove the certainty of faith of which they boasted. If they were so sure that their beliefs were true, they should teach them in defiance of the whole world. "This is what I did. When I wrote something, I said to myself: this is God's Word, let it happen as He wishes; it is His matter, He will take care of it properly. I hazard it on His name." And Luther warned the Strasbourgers to be on guard against mistaking reason for the Holy Spirit. Because of Zwingli's position on original sin, Luther contended that Zwingli had never known Christ. He laid out his position in these terms:

I shall hold all those who contend that the body is not present to be outside the faith. At the moment I do not intend to write against Zwingli or Oecolampadius. . . . I know that they think that I do not wish to yield because of shame. They are certainly mistaken. For there is God's Word from which I know the conquering argument. I have already preached God's Word six years, with what fruit is manifest I think. And they say that I [too] am a man. I confess that I am a man and but a single man, but I shall not yield Scripture so easily. They boast at length of having sought Christ's glory. Have I sought or do I seek mine? God is my witness that I have not.

Luther did not know how the matter might be healed. He would leave it to God's will.[28]

This report touches on several themes that run throughout the controversy. The sacramentarians, especially the Strasbourgers, would plead for concord, and Luther would insist that concord was an impossibility because of the extent of the disagreement. Luther would argue that they should not be so concerned about appearances, about dissension, about condemnation. Such concerns should be left to God. The important thing was to preach the truth with confidence. Again and again Luther complained about his sacramentarian opponents' accusing him of immoderation and abuse when they themselves engaged in abuse that was quite as bad, if not worse. The matter was not indifferent to Luther. As he put it in his instruction to Casel: "either they or we must be ministers of Satan. There is no room here for negotiation or mediation. . . . If they go on with their pretending it is our duty to confess that we differ from one another, that their spirit and ours are in conflict, for what agreement has Christ with Belial?"[29]

In December 1525 Luther shared with his friend Michael Stifel, a preacher in Mansfeld, his view of the growing controversy:

This error concerning the Sacrament has three sects, but they agree with each other. . . . This quarrel among the sects is a sign that their teachings are of Satan, since the Spirit of God is not a spirit of discord, but of peace.[30]

It was one of Luther's favorite arguments that his evangelical opponents revealed their error (and by the same token, their guiding spirit) by their disagreements with one another. This argument derived at least in part from Luther's initial judgment that they were united by one demonic spirit. But the demonic spirit, as Luther made clear, is a spirit of discord. So Luther lumped together opponents who claimed to have little if anything in common with one another, holding them responsible for the disagreements among them, and arguing that the very fact that they disagreed was a sign that their teachings were of Satan. When Karlstadt, Zwingli, or Oecolampadius turned the argument on Luther and pointed out that he and the papists disagreed in their understanding of the real presence, Luther was enraged.

In January 1526, at the request of a delegation sent to him, Luther addressed a letter to the congregation at Reutlingen, warning them against the sacramentarian error and its supporters. His argument is already familiar to us. The devil had first attacked the gospel by force through the pope, the emperor, and the rebellious peasants, and now through the fanatics he had launched an attack on baptism and the Lord's Supper. He repeated this to Stifel, alleging also that the sect now had three heads, and that this demonstrated their uncertainty and revealed the devil behind them all. He labeled Karlstadt's position the first head, and Oecolampadius' and Zwingli's the second. He did not identify the third head. This letter was later published, probably by the Reutlingers.[31]

During the following summer Luther wrote two forceful prefaces to translations of the *Swabian Syngramma*, which he said pleased him exceedingly. In these he condemned Zwingli, Oecolampadius, Karlstadt, and the other sacramentarians as false prophets possessed by Satan's spirit. He claimed now to find six heads of the sect, an even surer sign of their uncertainty and their satanic source since the true Holy Spirit is not a spirit of division. And he announced that his treatise *Against the Heavenly Prophets* had already refuted the arguments of this evil spirit and that none of his arguments in refutation had ever been met by his opponents. Given the time and opportunity, he would bring forth another treatise of his own.[32]

In August 1526, Oecolampadius replied to Luther's first preface to the *Syngramma*. In his *Reasonable Answer to Dr. Martin Luther's Instruction Concerning the Sacrament* Oecolampadius attacked Luther's position on the Supper and excoriated him for his intemperance and his unjust and uncharitable claims that the Swiss were false prophets and minions of the devil.[33] At the same time, Oecolampadius acknowledged Luther's accomplishments and the difficulty entailed in opposing him:

... I do not willingly oppose you [Luther] whom I recognize as a worthy and cherished servant of the gospel through whom God has opened the eyes of many to recognize the true path of truth. And yet God has also shown us that you, too, as a man, can err and fall.[34]

One of the central issues of Oecolampadius' *Reasonable Answer* is Luther's personal authority. Oecolampadius launched a predictable frontal assault, alleging that Luther was attacking them because his personal authority was being questioned. "But the Christian reader can well surmise," wrote Oecolampadius,

that these are words of an angry man who can not do otherwise. Since he has lost control of himself, he believes that there is no greater sin and unfair act in the world than that one attacks him. We have then a miserable creature [who] smashes heaven and earth because one has told him that he, too, as a man might err and that those who rely upon him might also miss the mark. Ah! thus one overturns the whole faith! Not so, my brother, we must only not get it into our minds that the Holy Spirit is bound to Jerusalem, Rome, Wittenberg, or Basel, to your person or to any other.[35]

Oecolampadius went on at considerable length on the tone of Luther's polemics and the specific accusations and charges Luther levied against his evangelical opponents, which he said constituted uncharitable conduct toward his fellow Christians. But in comparison with Luther's self-righteous censoriousness, Oecolampadius' complaints seem very restrained, and Oecolampadius himself gives the impression of a man frustrated and aggrieved about an awkward situation over which he has little control. "My dear [Luther]," Oecolampadius wrote, "if you wish to teach, leave your invective in Wittenberg. It does not improve your matter and we have no need of it either. I also do not know how you will answer for it before God."[36]

The difference in tone may be due in part to the difference in their respective "tactical" positions of the two opponents. Luther, not having to acknowledge any dependence on or debt to his evangelical opponents and not needing to appeal to their followers, could engage in unrestrained *ad hominem* attacks. His evangelical opponents, on the other hand, as in the case of Oecolampadius, may have felt a need to acknowledge some obligation to Luther, if for no other reason than to speak to his numerous followers, and therefore they could not afford to reciprocate Luther's extravagant polemics. One cannot treat an erring brother in the same way that one treats an out-and-out heretic. Furthermore, in the specific case of the Upper Germans and Swiss, their humanist concerns for modesty and temperance and their preoccupation with the effects as well as the substance of polemics made it difficult for them to go beyond sarcasm and the barbed remark to the full-blown condemnation, of which Luther was such a master.*

That same summer of 1526 several publications came to Luther's attention that fully confirmed his judgment of his sacramentarian opponents and heightened his fears that Satan would use the authority of his name to mislead the faithful. First, there were Martin Bucer's translations of Bugenhagen's *Psalter* into German and Luther's *Postil* into Latin. With the former, Bucer had used the license granted him by Bugenhagen to change and add as he saw fit in order to put forward a spiritual interpretation of the Supper. Since this *Psalter* had been issued with forewords by both Luther and Melanchthon, it could easily be thought that the Wittenbergers now supported

---

*I should at some point like to consider in detail the differing attitude toward polemics and edification that separated Luther from his humanist opponents and even supporters (e.g. Melanchthon).

the Swiss position, and an enterprising publisher in Augsburg issued excerpts from the translation with the intention of producing just this impression.[37] Bucer, not having permission to alter Luther's *Postil*, had added to his translation of the fourth volume a preface, annotations, and a commentary on 1 Cor. 10:4 in which he criticized Luther's position and advocated his own understanding of the Supper.[38] Still further confirming Luther in his conviction that the Swiss and Upper Germans were trading on his name to advance their error was a treatise he received written pseudonymously by Leo Jud, arguing that Luther and Erasmus agreed with Zwingli in their interpretation of the Supper.[39]

The extent of Luther's anger over these publications can be seen in the ferocious letter he sent to the Strasbourg printer of the *Postil*, John Herwagen, with the request that it be included in any future editions of the *Postil*.[40] Luther praised Bucer's skill at translation; his complaint was with Bucer's preface and notes, which "crucified" his work: "These miserable men are not content to spread their virus in their own books, already infinite in number, but spoil other men's books by smearing them with that poison." Luther specifically objected to Bucer's translation of Bugenhagen's *Psalter*—"a piece of special perfidy"—and the pseudonymous tract which asserted that Erasmus, Luther, Melanchthon, Bugenhagen, and all the others in Wittenberg agreed with the sacramentarians. "What will happen to us after we are dead," Luther asked, "if such things take place while we are still alive?" Luther then drew attention to his previous statements on the Supper and dismissed the arguments advanced against his position. He went to the heart of the matter in his conclusion:

To be sure he wishes it to appear that this is only a trifling disagreement and that it does no harm to faith. For this spirit thinks that faith is not lost if Christ is called a liar in respect of His own very words, which is sufficient proof of what he thinks of Christ and His whole kingdom. For since we both contend that Christ says thus and so, and our contentions are opposite, it follows of necessity that either we or they accuse Christ of falsehood and lying. But if to make Christ a liar is not to deny Christ and blaspheme His faith, what, pray, does blaspheming Christ mean? ... That is what I have always said, that those sacramentarian heretics make sport of Christ and have never seriously known Him or taught Him, however grandly they boast that they seek the gospel and the glory of God. A good man does not seek the glory of God by not knowing or making light of it when Christ is blasphemed.[41]

Once again Luther is attacking the spirit rather than the man, and finding proof of his contentions in his opponents' attempt to minimize the importance of the dispute. Bugenhagen also issued a denial of agreement with the sacramentarians, but in a more moderate tone.[42]

About the same time that Luther sent his letter to Herwagen, in September or early October, friends of Luther's published three of his sermons from the previous Easter on the proper reception of the Sacrament and entitled them *The Sacrament of the Body and Blood of Christ—Against the Fanatics*.[43] Despite the title, these three sermons were not properly speaking polemics, nor were they directed against the Upper Germans and Swiss. They were merely a stopgap while Luther prepared a detailed attack on his opponents.

Both sides to the dispute prepared treatises for the Frankfurt spring book fair in 1527. These treatises were the first major frontal attacks launched by both sides. Bucer published his reply to Luther's and Bugenhagen's charges that he had "poisoned" their books. Zwingli issued two works: *Friendly Exposition of the Eucharist Affair, to Martin Luther*, in Latin, and a German supplement, *A Friendly Rejoinder and Rebuttal to the Sermon of the Eminent Martin Luther Against the Fanatics*. Luther published *That These Words of Christ "This Is My Body," Etc., Still Stand Firm Against the Fanatics*.

In his defense of his additions to Luther's *Postil*,[44] Bucer acknowledged Luther's authority even as he attacked it. His introductory remarks expressed the now familiar qualified deference:

In all things on which the Christian religion truly rests, namely faith in Christ and love towards one's neighbor, I have always recognized and praised Luther as a superior servant of Christ and indeed perhaps as more magnificent than sufficed for God's honor and the edification of the brethren. . . . That we have not, however, taken everything in [Luther's] translation and exegesis of Scripture to be pure gold, as the saying goes, is because he obviously and in fact frequently stumbles, to be sure not in an intolerable fashion with an upsetting of the Christian faith, nevertheless in such a fashion that one can see that Luther, too, is numbered among those who can stumble and fall.[45]

Stressing Luther's fallibility was necessary if Bucer were to reach those who believed as they did because of Luther's authority: "Truly, if I had not seen that many were so beguiled by the brilliance of Luther's name that they regarded as true without scrutiny everything that he believed, I would not have responded to these so obviously human matters."[46] But Bucer must respond, for many do believe because "Luther was the first to restore the gospel to the world, [and] he had not erred in great matters: therefore he cannot be mistaken in anything."[47] Although Bucer wrote this as a general reproach and in a sarcastic vein, he was stating precisely the problem that he and Luther's other evangelical opponents had to contend with. Bucer could criticize Luther's treatises for their lack of charity. He could advance his own arguments. He could urge his readers to test his and Luther's arguments against Scripture. He could even suggest that the devil might use Luther's reputation to institute his trickery and deception. But he could not escape the dilemma of a man who wishes only to correct Luther's teachings, not to discredit them completely. In his closing words Bucer urged his readers to use judgment:

I beg once more, however, for the sake of God's honor and the redemption of Christ our savior that no one condemn on this account anything of Luther's that he has not recognized with certainty through the Spirit of God to be human [as opposed to divine]. God has allowed the gospel to be preached to us even from ancient times by mortal men and not by immortal angels, and we all sin manifoldly.[48]

Bucer's plea contrasts sharply with Luther's unqualified assertion that the "sacramentarian heretics make sport of Christ and have never seriously known Him or taught Him." Between Luther and his evangelical opponents there were differences not only in conviction, in personality, and in polemical style, but also in "tactical" position.

Luther's treatise, *That These Words of Christ "This Is My Body," Etc., Still Stand Firm Against the Fanatics,*[49] can be said to epitomize most of his treatises that were to follow. In it he set forth his understanding of the controversy, his convictions concerning the Supper, and his judgment of his opponents, and later statements would not show any great change or modification in the sentiments expressed here.

The treatise began with the assertion that throughout the history of the Church the devil had attacked Scripture through heretics and sects, causing it to be supplanted by man-made laws. Luther applied this generalization to his own day and, incidentally, asserted claims about himself and his accomplishments:

Now in our day, having seen that Scripture was utterly neglected and the devil was making captives and fools of us by the mere straw and hay of man-made laws, we have tried by God's grace to offer some help in the matter. With immense and bitter effort indeed we have brought the Scriptures to the fore again and released the people from man-made laws, freed ourselves and escaped the devil, although he stubbornly resisted and still continues to do so.[50]

"It is precisely the same devil who now assails us through the fanatics by blaspheming the holy and venerable sacrament of our Lord Jesus Christ, out of which they would like to make mere bread and wine as a symbol or memorial sign of Christians, in whatever way they dream or [their] fancy dictates."[51] And so Luther asserts, once again, that his primary opponent is the devil, who has possessed the fanatics: "Therefore I do not fix my attention as much upon them, as upon him who speaks through them—the devil, I mean—just as they regard me as full of devils."[52] He will attack some of the major arguments of his opponents, but his primary assault will be, as before, on the demonic spirit: "So I shall once more set myself against the devil and his fanatics, not for their sake, but for the sake of the weak and simple." Luther doubted the possibility that an "arch-fanatic" could ever be converted. In any case, he wished to be able to foreswear any responsibility for these men or their actions: "I will have made my testimony before God and all the world, and declared that I have nothing to do with these blasphemers of the sacrament and fanatics, nor have I ever had, nor will I ever have, God willing; and I shall wash my hands of all the blood of those souls whom they steal, murder, and seduce from Christ with their poison."[53]

Luther threw back in his opponents' faces their charges that the Lutherans were being "un-Christian," offending the common people, vilifying the servants of Christ, and rending Christian unity, love, and peace.[54] The matter of the real presence was no minor issue, for it divided Christ's church from the devil's: "One side must be of the devil, and God's enemy. There is no middle ground." And it was no use for them to assert that at all other points they had a high and noble regard for God's Word and gospel: "When one blasphemously gives the lie to God in a single word, or says it is a minor matter if God is blasphemed or called a liar, one blasphemes the entire God and makes light of all blasphemy."[55] Therefore, although Luther was willing to keep peace with his opponents in civil matters, in spiritual matters he intended "to shun, condemn, and censure them, as idolaters, corrupters of God's Word, blasphemers, and liars; and meanwhile, to endure from them, as from enemies, their persecution and schism as far and as long as God endures them; and to pray for them, and admonish them to stop."[56]

The central issue was how the words of institution should be interpreted. Luther was convinced that the words were to be understood literally, and he challenged Zwingli to prove that they must be understood figuratively, not that they could be figurative, or might be figurative, but that they must be figurative. As Luther interpreted the controversy, Zwingli's two basic arguments were that Christ's ascension to heaven to sit at the right hand of God removed him physically from the world and that John 6:63 ("The flesh is of no avail") made His physical presence unnecessary. Luther attacked the first argument by attacking reason. Reason, he said, cannot prove or disprove any matter of faith. God's right hand refers not to some physical location in heaven but to the "almighty power of God, which at one and the same time can be nowhere and yet must be everywhere."[57] This presence is not a circumscribed or local presence, but an essential presence that creates and preserves all things. Moreover, there is a special presence in the Lord's Supper, for there God is present *for you* and binds His presence through the Word:

Because it is one thing if God is present, and another if He is present for you. He is there for you when He adds His Word and binds himself, saying, "Here you are to find me."[58]

Such is the case in the Supper, when Christ said "This is my body." By partaking of Christ's body in the Supper, one nourishes not only the soul but one's body itself toward immortality.

As for the argument from John 6:63, "The flesh is of no avail," Luther insisted that this could not apply to Christ's flesh without simultaneously negating the incarnation. His fanatics, he contended, misconstrued the words spirit and flesh as presented by the Bible. There are spiritual and fleshly acts, but not spiritual and fleshly things:

> Thus, all that our body does outwardly and physically, if God's Word is added to it and it is done through faith, is in reality and in name done spiritually. Nothing can be so material, fleshly, or outward, but it becomes spiritual when it is done in the Word and in faith. "Spiritual" is nothing else than what is done in us and by us through the Spirit and faith, whether the object with which we are dealing is physical or spiritual. Thus, *Spirit consists in the use, not in the object*, be it seeing, hearing, speaking, touching, begetting, bearing, eating, drinking, or anything else.[59]

On the basis of this understanding of spirit and flesh, Luther turns the sacramentarian argument on its head:

> Our fanatics, however, are full of fraud and humbug. They think nothing spiritual can be present where there is anything material and physical, and assert that flesh is of no avail. Actually the opposite is true. The Spirit cannot be with us except in material and physical things such as the Word, water, and Christ's body and in his saints on earth.[60]

"So God arranges that the mouth eats physically for the heart and the heart eats spiritually for the mouth, and thus both are satisfied and saved by one and the same food."[61]

The misunderstanding on the part of Zwingli and Oecolampadius and their supporters links them with the spirit that motivated Karlstadt and Müntzer:

> ... they do not see the Word of God in the Supper, and simply gape and stare at the physical eating, thinking that the divine Word must set forth nothing but spiritual things. But this is the seed of Müntzer's and Karlstadt's spirit, who also wanted to tolerate nothing outward, until they were utterly drowned in flesh.
>
> God inverts this order, however, and sets before us no word or commandment without including with it something material and outward, and proffering it to us.[62]

It is from this premise that Luther refutes all the other arguments advanced to deny Christ's real presence in the Supper.

Having dealt roundly with Zwingli and Oecolampadius, Luther

turned in the last pages of the treatise to Bucer and his translations
of Bugenhagen's *Psalter* and Luther's *Postil*:

The devil saw clearly that his book [Luther's *Postil*] was being dissem-
inated everywhere. Therefore he seized it, and loaded and smeared it with
his dung. So I, an innocent man, must now be the wagon driver of the
devil's manure, whether I will or not.

This prompted a fear that persists in the years ahead: "What will
happen after my death, when they do this during my life, while I sit
here in Wittenberg looking on?" And he protested that he must bear
the charge of being a reviler and intolerant person while his opponents wished to be seen as "pure holiness" even though they despoiled
other men's books.[63]

In his concluding remarks, Luther finally answered the criticism
of his treatise against the peasants:

For what we are to make of this spirit who in a seditious way still com-
forts and exonerates the peasants and condemns me for writing against
them, is easy to see. The devil does not sleep, but ever continues to spit
fire. That is why I said above: This spirit is not good, and means no good
through these fanatics, although I think the preachers against whom I
write have no malice in mind. But dear God, they are not their own mas-
ters; the spirit has blinded and captured them. Therefore they are not to
be trusted. For any spirit that does away with Christ's flesh is not of God,
says St. John [I John 4:2–3]. . . . Now this spirit certainly does away with
Christ's flesh, because he makes of it a useless, perishable, and altogether
common flesh. . . . Therefore he cannot be honest. I warn, I counsel: Beware, watch out, Satan has come among the children of God![64]

United by the satanic spirit, all Luther's evangelical opponents must
bear responsibility for the misdeeds of the worst of them. Once again,
Luther was accusing specific opponents not only of the misdeeds they
had in fact committed but also of the misdeeds they were capable of
committing. He was labeling them with qualities they would be loath
to possess, and charging them with actions they had neither committed nor advocated. It is not surprising if they responded in an
injured tone, claiming that injustice had been done them. Luther's
recriminations made even the thought of reconciliation difficult and
provided obstacles beyond the formidable disagreement on the theological issues involved.

Instead of discussing Zwingli's two treatises that appeared at the 1527 Frankfurt spring book fair, except to say that they, too, dealt among other things with the question of Luther's authority,[65] I wish to skip to Zwingli's rejoinder to Luther's treatise *That These Words of Christ . . . Still Stand Firm Against the Fanatics.* This rejoinder appeared in June 1527 under the long title *That These Words of Jesus Christ, "This Is My Body Which Is Given for You," Will Forever Retain Their Ancient, Single Meaning, and Martin Luther with His Latest Book Has by No Means Proved or Established His Own and the Pope's View.*[66] It is, in parts, a paragraph-by-paragraph reply to Luther's treatise, which began, as previously noted, with a history of how the devil had subverted the Scriptures through heretics and sects, and with assertions about himself and recent events:

> Now in our day, having seen that Scripture was utterly neglected ["lay under the bench"] and the devil was making captives and fools of us by the mere straw and hay of man-made laws, we have tried by God's grace to offer some help in the matter. With immense and bitter effort indeed we have brought the Scriptures to the fore again and released the people from man-made laws, freed ourselves and escaped the devil. . . . However, even though he has had to let us go, he does not forget his tricks. He has secretly sown his seed among us so that they may take hold of our teachings and words, not to aid and assist us in fostering the Scriptures, but, while we were leading in the fight against human drivel, to fall upon our host from the rear, incite rebellion and raise an uproar against us, in order that caught between two enemies, we may be more easily destroyed.[67]

Zwingli's lengthy reply to this assertion is revealing, not only of Zwingli's awareness of the dynamics working to his disadvantage but also of his inability to escape the effect of these dynamics despite his awareness of them. To bring Luther's authority into question, as he wished, Zwingli had to acknowledge it at least in part. "You give yourself a great deal of credit, in my opinion unwarrantedly, how you brought forth the Scripture which was under the bench." Credit had to be given, Zwingli pointed out, to Erasmus and Valla for the linguistic tools to understand the New Testament, and to Reuchlin and Pellican for the tools to understand the Old. Furthermore, God had to be acknowledged as the true originator of the reformation. He added that he was, in fact, sparing Luther, for in many treatises, cir-

cular letters, and in other ways, too, Luther had boasted even more
conceitedly about himself. Zwingli went on:

For in truth, as you well know, at the time when you stood forward, there
was indeed a great throng of people who were much more talented in
reading and writing than you, although they had not stood forward, because of fear and because God had not awakened them and made them
courageous, to protect Israel and to fight against the giant Goliath of
Rome. (Now your praise follows as well.) But in all this you were called
by God no differently than was David. You confronted the enemy so comfortingly that all those who had previously been fearful how the abominable Antichrist would be endured [*wie der schmähliche Antichrist hin
würde genommen*] were strengthened and they sprang to your aid so that
the gospel had striking successes. For this reason we should justly thank
God that He had awakened you when no one dared [to attack the Anti-
christ]. And we should hold you in honor as a useful instrument, as we
also gladly do, although you do pervert the same in many ways.[68]

Zwingli conceded that Luther had stormed the papacy and exposed
it for what it was and that God had given Luther much power of
speech. But he criticized Luther's anger, charging that he had lost
control of his senses much as a madman does. "That you are now,
however, raging with anger," Zwingli wrote, "you cannot, God willing, deny if you just read your own book; for the countless words of
abuse and perverted opinions, as we will make clear, cannot come
from love and fit consideration [*Wohlbetrachtung*]."[69] Luther erred
in four ways, he said: by insisting on the necessity of absolution, by
still to some degree affirming belief in purgatory, by allowing the
intercession of saints, and by tolerating images in church.[70] He was
pointing out these errors, he said, so that "you may see that you have
not missed the mark on one issue but in many and [so that] you may
from now on restrain yourself about [your] great fame among Christians as if you alone had accomplished everything, which we would
indeed gladly grant you to the degree it is true." Luther was but one
upright Ajax or Diomedes among many Nestors, Odysseuses, and
Menelauses.[71]

Zwingli was well aware that Luther used the authority of his own
name to add weight to his arguments and at the same time used *ad
hominem* attacks to discredit the arguments of his opponents. Rather

than simply laying out God's Word and drawing conclusions from it, Zwingli accused him, "you always put forward first a long abusive section so that a simple person will be induced by your authority or name, in which he has much faith, to hate your opponents, and, as a result of such a temptation, he will not examine your unfounded opinion very carefully, rather he will be taken in by your abuse... and will rage and scream with you: 'Flesh and blood, the words are plain.' " To underline the unfairness of this tactic, Zwingli pointed out that it was the same maneuver that the papists used against Luther.[72]

In the course of his treatise, Zwingli touched on most of the accusations lodged by Luther against him and Oecolampadius: their uncertainty,[73] their possession by the devil,[74] their boasting about their love and forbearance,[75] among others. He defended Bucer from Luther's charges about the translations of the *Psalter* and *Postil*,[76] presented his own understanding of the principles of exegesis and how Scriptural passages should be compared, advanced his understanding of the words of institution, discussed his understanding of the relationship between Christ's two natures, and dwelt at some length on his understanding of John 6:63.[77]

One additional aspect of Zwingli's treatise should be noted. As the title itself makes clear, Zwingli maintained that Luther and the papists were essentially of one mind (...*And Martin Luther with His Latest Book Has by No Means Proved or Established His Own and the Pope's View*). This lumping together of Luther and the pope infuriated Luther, and, much as Luther's lumping together of the fanatics had done, made eventual reconciliation more difficult. Both Zwingli's rejoinder and Oecolampadius' rejoinder, *That Dr. Martin Luther's Misunderstanding of the Everlasting Words, "This Is My Body," Is Untenable. The Second Reasonable Answer of John Oecolampadius*, appeared in June 1527. Luther took nearly a year to frame his next treatise, *Confession Concerning Christ's Supper*. It was on sale at the Frankfurt book fair in the spring of 1528.[78]

This treatise began with an announcement that he had sufficiently refuted the sacramentarian argument in his *Against the Heavenly Prophets* and *That These Words of Christ...Still Stand Firm Against the Fanatics* and was publishing the present treatise only in order to strengthen the weak in conscience: this treatise would be his last, Luther said, for he did not intend to issue any further replies to the fanatics "lest Satan become still more frantic and spew out still more lies and follies, as he has been doing, besmearing paper uselessly and depriving the reader of time for reading something better."[79]

The *Confession* was divided into three parts. The first part—by far the longest—dealt mainly with refuting Zwingli and Oecolampadius and has the most bearing on this study. The second part was devoted to a careful examination of the four biblical texts that dealt with the Lord's Supper. In the third part Luther confessed all the articles of his faith "in opposition to this and every other new heresy, so that neither during my lifetime nor after my death will they be able to claim that Luther agreed with them—as they have already done in certain instances."[80] Except for this desire to forestall the misuse of his name or authority during his lifetime or after his death, which explicitly motivated the third part,[81] most of the comments with some bearing on our study appear in the first part.

Throughout the treatise Luther's attack was once again aimed primarily at the satanic spirit motivating his opponents. Zwingli, and especially Oecolampadius, had complained in their treatises about this tactic, and Luther responded directly to their complaints. Commenting on the charge that he had mentioned the devil seventy-seven times in his *That These Words of Christ ... Still Stand Firm Against the Fanatics*, he wrote:

> Well, I have declared that I write not against flesh and blood, as St. Paul teaches, but against the devil and his followers. Therefore I would do well if every other word I write were "devil." Shall I now become so timid for the sake of these delicate, highly spiritual, profoundly holy fanatics, that I must also avoid mentioning my enemy? I am quite willing to be called blasphemous and mad when I attack the devil pungently and pointedly in his messengers. For my frank, public, simple snapping at the devil suits me better than their poisonous, sneaky stabbing, which under the guise of peace and love they practice against the upright, as the Psalter says of these vipers.[82]

Luther was not to be dissuaded from his pungent and pointed attacks, especially against Zwingli, who "is completely perverted and has entirely lost Christ." He urged his readers to beware of Zwingli and to "shun his books as the prince of hell's poison":

Other sacramentarians settle on one error, but this man never publishes a book without spewing out new errors, more and more all the time. But anyone who rejects this warning may go his way, just so he knows that I warned him, and my conscience is clear.[83]

At another point Luther vented an even more severe judgment of Zwingli, and conjoined it with a disavowal of responsibility for the man, or his teaching:

I testify on my part that I regard Zwingli as un-Christian, with all his teachings, for he holds and teaches no part of the Christian faith rightly. He is seven times worse than when he was a papist. . . . I make this testimony in order that I may stand blameless before God and the world as one who never partook of Zwingli's teaching, nor will I ever do so.[84]

With a mixture of Scriptural exegesis, logic, sarcasm, *reductio ad absurdum*, ridicule, and *ad hominem* denunciation, Luther proceeded to attack Zwingli's figurative interpretation of the biblical texts, to rebut Zwingli's criticisms of his own interpretation, and to question Zwingli's grammatical analysis. Then, once again, he tackled Zwingli's two major arguments: his understanding of Christ's two natures and his interpretation of John 6:63. In the course of this discussion he repeated his understanding of the ubiquity of Christ's glorified body and restated his understanding of the spirit-flesh dichotomy.[85]

After finishing with Zwingli, Luther went on to deal with Oecolampadius. The tone in this section is considerably more moderate, perhaps because Luther still had some hope for him, "that he does not agree with Zwingli in all points but only in the sacrament [of the altar] and baptism,"[86] but Luther firmly rejected Oecolampadius' arguments. In the last few pages of part one he also disputed the arguments of the Silesian nobleman Kaspar Schwenckfeld and his disciple Valentine Krautwald, and attacked John Wycliffe, whose arguments concerning "identical predication" had been cited by Zwingli and Capito.[87] Some six months later, in the autumn of 1528, Zwingli and Oecolampadius published their carefully coordinated reply: *Concerning Dr. Martin Luther's Book Entitled "Confession": Two Answers, by John Oecolampadius and Ulrich Zwingli.*[88] Luther, true to his announced intention in the *Confession,* did not respond. The next important stage of the dispute came in 1529 at the Colloquy of Marburg.

On 22 April 1529 at the second Diet of Speyer, three days following the famous "protestation," the Landgraf Philipp of Hesse concluded a secret alliance with Electoral Saxony, Nuremberg, Strasbourg, and Ulm. But Philipp nursed plans for a wider alliance, as he implied in a letter to Ulrich Zwingli written that same day: "We are endeavoring to bring together at some suitable place Luther and Melanchthon and some of those who hold your view of the sacrament, so that if a merciful and almighty God grants us His favor, they may come to some Scriptural agreement about that doctrine and live in harmony, as becomes Christians." He requested Zwingli to help to bring this colloquy about.[89] This was the first step toward realizing a project that Philipp had championed for several years: a religious conference leading to an agreement on which an alliance of evangelical states could be built.* Zwingli greeted the plan enthusiastically.[90] Only then did Philipp write to the Wittenbergers about the proposed colloquy, carefully omitting, as he did throughout his correspondence with the Lutherans, any suggestion that Zwingli himself had been invited, much less that he had been the very first to be invited.†

In Wittenberg, however, Philipp's plans for an alliance and for a religious colloquy were to meet with determined opposition. When Luther learned of the proposed alliance from Melanchthon, he immediately sent the Elector a letter in which he laid out weighty theological objections. He saw Satan once again hard at work. Such an alliance was not of God and did not come of trust in Him, but was a device of human wits. If there were to be an alliance, God would provide for it without their seeking it. The gospel was not to be defended by human arms or calculations. Furthermore, Luther har-

---

* My summary of these events necessarily omits many of the details and especially the political maneuvers and calculations involved. For a full account, see Walter Köhler, *Zwingli und Luther* (Gütersloh, 1953), 2: 1–163.

† Reference was always to "Oecolampadius and those of his opinion" (e.g. WABr 5: 108 [S-J 2: 485]) when names were mentioned at all. Philipp realized that Luther's and Melanchthon's opposition would have been even greater if they had known that Zwingli had been invited.

bored serious doubts as to the wisdom of relying on Philipp of Hesse, who, in the previous year, had almost drawn Electoral Saxony into war on the basis of a forged letter.[91] Of Luther's three major objections, the most significant for our study is the second:

> The worst thing of all is that in this league most of the members [e.g., Strasbourg and Ulm] are those who strive against God and the Sacrament, willful enemies of God and His Word. By making a league with them we take upon ourselves the burden of all their wickedness and blasphemy, become partakers in it and defenders of it. In truth, no more perilous league could be proposed for the shaming and the quenching of the gospel and for our own damnation, body and soul. That is what the devil, sad to say, is seeking.[92]

This advice, seconded by Melanchthon and others, and reinforced by the Elector's own political and theological scruples, led Electoral Saxony to insist that a common religious confession was the prerequisite of any political alliance. Later in the summer, articles that were to be known as the Schwabach articles were drawn up by Luther and the other Saxon theologians as a basis for such a confession.*

Despite their extreme misgivings, Luther and Melanchthon, at the urging of the Elector,[93] accepted the Landgraf's invitation. Luther's pessimistic evaluation of the whole enterprise is apparent in his letter of acceptance, especially in what seems to have been the first draft, later modified, very likely at the request of the Elector.[94] Although he entertained little hope for concord, he praised the Landgraf's concern and declared his willingness to perform this "vain and for us, possibly dangerous service." Luther explained why he would nevertheless come: "For I truly do not want (God willing) to allow our opponents to boast that they were more well disposed to peace and unity than I." Several times he voiced the suspicion that his opponents were going to use the conference to attack the Lutherans once more as enemies of peace and unity. He requested the Landgraf to consider or at least to find out whether the other party was inclined to give ground. "For I know well," he declared, "that I simply will not and

---

* See Köhler, 2: 1–66, for a detailed discussion of the political and confessional maneuverings. About the same time that Luther and the other theologians drew up the Schwabach articles, Luther renewed his objections to an alliance. See WABr 5: 78–81.

can not yield to them, because I am personally so certain that they err and, what is more, that they are themselves uncertain of their opinion."

Luther also asked the Landgraf to consider whether more good than harm would come of the colloquy, for it was inevitable that if Luther's opponents did not yield, the participants would go their separate ways without having accomplished anything, and the Landgraf would be out money and effort for nothing. Matters would likely be even worse than before. "That is what Satan wishes and seeks," Luther warned. When discussing the Landgraf's concern that the disagreement might eventually lead to bloodshed, he repeated the now familiar denial of responsibility. God shall reveal the Lutherans' innocence: "If the fanatical spirit causes bloodshed, then it does so as it previously did with Franz von Sickingen, Karlstadt, and Müntzer; and afterwards, by God's grace, we remained [i.e., we were found to be] innocent and [our] opponents guilty."[95] Luther suspected the worst of his opponents and was determined from the outset not to budge an inch on the central issues.

Although Luther had given his acceptance, reluctantly, he was still pessimistic about the enterprise. In a letter to a friend he likened the forthcoming colloquy to the meetings "in the days of Arius" that "did more harm than good," allowing the boastful Arians to spread their teachings all the further. He also reported that the Nuremberg preacher Andrew Osiander, John Brenz, and others had "manfully" declined to attend.[96] As this was not in fact the case, he was perhaps indulging in wishful thinking. In any case, he urged Brenz not to come and thereby to give the Wittenbergers themselves an excuse not to do so.[97] Both he and Melanchthon suggested that "honorable papists" should also be invited "as witnesses against the future bragging of these boastful saints."[98] It seems clear that Luther's suspicion that his opponents would use the conference to malign him and his party as enemies of concord had a great deal to do with his opposition to the colloquy and his attempts to scuttle it.

Whatever Luther's and Melanchthon's reservations, Philipp was not to be dissuaded. Invitations went out to other theologians, most notably to Oecolampadius and Bucer, Brenz and Osiander. The plan was to have only the four major theologians take active part in the discussions, Luther and Melanchthon opposing Zwingli and Oecolampadius, but other theologians were to be allowed to view the proceedings, and several of the states decided to send political as well as theological representatives. Though the theologians may have wished to separate the religious issues from the political, the secular authorities, especially Philipp himself and the Strasbourgers, saw them as closely interrelated.[99]

Even Karlstadt, who had in recent months finally broken once more with Luther and left Electoral Saxony, tried to gain admission to the colloquy but was turned down.[100] All the other major principals in the preceding years of dispute agreed to come to what was to be their first and only face-to-face meeting.

Since Luther insisted that no official minutes be recorded, we must reconstruct what went on at the colloquy from the notes and later recollections of participants. My account which follows is based on several such reconstructions that have been attempted as well as on the texts themselves.[101]

Luther and his party arrived at Marburg on Thursday, 30 September 1529. The Zurich, Basel, and Strasbourg delegations had arrived several days earlier, and the next day private, two-man discussions were held between Luther and Oecolampadius as one pair and Zwingli and Melanchthon as the other. It appears that Luther and Melanchthon pointed out to Oecolampadius and Zwingli a number of errors in their teachings over and above their denial of the real presence.[102] There is no detailed account of Luther's conversation with Oecolampadius, although it was apparently strained, for Oecolampadius is said to have told Zwingli later that he had come upon another Eck.[103] The next day the colloquy proper began, with Zwingli and Oecolampadius upholding their side of the argument while Luther did most of the speaking for his.[104]

In his opening statement Luther announced that he had turned down a proposal for a colloquy two years before because there were no new arguments to be presented and his own opinion was firmly established. He was participating in the present colloquy at the request of the Landgraf, for his conviction was still firm and he had no desire to change it. He did wish to present the foundation of his faith and show where the others erred, but first he asked his opponents to express their views on seven other issues on which they seemed to him to be in error. Zwingli and Oecolampadius objected to this procedure on the ground that the purpose of their being there was to discuss the Supper. Luther then challenged them to prove that Christ is not present, and chalked on the table the words "This is my body," his proof-text throughout the colloquy. Both sides agreed that there was a spiritual eating, but whereas Luther insisted that this did not exclude a bodily eating as well, the Swiss insisted that it did. At the close of the morning session Zwingli and Luther exchanged heated words on John 6:63. Zwingli warned that this passage would break Luther's neck, but when Luther countered that necks did not break so easily in Hesse as in Switzerland, Zwingli explained that this was just a figure of speech in his Swiss dialect and apologized.

Zwingli returned to John 6:63 in the afternoon session, warning Luther and Melanchthon to beware lest the papacy be reintroduced through their interpretation. He was obviously disturbed by the idea that an unworthy person (e.g. a papist) could cause the body of Christ to be present in the Sacrament. Luther met this argument with the contention that it was God through His Word that caused Christ to be present, not the priest or celebrant, since the worthiness of the minister in no way affected the efficacy of the sacraments. Oecolampadius then continued with his argument that the eating of Christ's body was not necessary; he cited various passages showing that Christ had left the world and discussed the properties of a true body with which Luther's understanding was inconsistent. Luther rejected these arguments and presented his interpretation of the spirit-flesh dichotomy. Zwingli came to Oecolampadius' support, and each side insisted that the other prove its position from Scripture. Luther finally lifted the tablecloth and read the chalked words, "This is my body." Zwingli, very agitated, insisted that Luther was advocating a local presence, and Luther retorted that he did not want to know whether it was there locally or not, he would stand by Christ's words. The first day's session ended with Zwingli's bitter question, "Should, then, everything go according to your will?"

The second day's session began with Zwingli arguing that the properties of a body required that the body of Christ must occupy a certain space and must exist locally.[105] Luther replied that the words of institution proved the presence of the body in the bread. Christ's body could be many places simultaneously, and once again Zwingli claimed that Luther was reestablishing the sacrifice of the mass. In the afternoon session both Luther and Oecolampadius made an attempt to move toward each other as far as possible. Luther admitted that the sacraments were sacred symbols and that as such they stood for something that was beyond themselves and that transcended man's intellect, but that they were not mere signs. Oecolampadius admitted that the sacrament was not merely a sign and that in the Lord's Supper there was the true body of Christ but only through faith. Neither side could go further and it was agreed to cease the discussion.

Luther thanked Oecolampadius for having made plain his views in a friendly manner, and Zwingli as well although he had spoken more bitterly. He asked that any bitter words of his own be forgiven. Zwingli in his turn asked Luther to pardon his bitterness and tearfully confessed that it had always been and still was his eager wish to have Luther as his friend. To this Luther replied that Zwingli should ask God for enlightenment, and Oecolampadius countered that Luther needed enlightenment no less. Then Jacob Sturm, the Strasbourg city secretary, reminded the participants that Luther had raised questions about other doctrinal issues and requested that Bucer be allowed to outline their beliefs so that Luther's suspicions would be removed. Bucer did so and then asked Luther to tell them whether their doctrine was orthodox. This Luther refused to do, saying that he was neither their lord nor their judge:

Since you do not want to accept me or my doctrine I cannot allow you to be my disciples. Indeed, we have previously noticed that you desire to spread your teaching in our name. I hear what you say now, but I do not know whether or not you also teach the same way at home, etc. That is why I shall not testify on your behalf.[106]

Once again Luther's fear that his name might be misused to promote heresy is evident. Then Bucer asked if Luther would recognize him as a brother. Luther's reply was decisive:

Our spirit is different from yours; it is clear that we do not possess the same spirit, for it cannot be the same spirit when in one place the words of Christ are simply believed and in another place the same faith is censured, resisted, regarded as false and attacked with all kinds of malicious and blasphemous words.[107]

Luther once more commended them to the judgment of God. Negotiations were also held that night, but agreement on a compromise wording on the Supper suggested by Luther was rejected by Zwingli.

On Monday, 4 October, at the request of the Landgraf, Luther drew up fifteen articles based on the previously formulated Schwabach articles. Much to Luther's surprise, his opponents accepted fourteen of the fifteen with only minor modifications. The only point of disagreement was the article having to do with the Supper, and even here their positions were noticeably closer than before. All parties, including Zwingli, now agreed that there was a spiritual partaking of the true body and blood of Jesus Christ. The only disagreement remaining was whether or not the true body and blood were bodily present in the bread and wine.[108] Before parting, all parties agreed to refrain from further public controversy.

Luther's evaluation of the colloquy is expressed clearly in his letter to Gerbel in Strasbourg:

We defended ourselves strongly and they conceded much, but as they were firm in this one article of the sacrament of the altar we dismissed them in peace, fearing that further argument would draw blood. We ought to have charity and peace even with our foes, and so we plainly told them that unless they grow wiser on this point they may indeed have our charity, but cannot by us be considered as brothers and members of Christ. You will judge how much fruit has come of this conference; it seems to me that no small scandal has been removed, since there will be no further occasion for disputation, which is more than we had hoped for. Would that the little difference still remaining might be taken away by Christ.[109]

Luther's judgment that the sacramentarians had yielded to the Lutherans on all issues but the Supper only further confirmed his belief in the correctness of his own position.[110] He described the sacramentarians as "clumsy and inexperienced in argument" and thought they had refused to yield on the Supper "from fear and shame rather than from malice."[111] And as for their humility and their pleas to be considered brethren, this behavior only confirmed the judgment, of Luther and the other Lutherans as well, that they lacked assurance about their position.[112] Melanchthon expressed this feeling clearly:

When it was all over Zwingli and Oecolampadius earnestly desired that we should acknowledge them as brethren. This we were not willing to grant by any means. They have attacked us so severely that we wonder with what kind of a conscience they would hold us as brethren if they thought we were in error. How could they permit our view to be taught and held and preached alongside their own?[113]

The answer was that by their request they demonstrated that they did not have a quiet, certain conscience. Melanchthon and Luther did not understand how the Swiss and the Upper Germans could sincerely believe that this disagreement did not of necessity separate the true church from the false. Luther stated the mood of his party in a letter to Link in late October:

They were humble enough, nay, more than enough, and tried to gain recognition as our brethren. Nicholas Amsdorf is exulting greatly and praising the work of God because, although they sought to be recognized as our brethren, they did not succeed. He thinks Osiander's prophecy has been fulfilled ... that within two years either he [Zwingli] would be confounded, or he [Osiander] was not "speaking in the Lord," and now they, who condemned us as idolaters, cannibals, Thyestians, worshipers of an impanate and edible God, Capernaites, etc., are seeking the fellowship of such people and are not considered worthy to have it. His story is true, and so is his boast, as we ourselves see.[114]

In addition, Zwingli's repeated use of Greek during the discussions and his sermon during the colloquy confirmed Luther's belief that his spirit was a conceited one, much taken with itself.[115]

As is hardly surprising, the Swiss and Upper Germans did not agree with these opinions of Luther's and felt, in fact, that it was their position that had carried the day.[116]

⁘⟨ 5 ⟩⁘

The Mature Paradigm

Luther's view of himself as he entered the 1530's was in some ways different from the one he had held a decade earlier. He now saw himself as more than a doctor of theology, more than a professor at the University of Wittenberg.[1] The events and experiences of the last ten years had caused him to view himself differently, to elaborate his characterization of his evangelical opponents, and to act in accordance with these new views.

In 1531 Luther lectured on St. Paul's letter to the Galatians,[2] often drawing comparisons between Paul's experiences with the false apostles at Galatia and his own experiences with evangelical opponents. In some instances he used Paul's experiences to explain his own; in other instances he used his own experiences to fill out his interpretation of Paul's ministry.* These lectures show convincingly that Luther believed that his and Paul's experiences were substantially alike and that he could legitimately model his own behavior on the example set by Paul.

He had embraced a world view that posited a perpetual, unchanging struggle between the true and false church. He saw this struggle as involving a recurrent contest between true and false prophets and apostles. The men of the biblical accounts were real men involved in real struggles. They were not primarily "types" or "figura," for Luther had long abandoned the traditional *sensus tropologicus*.[3] And so, believing that mankind did not change and that the devil never slept, Luther saw the struggles that went on then as being no differ-

---

* A student of Luther's exegetical practices should attempt to sort these two out sometime.

ent from the struggles going on in his own time. What happened to the prophets and apostles in their day could and would happen to the church of his day. Their experiences established a paradigm of the dynamics of all sacred history.

Also, from his first encounter with evangelical opponents, Luther had equated them with the false prophets and apostles who had plagued the true prophets and apostles. In the course of his struggles with the fanatics during the 1520's he found many parallels between them and the biblical false brethren. It was only natural that he would see the true prophets and apostles as having provided a precedent for the way in which one should deal with such opponents. In time, these parallels between his evangelical opponents and the false brethren of the biblical accounts influenced his view of himself. Finding so many parallels in his own experience, gradually he came to see himself as occupying in his time the role occupied by the true prophet or apostle in the biblical accounts. This view of himself was sustained by his belief in the unchanging struggle between the leaders of the true and the false churches.

Luther contended that from the time of the Fall an enmity had existed between the seed of the woman and the seed of the serpent.[4] The seed of the woman was Christ and, by extension, the true church; the seed of the serpent was the false church. "There is no peace between Christ and Belial or between the seed of the serpent and the seed of the woman."[5] Luther believed this struggle to be taking place in every age. It began when Satan persuaded Adam and Eve to forsake their faith in God, and it continued into Luther's day:

Generations come, generations go. If one heresy is overthrown, another soon arises, for the devil neither sleeps nor is drowsy. I, although I am nothing, have been in the ministry of Christ twenty years already, and I can truly testify that I have been assailed by more than twenty sects. Some of these have completely gone to ruin, others still twitch like insect limbs.[6]

Cain and Abel were the founders of the false and true churches. Cain's murder of Abel was the first act of persecution of the true church by the false, and the sons of Cain had continued this persecution until God had been forced to destroy the world, saving only Noah, "the herald of faith and righteousness." Throughout the history of Israel,

Satan made headway, killing all the prophets and finally Christ Himself:

From the beginning this has been the fundamental principle of the devil and the world: "We do not want to seem to be doing evil, but whatever we do must be approved by God and agreed to by all His prophets. If they do not do this, they must die! Down with Abel, long live Cain! That must be our law."[7]

As long as there is life there will be no peace, for Satan and his apostles never rest:[8] persecutions, sects, and disturbances always follow the preaching of the gospel,[9] the devil always sends false apostles among those who love the gospel;[10] the minister of Christ knows, therefore, "that as long as he teaches Christ purely, he will not lack perverse men who desire to disturb the church, even from among our own [sic]."[11] This struggle is unavoidable as long as Christ is preached.[12]

Luther could even contend that the more the world raged against the gospel the better. Since suffering always follows the preaching of the gospel, the *lack* of disturbances and suffering is, at the very least, a sign that the Word is not being preached. "Yes, if there are no disturbances and the devil is not enraged, then we do not have the Word. The world loves a lie and persecutes the truth when it hears it."[13] From this it follows:

Therefore we must become accustomed to those diabolic evils because he always defiles [the church] with the greatest scandals about doctrine. He sows various opinions and discords about doctrines and thinks he has conquered. But by this very thing we test our true doctrine.[14]

And so the minister of Christ should "rejoice that he endures sects and those seditious spirits who perpetually follow after him." This is the glory of the Christian: "the testimony of our conscience that we are found standing and fighting on the side of the seed of the woman against the seed of the serpent."[15]

Luther's Genesis Commentary, which is based on lectures from 1535 to his death, makes his view of the struggle between the true and false churches even clearer, for Luther saw the beginning of this struggle recounted early in the Bible.[16] He believed that the true church was established even before the Fall when God commanded

Adam to eat from every tree except the tree of the knowledge of good and evil.[17] Satan tempted Adam and Eve, and they fell, yet even as they fell, God announced the promise of the blessed seed that would crush the head of the serpent.[18] The saints of the Old Testament lived and taught this faith in the promise of the seed of the woman.

They delivered the very same sermons we set before the church today, except that they taught about the Christ who was to come and be revealed. But we speak in the past tense. We say: "Christ has come," whereas they said: "He will come."[19]

Because every promise of God includes Christ, Luther could claim that "the only difference between Abraham's faith and ours is this: Abraham believed in the Christ who was to be manifested, but we believe in the Christ who has already been manifested, and by that faith we are all saved."[20]

The true church began with Adam and with Abel, and Cain was the first member of Satan's false church.[21] Luther believed that the history of every age bore witness that the true church must always endure hardships and the persecution of the false, hypocritical church. "Therefore there is no doubt among us today that the church of the pope is the church of Cain," Luther said. "We, however, are the true church."[22] Once the purer doctrine of the gospel came to light, several kinds of opponents arose.[23] Satan raged, and through the pope, the bishops, and tyrannical princes, filled the entire world with poor people and exiles.[24]

Within the true church false prophets and false apostles arose and created sects and disturbed the peace of the church, "For Satan leaves the saints and the church of God no peace, when one sect has been either overcome or humbled, another springs up." The experiences of Adam, Abraham, Isaac, Jacob, Paul, and Christ all attest to this.[25] The reason was the same:

This evil has its origin in a loathing of the Word, and Satan originates this loathing with outstanding skill. Thus in our time Müntzer departed from the Word and kept stirring up rebellions. When these had been put down, Karlstadt and the sacramentarians disturbed the church. When they, too, were already giving way, the Anabaptists arose. Thus the church is never without a trial.[26]

Just as Abel did no harm to Cain, the Lutherans did no harm to the papists but allowed themselves to be harassed, condemned, and slain by them.[27] But rather than lose heart on account of condemnation and persecution by their adversaries, Luther urged himself and his followers to "gain the conviction that the cross and those verdicts are true and infallible signs of the true church."[28]

Convinced that this struggle between the true and false churches was continuing in his own day, Luther noted in his lectures on St. Paul's letter to the Galatians specific parallels between his experiences and those of the prophets and apostles, especially those of St. Paul, even finding parallels in the ways that he and Paul had come to the gospel.

In commenting on Gal. 1:13, where Paul reminds the Galatians that he had once been a strict Jew and a passionate persecutor of Christians, Luther has Paul say, "I adhered more strongly than did you and your false apostles." Then he draws this comparison: "Thus I was more deeply stuck in monasticism to the point of delirium and insanity. . . . I was an extraordinary man for my brethren, and we were better papists than the papists themselves: we prayed and performed the mass diligently."[29] Until God rescued him, Paul was a zealot and persecuted Christians, thinking it was meritorious. "In similar fashion, I lived in poverty and chastity, caring nothing about the things of the world. Meanwhile underneath this sanctity, this trust of mine, I nursed blasphemy and a distrust of God, and I experienced fear." And even as Paul persecuted the Christians, Luther confessed, he himself would have assisted gladly in the burning of Hus, if not by carrying the wood and straw to the fire, at least by consenting to it in his heart.[30]

These two men, who had once been staunch supporters of the old faith, came to preach another gospel. In the face of determined criticism by members of the old faith, Paul had argued that he received his apostleship and doctrine not from men but directly from God. "Thus it is for me," Luther said. "I do not have what I teach from the Pope. External symbols and Holy Scripture, yes, but I do not have my doctrine from him."[31]

Luther made numerous comparisons between Paul's suffering and his own. He compared Paul's temptations and tribulations with the "stigmata of glory" that gave a person a reputation among men, such as those of St. Francis. Such stigmata were monastic follies. The *true* stigmata were hunger, imprisonment, accusations of sedition, dangers, and false brethren (2 Cor. 6:5; 11:26ff). "Thus it is for us," Luther said:

We are killed all day; the devil attacks us in our heart. Externally he vexes us through evils and fanatics, and all on account of Christ. These things are stigmata. Thus the kings and nobles give us good marks and stigmata as do our adversaries, the devil, the world, and the flesh.

St. Francis' stigmata, even if they were genuine, were worthless in Luther's eyes, for they were corporal sufferings and were not suffered on God's account. "But to be frightened by the devil and his darts," Luther said, "those are stigmata that we do not want, and yet I am forced to suffer because the world rends [me]."[32]

Both Luther and Paul suffered the charge of causing scandal and splintering the church into sects. Luther was held responsible for Müntzer and Karlstadt and their factions,[33] and he had to endure as Paul had the *tentatio* that when people saw so many sects appearing in the wake of the new teaching, they asked themselves if it might not have been better to remain within the old faith.[34]

Both men had to suffer with those who thought that since they were not justified through the law, they should be able to live without the law:

This is what happened to the Apostle Paul. This is what happens to us. It also happened that way with the peasants of Wittenberg.... Therefore they said to Paul: we shall do nothing. And thus it is today.... It happened to Christ and to Paul so why shouldn't it happen to us?[35]

Both Luther and Paul had to endure the hatred of those who were of the old faith as well as the hatred of those who were once their followers but had fallen away from the gospel:

Consider those who were seduced by the fanatics. They are more hostile to us than to the Pope, although we do not merit this ill-will from them and they have everything good from us. But the fanatic comes along and excites them so much that they work against us, whom they [once] willingly listened to, with the most bitter disposition and hatred. And nothing is brought forward more harshly than that they should have another teacher. Such was the case with Paul.[36]

When the Galatians accepted Paul, they earned bitter hatred from both gentiles and Jews, and from this Luther drew another parallel: "Just as my name is most bitterly hated, whoever praises me participates in this hatred."³⁷ The sacramentarians were once united with the Lutherans in zeal and love, but now they were impatient with them. "Thus it occurred with the Galatians: when they were subverted by the false apostles, they then no longer recognized Paul as their teacher, just as our fanatics wish to force us to be slaves."³⁸ To the preceding quote George Rörer appended to his notes of the lectures a comment that Luther had made at the table:

This hatred of the adversaries is satanic and beyond human nature. Moreover, these two things, the ingratitude of our people who desire avidly to kill the ministers of the Word and the hate of the adversaries, are most certain signs to us that our doctrine is the true Word of God which Satan thoroughly hates and persecutes.³⁹

Both Luther's and Paul's false brethren sought contradictions in their writings,⁴⁰ and the false apostles boasted that they "had fetched back from the heretic Paul many who now lived in the bosom of mother synagogue." "So it is today," Luther said. "They boast, 'we have led back [many] to the bosom of the Church.' "⁴¹ If Paul had remained quiet and had not preached against circumcision, the Jews would have praised him. But because he had preached against circumcision, all of Judaism had been in an uproar and he had suffered persecution. Similarly, if Luther were willing to adore the pope and teach his doctrine, then Satan and the pope would be quiet. Because Luther was not willing to do this, there was scandal and uproar everywhere. This was the inevitable result of Luther's and Paul's teachings.⁴²

Luther and Paul had their authority impugned on the same grounds. Both were attacked for being a single individual opposing an institution with a long, venerable tradition. The false teachers who crept in after Paul boasted that they were of the Jewish race, the holy people, the seed of Abraham, and that they had the promises of the fathers. They were the disciples of the apostles and had seen them perform signs, and they had, perhaps, even performed signs themselves. They were led to ask "Who is Paul?" and they answered the question themselves:

He is the most recent convert to Christianity while we are disciples of the apostles. We saw Christ and heard him preach. ... And we are Jews, and it is impossible that God would abandon us, who are of the holy people. Finally, we are many while Paul is one.

For Luther, this was "just as the pope does with his argument, '[We are] the Church! Do you think that God would allow the Church to err for so many centuries?' "[43] But Luther found it a marvelous thing that one man such as Paul *could* be the church. When Barnabas and Peter strayed, for example, Paul maintained the true church and called the others back to the true way.[44] On other occasions, Luther expressed a similar wonder in talking of Abraham's faith, and he was particularly moved by the example of Noah.*

Luther also believed that he and Paul had both suffered the accusation of not going far enough. Paul, the false apostles had argued, had begun well but he stopped short of advocating circumcision:

Such is the case today. They say of us that we have a timid spirit, that we ought to go beyond faith in Christ. That is the beginning, [they say,] but the beginning, middle, and end belong together.[45]

Karlstadt and Müntzer had made this charge: "We began well, but because we did not advance, we are considered to be worse than the papists."[46]

---

* Luther thought that his own experiences allowed him to understand the trials and tribulations that Noah experienced. "From the character and nature of the world and of the devil, from the experiences of the apostles and prophets, and from our own experience we can infer how great an example of patience and of all virtues Noah was." Noah was an amazing man because he alone defied the entire world and condemned it as evil. The world must have hated him intensely and harassed him, asking: "Is it you alone who are wise?" Similarly, Luther claimed, the papists assailed him and his followers with the same question: "Do you think that all the fathers were in error?" The sacramentarians and the Anabaptists and "a thousand others" also condemned the Lutherans but, Luther pointed out, this was all child's play, for he and his followers had many churches that were in agreement and princes who supported them. But Noah had been alone and had had no such supporters or protectors. "If I had been aware that so many men in the generation of the wicked were opposing me," Luther confessed, "I surely would have given up the ministry in despair. No one believes how difficult it is for one man to oppose the common opinion of all other churches, to contend against the views of very good men and very good friends, to condemn them, and to teach, live, and do everything in opposition to them." Noah remained for Luther an example of incredible faith, a person, like Paul, who alone stood up for the true gospel against all the world. For these arguments see WA 42:

On still another score, it seemed that Luther and Paul both had to suffer the charge that they sinned against charity by stubbornly insisting on a trifle.[47] The sacramentarians accused Luther of being stubborn and disturbing the peace of the church over one insignificant doctrine despite their agreement on all other points; the Galatians asked Paul why he did not tolerate their conduct and weaknesses (*mores et infirmitatem*).[48] "I believe," Luther said,

that by this argument they subverted many good men, for it is designed to excite ill-will against us and to subvert doctrine. Thus they say: "Why are we agreed in all articles and only in this one still uncertain article not of one mind? You, who thus stubbornly maintain that one uncertain article, seem therefore not to have regard for doctrine and harmony."[49]

It was Luther's belief that he and Paul had suffered similar attacks from false brethren who were bewitched by Satan and motivated by vanity and a desire to avoid persecution. In Gal. 3:11, Paul asked the Galatians who had bewitched them so that they no longer obeyed the truth. When Luther came upon this question he answered that it was the devil.[50] Great men such as Zwingli, Oecolampadius, and the Anabaptists suffered under the same sort of "spiritual bewitchment."[51] Once ensnared in this bewitchment, they could not easily escape:

Just as it is impossible in [deceptions of] the senses for a man to extricate himself . . . in like fashion Zwingli and Oecolampadius cannot be freed unless they are illuminated by us. Otherwise, [they think they have] the most certain truth. If I adduce the Holy Scripture, they have 100 glosses prepared to elude it and not to admit it.

It would have been hard for Luther to believe that the devil could make his transformation into the form of Christ so realistic had he not observed it himself.[52] The human authors of this spiritual bewitchment would probably never be recalled to the truth. Luther believed on Paul's authority that people so thoroughly possessed by the devil were not likely to recover.[53]

It was Luther's contention that Paul's false brethren and his own

300–302, 323–24 (LW 2: 54–57, 87). See also Jaroslav Pelikan, *Luther the Expositor* (Philadelphia, 1959), pp. 97–99, and John M. Headley, *Luther's View of Church History* (New Haven, 1963), pp. 264–65.

were consumed by pride and a desire for popular approval.[54] He charged that Karlstadt, Zwingli, and "all those spirits" did everything to gain applause and fame among the common people. They wanted it to be thought that they had discovered a distinguished dogma that had conquered the Lutherans and the papists. This was in the nature of false brethren: "where there is applause, nothing is more confident, or rather foolhardy." It was particularly true of Karlstadt. Such men "wish to be praised and held [to be] the greatest and most erudite teachers." They

place themselves under our doctrine and are united with us for a time. [Then] they say that they have breathed the spirit, but they do not remain orderly but set something off. As Paul once had, so now we have several such men who place us in obscurity and glorify themselves.

Pride of this kind was such a poisonous and evil blasphemy that Paul had dedicated a chapter to it.[55] "That is the wretched pride," Luther said in his typically colorful fashion, "on which the devil wipes his ass."[56] Karlstadt, Zwingli, Oecolampadius, and Erasmus, he said, burned with hatred when he did not do what they wished.[57] They sought fame and wanted to claim credit for the reformation, while at the same time they wished to seem humble brethren who were zealous for the glory of God. Just as the false apostles tried to improve on Paul's work by advocating circumcision, the sacramentarians tried to improve on the doctrine of justification by faith, for they wanted the credit for bringing down the papacy.[58] But they were using God's name to cover up their vainglory. "My fanatics," Luther said, "brought vainglory into the land."[59]

Combined with their zeal for glory Luther saw a desire to avoid persecution. False brethren always insinuated themselves among those who loved the gospel, even in the territories of the impious princes such as Archduke Ferdinand and the King of Bavaria. "They don't wish to bite the fox, only the sheep." Instead of going where they might be persecuted, they "sprinkled their poison" in places where the gospel was tolerated. And so it was in Galatia: when it had been prepared for Christ, the false brethren poured in. "Why didn't they go to Jerusalem or Rome where no one yet had been, as Paul and the apostles did with great danger to themselves?"[60]

When Paul rebuked Peter in the presence of the church at Antioch (Gal. 2:11–14), he provided an example that Luther would use many times to justify both his own refusal to yield on points of doctrine and his rebuke of his opponents. In discussing this famous confrontation, Luther pointed out that Julius, Celsus, Porphyry, Jerome, and Erasmus all accused Paul of pride in that he rebuked the greatest of the apostles in the presence of the church. They felt that Paul had exceeded the bounds of Christian modesty and humility. As Luther saw it, their accusation simply showed that they did not understand what was at stake. Paul was not dealing with something trivial, but with the supreme article of Christianity: justification by faith. This article must not be corrupted, and Luther's conclusion from Paul's example was that even if an angel preached a doctrine different from justification by faith, he was to be condemned. Paul's critics were considering the importance of the person, namely Peter; but Paul was properly considering the importance of the article of faith, which Luther believed had to take precedence over the person.[61] He stated this principle succinctly: if you are defending this doctrine, it matters not "if you tread on Peter's foot or even slug an angel in the mouth."[62]

It was Luther's contention that Paul had been proud and conceited through "divine necessity." His critics might think that he had become haughty with (self-)pride, but in fact he was being proud for the glory of God. "In matters of faith," Luther concluded, "we must be inflexible, unconquerable, and as unyielding as adamant. But in matters of charity, we should be as flexible as a leaf and reed, yielding in all things."[63] When Paul claimed that he had not obtained his teachings from men (Gal. 2:6), this, too, was a necessary pride. Luther modeled and justified his own behavior on this example:

I ought to be humble, but against the pope I should have a holy pride [and say]: I do not wish you as a teacher, for I know this [teaching] is true, and I can give rational arguments for it. But they do not wish to listen. . . . If we were not proud and did not in the Holy Spirit condemn the devil and all his [teachings], we would be unable to retain the article on justification by faith.

If the pope would allow this article of faith, Luther said, he would not only kiss his feet but carry him on his shoulders. But since the pope opposed this article, Luther remained firm:

I shall not yield to all the angels in heaven or to all the emperors and a thousand popes, for they wish to rip from me my sacred glory, the God who created me [and gave me] body and life, money and goods. . . . Here I wish to be the hardheaded, stubborn fool, and I am proud to be called such, for one may not yield here.[64]

And as for the sacramentarians who charged that Luther sinned against charity and disturbed the concord of the church in the dispute over the Lord's Supper, he cited Paul's saying that "A little yeast leavens the whole loaf." In matters of charity one could and should yield, but in matters of faith one must remain firm.[65] It was the devil who would willingly render doctrine impure by injecting these arguments about concord.[66]

Because of Paul's example and counsel, Luther felt certain in his judgment of his opponents. Putting Paul's words in the form of direct discourse,[67] Luther has him say:

I seek to please not man but God. Therefore I say that to teach other than I teach is anathema, for in this, pure doctrine can be recognized: if someone teaches that which He commands, and glorifies his creator and the one who sent him [then he is teaching pure doctrine].

All doctrine that teaches against grace must necessarily be unpure, so Luther felt he could state with the utmost confidence:

All doctrine that teaches other than what we taught is accursed, for we do not seek wisdom or the favor or grace of princes and bishops, but [we seek to please] God so that He favors us because we preach His gift, son, and grace, and we tread under foot all our own things. Those things that are different or contrary we say are from the devil, and we pronounce them to be anathema with utmost confidence.[68]

It was Luther's view that Paul did not disparage his opponents but that he judged them by his apostolic authority. And Luther then added: "Just as it is proper for us [so to judge]: we are not simply insulting them when we judge that the pope, Oecolampadius, and Karlstadt are diabolical."[69] Since Luther and his followers had received the Holy Spirit, they had been made different men with a new sense and judgment. They were capable of judging all laws and doctrines, whereas those who were without the article on justification by faith were incapable of judging anything. This new spirit and competence to judge was not a human virtue according to Luther, but was a gift from God that came with the preached word and made them new men.[70]

It was from Paul too that Luther learned the proper way to rebuke an opponent. Paul's treatment of the Galatians who had been misled was mild, but his full anger was turned against the false teachers.[71] Luther claimed that his rebukes were like Paul's: they were harsh but not bitter. He, too, did not wish his adversaries to perish but wished them to return to the proper way.[72] Paul's example even showed that Christians might curse those who taught doctrine different from the doctrine of justification by faith, for Paul had cursed those who were so ardent about advocating circumcision, and had recommended that they go the whole way and make eunuchs of themselves.[73] But this was not all. He learned from Paul that the law should be cursed when not functioning in its proper sphere,[74] that ceremonies should be done away with when they were interpreted as contributing to eternal life,[75] that respect of persons should be observed only outside affairs of religion,[76] and that Christian freedom should not be misused to gratify the flesh.[77] He learned also from Paul that all those who taught salvation by works and observance of the law were disturbers of the church, including the pope and the monks,[78] and that he should condemn them accordingly.

In his lectures on Genesis, when discussing the descendants of Ham, Luther is reported to have enunciated this revealing exegetical principle:

Even though there is no written record of what they attempted against the true church, against Noah himself, the ruler of the church, and against his pious posterity, it can nevertheless be surmised by analogy if we carefully consider the actions of our opponents at the present time. For Satan, who incites the ungodly against the true church, is always the same.[79]

It should be obvious from what we have seen of his lectures on Galatians that Luther was following this principle in his consideration of St. Paul's letter. Luther felt secure following this principle because he believed that the devil was motivating his opponents and the devil never changed. The struggle between the true and false churches and between the true and false prophets and apostles continued in the same pattern because of the unchanging nature of Christ and of Satan, who, in the ultimate analysis, were the true protagonists.

By 1531 Luther had come to believe that he occupied in his time the same role that the true prophets and apostles had occupied in biblical times. This does not mean that he thought that he was a prophet or apostle on the same scale as his biblical predecessors. His sense of his own limitations was such that he would have felt very uncomfortable making a claim of this kind, for he did not feel in any way the equal of these men of God. Nevertheless, he did see himself as occupying the same role, however unworthy he might be. He felt that he bore most of the true stigmata that Paul also had had to bear: internal doubts and temptations, external afflictions and persecutions. And Luther feared that when he died Germany would enter a period of disorder and darkness, and that false teachers would arise and subvert everything, as had also happened in the time of Paul.[80]

It is evident that although Luther might be unwilling to claim equality with the biblical prophets and apostles, he nonetheless had a keen sense of his importance in the affairs of the church of his age. The startling parallel he drew between his background in Catholicism and Paul's background in Judaism suggests that he identified himself with Paul on a very personal level as well. The many similarities he saw between his own afflictions and Paul's reinforced this identification, as did the similarities he saw between their respective opponents.

The significance Luther attached to these similarities was brought out forcefully when he argued that he was able to understand St. Paul only because they had experienced similar sufferings. He made the point that St. Jerome did not understand Paul because he had lived at a time when the church was experiencing temporal success, when the bishops were tyrants, when few of them preached, and when those who did preached their own traditions. There was also no persecution:

Therefore it was impossible for Jerome to understand Paul. It is for that reason that we understand Paul. If we did not have the temptations of the devil through force and trickery, we would not understand, just as the previous ages did not understand. Hence [there are] internal temptations.[81]

This line of reasoning suggests that the parallels Luther saw between himself and Paul were reassuring to him. In the preceding section we saw several other indications that Luther believed that the parallels between himself and Paul, and between his opponents and Paul's, confirmed his doctrine as the true doctrine. His sense of certainty and righteousness was undoubtedly bolstered by these parallels.

Once Luther saw himself in the role Paul had occupied, he had an explicit model for his behavior toward opponents. He could explain and justify his polemics and his stubbornness on points of doctrine by pointing to the example set by Paul. When critics charged, as they frequently did, that Luther violated the requirements of charity and modesty in his polemics, there was no need to be disturbed, for he had a cogent rationalization for his behavior.

Finally, by equating his evangelical opponents with the biblical false prophets and apostles and by linking them all to Satan, he justified his characterizations of them as vain, lying hypocrites who were wantonly violating their own consciences. Apparent differences between them were a deception, for the devil rode them all. Because they shared a common devilish spirit, the misdeeds of one were potentially the misdeeds of all.

By occupying the role previously occupied by the biblical prophets and apostles, Luther bolstered his own authority and thus validated his teachings. A true prophet could not advocate false teachings; God would not allow it. By equating his evangelical opponents with the biblical false prophets and apostles, he discredited them and, by association, the beliefs they held. A false brother was a vain, self-serving man whose every utterance should be held suspect. Both roles with their attendant characteristics and behavior were embedded in the paradigm of the unchanging struggle between the true and false churches. Much of their vitality, elaboration, and justification came from this larger world view.

⚜ 16 ⚜

The Wittenberg Concord

With the failure in Marburg in 1529 to reach agreement on the Lord's Supper, Philipp of Hesse's plans for an evangelical alliance that included the Upper German cities (and even the Swiss evangelicals!) could not be realized. In mid-October the parties to the secret alliance formed at the Diet of Speyers met in Schwabach to decide whether their alliance should continue. At this meeting Electoral Saxony and the Margravate of Brandenburg insisted that the prerequisite to a political alliance was a common confession. As a basis for this confession they offered the seventeen Schwabach articles drawn up by Luther, Melanchthon, and Jonas prior to the trip to Marburg. These articles were unequivocally Lutheran in their formulation and, as a result, could not be accepted by the Upper German cities.[1] Further negotiations were scheduled for later in the year at a meeting to be held in Schmalkalden.

In preparation for this meeting, the Elector requested an opinion from his Wittenberg theologians on the propriety of concluding an alliance with the Upper German cities. On 18 November 1529 Luther sent the Elector the theologians' opinion together with a letter of his own. The theologians advised strongly against concluding such an alliance. They listed several reasons "why one should not reach an agreement or arrangement with the fanatics for the protection of their error." Central to their argument was the assertion that by offending against one article of faith, the fanatics were guilty of offending against them all. They brushed aside all the arguments advanced by the Landgraf in favor of the alliance. "Better to form an alliance with pagans than with apostates!" they concluded.[2]

In his accompanying letter Luther confined his discussion to the political aspects of such an alliance. He saw the possibility that it might eventually result in bloodshed and he did not wish such a burden on his conscience. He advised the Elector to rely on Christ's protection and repeated the offer he had made years earlier to Frederick the Wise:

And if it should come to the point (which I doubt) that the Emperor should continue to press and demand my extradition, or any others', then by God's grace we shall stand up for ourselves, [and] shall not expose Your Electoral Grace to any danger in our behalf. . . . For Your Electoral Grace is not to defend my faith, or that of anyone else.[3]

On 28 November the evangelical princes and cities met in Schmalkalden and once again a common confession of faith as expressed in the Schwabach articles was presented as the prerequisite to a political alliance. None of the cities, including Nuremberg and Strasbourg, could accept these conditions. Therefore another meeting was scheduled to be held in Nuremberg in early January, and this time only those willing to subscribe to the Schwabach articles were to send representatives.[4] At this meeting several cities, including Nuremberg, accepted the Schwabach articles, but Strasbourg, Constance, and the other "sacramentarian" cities of Upper Germany were left out of the alliance.[5] With the Emperor returning to Germany and calling for an imperial diet to meet in Augsburg in the spring, these cities were faced with the danger of perhaps having to deal on their own with an angry Emperor determined to reestablish the Roman Catholic faith within his empire.

This danger led the Strasbourgers to conclude an alliance with Zurich and several other Swiss cities, thereby confirming Luther's harsh judgment of them. "The people of Strasbourg," Luther wrote Hausmann in early February,

have defected from the Empire to the Swiss people, and are planning to resist Emperor Charles. I have been a prophet since I always have said that the spirit of the sacramentarians is full of hidden [leanings toward] insurrection. This spirit now comes to the fore and betrays itself. Unless God intervenes they will give us a new Müntzer, but they will do this to their own ruin, so that they, the violators and defilers of the sacrament and the gospel, may receive their punishment.

He also told Hausmann that since the colloquy at Marburg the sacra-mentarians were burning with a worse hatred for the Lutherans than ever before.[6]

Luther's suspicions of the Strasbourgers were increased when he had word from Gerbel at the end of February that his old opponent, Karl-stadt, had arrived in the city and was receiving a friendly reception from the Strasbourg clergy. Gerbel feared that Karlstadt might ignite another dispute.[7] Luther took the news badly. To Melanchthon he wrote: "Look what the Strasbourgers are doing! But Karlstadt will fulfill my prophecy that he does not believe there is a God."[8]

On 11 March 1530 the imperial summons to a diet in the city of Augsburg reached Electoral Saxony. The Elector ordered his theo-logians to draft articles expressing the Saxon position on matters of faith and ecclesiastical practice and to make ready to accompany the Elector to the diet. Melanchthon, Jonas, Luther, and Veit Dietrich, Luther's famulus, left Wittenberg on 3 April. They met the electoral party in Torgau and the entire Saxon contingent traveled to Coburg, the southernmost electoral residency and castle. Lacking a safe-con-duct for Luther, who was under both imperial and papal bans, the electoral party left him and Dietrich in the Coburg castle while they continued on to Augsburg. During the months of the diet, Luther followed the proceedings from the Coburg castle through letters from friends and reports from Nuremberg.[9]

A few days after his arrival in Augsburg, Melanchthon reported to Luther on the situation there. In the course of his letter, he described a discussion he had recently had with the Hessian theologian Erhard Schnepf about the Landgraf's position on the Lord's Supper and the frequent correspondence between the Landgraf and the sacramen-tarians, especially the Swiss and the Strasbourgers. Melanchthon sug-gested that it might be useful for Luther to write to Philipp in order to strengthen his heart against improper teaching,[10] and on 20 June Luther followed Melanchthon's suggestion.[11]

In his letter, Luther expressed concern for the Landgraf because he was being urged by the sacramentarians to join their party. "And even if their attempts and search for a contact might not be harmful to Your Sovereign Grace," Luther explained, "yet I know well what a mighty one and [what a] conjurer the evil spirit is, [who] insinuates [evil] with all kinds of cunning thoughts, and if he cannot win with force or cunning, he finally is able to wear people down with his incessant pushing, and thus to dupe them." Once again seeing Satan's spirit behind his opponents, Luther admonished the Landgraf not to be moved by the "sweet" words of the sacramentarians "or rather . . . the devil's cunning insinuations and thoughts, which St. Paul in Ephesians 6 calls 'flaming darts.' " He then denounced the sacramentarians and their arguments in a striking passage:

I know for a fact that [our] opponents themselves cannot silence their consciences with [the poor biblical passages they quote], and I am convinced that, were the beer in the barrel again, they would now let it remain there. This was very obvious to me on several occasions at Marburg. But since they have arrived at a negative position, they are unwilling and unable to retreat. Beyond this, Your Sovereign Grace at that time heard that their two best arguments were based on the following: Since the sacrament is a sacrament or sign, it could not be Christ's body itself, as Oecolampadius argued; and since a body would need some room, Christ's body could not be present there, as Zwingli argued. These certainly are absolutely rotten and unsound arguments, and we can hear them ridiculed even by the papists and sophists. Dear God, how many Scripture passages did [our opponents] quote in which they were openly caught as having erred and failed, and now they have to abandon them! Certainly this demonstrates sufficiently that there is no solid foundation [for their position], but only their own mere folly. Your Sovereign Grace knows further that [our opponents] did not remain with only this [one] error, but have [also] taught inappropriate things concerning baptism, infant baptism, hereditary sin, the usage of the sacraments, and the external Word; and yet they were so fickle in [these teachings] that (as Your Sovereign Grace knows) at Marburg they conceded all to us, and talked [quite] differently.[12]

Luther warned the Landgraf that all who accepted the sacramentarians' faith must assume responsibility for all their errors and more. Furthermore, he pointed to the Strasbourgers' reception of Karlstadt, and alleged that the Strasbourgers believed all the "obvious lies which that wretched man dreams up about us" and that they were defending him "God knows for how long." Luther spoke of the sorrow he would suffer if the Landgraf became a participant "in all their unfounded matters, evil folly, and grossly wrong teachings and actions." This would be a tremendous burden on the Landgraf's conscience, and also the Landgraf would thereby strengthen many in their error so that they might never recover. In his closing words Luther wrote about himself:

It is true that I have suffered such great torment and danger for my teachings that I certainly would not want to have done such sour labor in vain, nor [continue] to do it. Therefore I certainly would not resist them because of hatred or arrogance; God, my Lord, knows that I would have accepted their teaching a long time ago, if only they could demonstrate [a sound] foundation [for it]. But [the foundation] on which they stand is something on which I am unable to base my conscience. And so I hope that Christ, our Lord, has accomplished something through me, poor instrument [that I am], so that [our opponents] cannot in any way consider me as someone who has [done] nothing against their actions.[18]

As before, Luther wished no one to hold him responsible for the sacramentarians or their errors.

Several days later in a letter to the Bremen pastor Jacob Probst, Luther dealt at length with the sacramentarians' claim that they had conquered Luther at Marburg. This claim was just like them, Luther said, "for they are not only liars but are themselves lies, counterfeit, and pretense, which Karlstadt and Zwingli attest to by their words and deeds." They had renounced their previous position on baptism, the use of the sacraments, the external Word and the like, while the Lutherans had not renounced anything. But when they were also defeated in the matter of the Lord's Supper, they were unwilling to renounce this article although they saw that they could not maintain their position. This, Luther said, was because they were afraid of their populace and that they would not be permitted to return if this last article was also renounced.

Luther then characterized Zwingli's and Oecolampadius' positions much as he had done in his letter to Landgraf Philipp, and described how earnestly they had wished to be considered brethren by the Lutherans. Zwingli, with tears in his eyes, had said: "There are no people in the world with whom I would rather be united than with the Wittenbergers." And Luther had answered, much to their disappointment, that they had a different spirit from the Lutherans. Finally, the Lutherans had told them that although they were not brethren they should not be deprived of the Lutherans' love, which is due even an enemy, "So they were most indignant that they could not obtain the name of brother and were forced to depart as heretics." Luther assured Probst that this was an accurate account of the meeting and could be repeated with confidence to refute the sacramentarians' lies.[14]

In the following months of the diet Luther was primarily concerned with the negotiations with the Roman Catholics. Occasionally Melanchthon, Jonas, and John Agricola digressed from their accounts of the more important affairs of the diet to tell him about the activities of the Upper Germans and Swiss.[15] Melanchthon wrote about the treatises that Zwingli and Oecolampadius had prepared for the diet, and in reference to Zwingli's *fidei ratio* he wrote:

> Zwingli has sent here a printed confession. You would swear that he has lost his mind. He has publicly renewed his old errors on original sin, on the use of the sacraments. Concerning ceremonies he speaks entirely "Helveticly," that is most barbarously: he wishes to abolish them all. He vigorously pushes his case on the Supper. He wishes to destroy all the bishops.[16]

Oecolampadius' *Dialogue* fared much better in Melanchthon's estimation. This was because, as Melanchthon conceded, Oecolampadius had written against him more carefully than was his wont.[17] By 14 July Luther had a copy of Zwingli's treatise and on 21 July he wrote sarcastically to Jonas:

> Zwingli and Bucer really please me! So they should bring God into the light! Of course we should enter into fellowship with them! But after the departure of the Emperor they will be other people once again.[18]

Luther wished to have nothing to do with them.

Martin Bucer, however, was hard at work attempting to bridge the gap between the Lutherans and the Upper German cities which because of the disagreement had been forced to submit a confession of their own, the Tetrapolitana, to the Emperor while the Lutherans were submitting the Augsburg Confession.[19] Melanchthon, clearly reluctant, at last met with Bucer on 22 or 23 August, and on the twenty-fifth he sent word to Luther that Bucer was writing him a letter about the Lord's Supper and wished to accede to the Lutheran position.[20] Bucer's letter, sent the same day, stated his position and expressed a conviction, one that would be repeated in the years of negotiation ahead, that there was no real disagreement between the positions held by Luther and the Strasbourgers. This Bucerian formula, one of a long series that ended with the Wittenberg Concord in 1536, is representative of its genre.

With exaggerated deference, Bucer addressed Luther in his salutation as the "preeminent lover of pure doctrine." Then he went on to explain his position:

Indeed, it has always seemed [to me] that there was by no means so great a difference between your and our opinions on the real presence of Christ in the Supper as was commonly believed. But after having recently read Oecolampadius' *Dialogue* in which he examined the opinions of the ancients on this issue, I believe that I can conclude with certainty that there is absolutely no difference between us. For since you do not wish to maintain that Christ is in the bread locally and you acknowledge that although Christ is bodily [*corporis modo*] present in one place in heaven, he can nevertheless be exhibited as truly present in the Supper through the words and symbols, I simply do not see what conflict there is between your opinion and what our people assert [namely], that the bread is a sign and a figure of Christ's body and that he is located somewhere in heaven. For they indeed acknowledge that the bread is a sign and a figure of the present Christ not the absent Christ and that through the sacred symbols is produced not merely the memory of him but also Christ himself truly present.

Bucer said that he had discussed this matter with Melanchthon, who had helped him formulate his position in a set of articles which Melanchthon would send to Luther. He enclosed with his letter another set of articles, however, "in which I have set down the same opinion and also added the manner in which Christ is perceived to be present in the Supper, namely by the mind's eye [*oculis mentis*]." Bucer was sure that the contest was over words rather than substance. And, to add urgency and force to his appeal, he pointed out the damage the dispute was doing to the evangelical cause in France.[21]

In his articles Bucer came as close to the Lutheran position as was possible without giving in on the point that was of crucial importance to the Upper Germans and Swiss, namely, that Christ was truly present only to believers. Bucer argued that participants who believed could deal with the sacrament from unbelief so that they were guilty of sinning against the body and blood of Christ as had happened to the Corinthians (1 Cor. 11:27). This allowed for the real presence also for the unworthy who nonetheless believed. But Bucer was still at odds with Luther's central tenet in that he still tied the real presence to the faith of the participants rather than to Christ's promise. Furthermore, in his careful formulations Bucer sidestepped the assertion that Christ was "essentially" present, a significant point which he had conceded in the theses Melanchthon had drawn up during their discussion. As his later explanation of the articles shows, he was basically still advocating a spiritual rather than a real presence.[22]

It is hardly surprising, therefore, that Melanchthon commented to Dietrich: "Those propositions, which he is sending, do not at all seem to correspond with those I wrote down according to his opinion [i.e., at his dictation]"; perhaps, he said, Bucer was not being entirely candid.[23] Luther's reaction was similar and on 11 September he wrote to Melanchthon that he was not going to answer Bucer's letter:

> You know that I hate their tricks and subterfuges; they do not please me. They have not taught in such a fashion up to now, but they do not wish to acknowledge [this] or do penance, rather they proceed to assert that there was no disagreement between us, to wit, that we should confess that they had taught properly [and] that we had attacked [them] falsely or, more likely, that we have been insane. Thus the devil sets traps against our Confession from all sides, since he was unable to accomplish anything by force and was overcome by the truth.[24]

Bucer was not to be put off so easily, however. At the suggestion of Duke Ernst of Lüneburg, he decided to visit Luther.[25] On 25 September he arrived in the city of Coburg and the next morning he went up to the castle where Luther invited him to breakfast and discussion.

According to Bucer's report, Luther began by expressing his dissatisfaction with Bucer's statement that (only) the soul received the body of Christ. Bucer countered that, as Luther himself had taught, the oral manducation referred only to the bread and could only be attributed to Christ's body through the sacramental union. Then Luther argued a bit over the issue of the reception of Christ's body and blood by the impious, since he did not believe that Christ's presence depended upon the faith of the recipients but rather depended solely upon Christ's promise in the words of institution. To this Bucer replied that Christ's promise was made only to his disciples.

Luther was totally opposed to the formulation of new articles that they could both sign, since each side would interpret them differently from the other, as he had learned with the Marburg articles. He thought it would be better if Bucer and the other ministers gradually, in sermons and treatises, disabused the people of the notion that there was only bread and wine in the Supper, for he was certain that that was what the ministers had previously taught. And Luther added: "I shall not confess that I had misunderstood you people." The day's discussion ended with Luther assuring Bucer that he wished concord with his whole heart as long as the concord was arrived at truthfully.

The next day Bucer was unable to persuade Luther that he and his fellow ministers had taught about the Supper in the proper way, and Luther persisted in his opinion that it was necessary that they call their congregations back to the true way, but gradually, in order to avoid the offense that would accompany a sudden change. Bucer agreed to admonish his fellow ministers to this effect, and committed himself to visiting a number of the Upper German and Swiss cities before returning to Strasbourg. He also promised to compose a confession under his own name which he would send to Luther for Luther's evaluation, and which would include an appropriate apology (*excusationem*) for the dispute. Luther felt that such an apology was necessary, since he doubted that there could be a genuine agreement signed by both parties unless one or both recanted their previous beliefs. This condition and Luther's stubbornness caused Bucer to comment to Strasbourg friends: "As you well know, although he [Luther] often runs off the [true] way, nevertheless he does not tolerate [*sustinet*] running back." And he summed up his evaluation of the Saxon reformer in a few phrases:

He truly fears God and seeks God's honor from the heart, but is nonetheless more excited by admonitions. Thus God has given him to us and thus we must use him. . . . Peace cannot be reestablished in the church unless we tolerate many things in this man.

Bucer judged that everything depended upon an appropriate formulation of the concord so that it would not seem that Luther had conceded anything, and he added the frank observation that "no one perhaps except me will undertake to issue a formulation that will satisfy Luther."[26]

Luther was suspicious of Bucer and his slippery formulations, but he now nursed some hope for eventual reconciliation. In November he wrote to Briessmann:

There is hope that the sacramentarians, or at least the Strasbourgers, will return to grace [*in gratiam redire*] with us. For Bucer was sent to discuss this issue with me in a friendly colloquy on the Coburg and if what he said is not a deception (for I warned him not to dissemble) then there is no little hope.[27]

Bucer, meanwhile, was making his rounds among the Upper German and Swiss cities seeking an acceptable formula for agreement. For the next six years he was to make many such trips before his quest for concord was finally successful.

Upon his return to Strasbourg, Bucer immediately composed his promised confession.[28] Once again he maintained that the controversy was more over words than over substance, and repeated his formula that the true body and the true blood of Christ were truly present in the Supper and were offered with the words of the Lord and the Sacrament as food for the soul. His exposition skillfully combined Zwinglian and Lutheran formulations, and was another Bucerian masterpiece of ambiguity.[29] The treatise was finished on 9 November 1530 and circulated first among the Swiss and Upper Germans. Oecolampadius accepted it with its ambiguities, but Zwingli refused to give it his approval. Undaunted, Bucer sent the treatise, slightly revised, to Luther and the Landgraf and a number of others. The Landgraf passed a copy along to the Elector, who forwarded it to Luther with a request for Luther's opinion.

Luther's reply on 16 January 1531 pointed unerringly to the clear deficiencies in the treatise. Although he expressed his pleasure on reading that Bucer and his party agreed with the Lutherans that the true body and blood of Christ were present in the Sacrament and were offered with the words as food for the soul or for the strengthening of Christian faith, he doubted that Zwingli and Oecolampadius were of the same belief as Bucer since they had attacked this belief in their writings. Then he noted that Bucer had not discussed oral reception by the godless, although at Coburg he had presented a tolerable position on this point that had greatly pleased Luther. Luther believed that if the Strasbourg faction could agree with him on this issue then he and they would be united and a "lofty work and miracle of God" would be accomplished.[30] But, as we have seen, if Bucer were to accept the oral reception by the godless, he would have to give up his belief that Christ was present only spiritually and only to believers. The concord was still a long way off.

Writing directly to Bucer, Luther expressed his doubt that Zwingli and Oecolampadius believed what Bucer said they did, and made plain his reservations about the confession itself:

Now if we confess that Christ's body is truly offered to the soul as food, there is no reason why we cannot say that it is also offered in this fashion to a godless soul, although it does not receive it, just as the light of the sun is offered equally to the sighted and the blind. So I wonder why it bothers you to confess of your own accord that [Christ's body] is offered with the bread externally to the mouth of the pious as well as the impious.

But since it seemed that Bucer could not yet admit this, he suggested that efforts toward concord should be temporarily postponed. He explained:

I am not able to abandon this opinion, and if you do not feel this is demanded by Christ's words, as you write, nevertheless my conscience feels that it is demanded. Therefore I cannot acknowledge a solid and complete concord between us without doing injury to my conscience, nay, without sowing the seed for a much greater disturbance of our churches and for a more atrocious disagreement among us in the future.

He wished particularly to avoid the problems, as he saw them, that were entailed in intercommunion among people holding different conceptions of the Supper. His thinking was apparently this: that a person who believed in the real presence and communed at the hands of a minister who did not received mere bread and wine; whereas a person who did not believe in the real presence and communed at the hands of a minister who did received the true body and blood, and this was a sacrilege. In other words, Christ's presence was dependent upon the belief of the minister. This idea was totally objectionable to the Upper Germans and Swiss, and it seems also to differ significantly from Luther's usual insistence that Christ's presence was determined solely by Christ's promise.[31] However that may be, Luther felt that as things were, intercommunion would be worse than the present disagreement. As much as he wished for concord, he could not agree to it under the existing conditions, and he asked Bucer to attribute his refusal not to stubbornness but to conscience.[32] He repeated much the same sentiments in his letter to Duke Ernst of Lüneburg.[33] Nonetheless, it is apparent that he still had some hope of an eventual agreement through the intervention of God's grace.[34]

On 16 February Luther reported to the Elector that he was awaiting Bucer's reply to his letter. He put his finger on the issue still dividing them: the belief that the body and blood of Christ were externally present in the bread and wine and were received by the impious and pious alike. He could not yield on this point, and he felt he had already done a great deal. "Dear God," he exclaimed in exasperation, "is it such a hard thing [for them] to believe that a godless person may receive the body and blood of Christ, when they must believe that the devil led Christ bodily atop the temple and the high mountain, and afterwards the Jews seized and crucified Him?"[35]

Bucer had in fact written to Luther on 9 February. He vouched for Oecolampadius' sincere acceptance of his confession and briefly justified Zwingli's position. Then he attempted with difficulty to satisfy Luther's demand that he admit that even the godless could receive Christ's true body and blood. He confessed that those who knew that Christ's body was offered also received it, even though their souls might receive it to their destruction rather than as nourishment. As for the godless, who have no faith and regard the bread as no different from any other bread, Bucer saw them as no different from mice who happened to nibble at the bread. In effect, Bucer was still arguing that the reception of Christ's body and blood depended on the recipient's faith in, or at least his knowledge of, Christ's presence.

He also took issue with Luther's argument that intercommunion would lead to the sacrilege of some receiving Christ's body and others not, depending upon the belief of the officiating minister. Bucer held that God's gifts did not depend upon the faith or merit of the minister or even of the communicants. Those who accepted Christ's promise with faith as well as with their ears simply could not be frustrated in their hope, and as much as they believed, so they received. Moreover, he argued that even Christ's promise was given only to His disciples, who were believers, and thus there was no reason to worry about what unbelievers received. He agreed, however, to keep the negotiations and his confession secret for a while longer, and he suggested again that the dispute had to do more with words than with substance.[36]

Luther reacted favorably to this letter from Bucer. In the second half of March 1531, he wrote to the Eisenach pastor Justus Menius that it was true, as Menius had heard, that "Bucer has indeed begun to believe with us concerning the Sacrament unless his letters to me and Philipp [Melanchthon] are deceptive, which I have difficulty believing." It was still uncertain whether the other sacramentarians also were in favor of Bucer's position. Bucer had managed to get all of them to concede that the Lord's body was truly present and offered in the Supper, even corporally. "But the others," Luther added, probably with Zwingli and Oecolampadius in mind, "concede this offering and presence only to the believing and pious souls; but Bucer agrees that it is offered and received by the hand and mouth of the godless, for his letter clearly testifies to this."[37] He had interpreted Bucer's letter as "clearly" agreeing to the oral reception by the godless despite Bucer's many qualifying phrases.

Another letter written in late March to the Lutheran preacher John Frosch in Augsburg makes clear, however, that Luther still disagreed sharply with Zwingli and that he saw concord as possible only if Bucer and the others renounced their previous error. "I have heard of the boasting of your Michaelists," he wrote, referring to the Zwinglian Michael Keller and his followers in Augsburg,

that a concord has been reached between us and the Zwinglians so that the rumor has it that we have completely yielded to their belief. But you and your colleagues, my dear Frosch, believe steadfastly that we have yielded nothing of our belief.

Luther said that Bucer was diligently and sincerely disposed to believe and teach with the Lutherans, so that he had good hope that Bucer, at least, would return to the true way. As for the others, Luther had no certain information, but he was willing, if they sincerely wished concord, to be forbearing with them so that they might gradually move toward the Lutheran position. Meanwhile, Frosch should remain firm and not be swayed by the opposition's boasting, and, God willing, he would not change his belief and faith.[38]

So things stood through the summer and autumn of 1531 when Luther delivered the lectures on Paul's letter to the Galatians. Strasbourg and other Upper German cities had been accepted into the Schmalkaldic League on the basis of the Tetrapolitana and the "understanding" reached between Bucer and Luther, but their acceptance rested on very insecure foundations.[39] As for Luther, he felt some hope for eventual agreement with Bucer and the Strasbourgers, but he still believed Zwingli and Oecolampadius to be unrepentant and firmly stuck in their satanic error. Zwingli's death and the defeat of Zurich at the second battle of Kappel in 1531, followed soon after by Oecolampadius' sudden death, stripped Strasbourg and the other Upper German cities of their Swiss allies and dramatically increased the pressures to reach a more substantial agreement with the Lutherans. Bucer and the other Upper Germans were forced to accommodate themselves, whether they liked it or not, to the convictions of the uncompromising Saxon reformer and his Elector.

Much as in the case of Müntzer's death, Luther saw Zwingli's violent end and Zurich's defeat as a sure sign that Zwingli's teachings were blasphemous. Toward the end of December 1531, Luther wrote to Amsdorf:

The Zwinglians have reached an accord with the other Swiss but under the most shameful conditions in addition to the ignominy and disaster of so unhappily losing the leader of their doctrine. But this is the end of the glory which they sought by blaspheming Christ's Supper. And they still are not repentant, although they revoked practically everything in the peace conditions and justified the papists in everything. Indeed, they were forced to rescind all alliances with foreign princes such as the Landgraf. It says [Phil. 3:19]: "[they are the enemies of Christ's cross...] whose glory is in confusion."[40]

On 3 January 1532 Luther wrote that they had even appointed Karlstadt as Zwingli's successor.[41] This was not in fact the case, but Luther would have had no trouble believing such a rumor since it was in accord with his judgment of both Zurich and Karlstadt. On the same day he wrote Link in Nuremberg that they had now seen God's judgment a second time, first with Müntzer, now with Zwingli:

> I was a prophet when I said that God would not long tolerate these rabid and furious blasphemies, of which those people were full, ridiculing our "breaded" God, calling us carnivores and blood drinkers and bloody Thyesteans, and naming us other horrible names.[42]

Luther also suggested, in 1533, in a treatise directed for the most part against the papists that Oecolampadius had probably died of Satan's flaming darts, a suggestion that created a considerable uproar among the Swiss.[43]

In the meantime the disputes in Augsburg between the Lutherans and Zwinglians had continued, with the Zwinglians faring much better than the Lutherans. On 3 January 1532 Luther wrote to the Lutheran Kaspar Huber in Augsburg warning him against the Zwinglians and advising him and his coreligionists not to partake of the Supper with the Zwinglians. It would be better if they abstained from the Supper entirely. As for baptism, they should practice private baptism or, if that were forbidden, it would be better to accept baptism from the papists, for the fanatics had no baptism or sacrament at all.[44] When the content of this letter got about, it caused great excitement and bitterness in Augsburg and in Switzerland.[45]

Then in February 1532 Luther published an open letter to Duke Albrecht of Prussia which agitated the Zwinglians even more.[46] He announced that this letter was to be his last word on the subject of the sacramentarians and their teachings. In it he denied again that John 6 referred to the Supper, for it dealt with faith, which is the spiritual eating and drinking of Christ's body and blood. In the Supper, he asserted, both the worthy and the unworthy eat Christ's body. The worthy eat both bodily and spiritually, the unworthy eat only bodily and to their own destruction. Although the fanatics babbled on a great deal about spiritual eating, none of them understood what spirit, or spiritual eating, or faith really was. The Holy Spirit had warned Christians against these fanatics:

> For we have indeed seen how It struck Müntzer and his comrades and made of them a horrible example for all fanatics and enthusiasts, for

among them there was vain boasting about the spirit and contempt for the Sacrament, but it became apparent in the end what sort of spirit it was. In the same way It has chased Karlstadt here and there in the world, since he began the game, and not allowed him a place [*stat*] for his body or peace in his heart, like a true Cain marked and plagued by trembling and fear. And now recently It has punished the poor people in Switzerland, Zwingli and his people, clearly enough. This should be a warning to the fanatics [*dar an sich die Rotten geister billich strossen solten*] but they are impenitent, perverse, and self-condemned as St. Paul says.[47]

But the Zwinglians do not want to acknowledge these warnings, he went on to say, and they try to make out Zwingli, a man punished by God, to be a martyr! Luther was disappointed that the peace accord following the defeat of Zurich had allowed the Zwinglian doctrine to be tolerated. Since God had intervened so forcefully in the dispute, it was time to cease discussing the matter lest God punish the Lutherans as well. From the beginning of the church there had been a constant witness to the proper understanding of the Supper. Whoever denied this understanding cut himself off from the church. In closing he urged the Duke not to tolerate the sacramentarians within his lands. Karlstadt and the Zurichers wished to reply to this treatise publicly and Bucer dissuaded them only with difficulty. He had his hands full for a time calming the storm.[48]

No sooner had this turmoil quieted down, when in the last month of 1532 Luther loosed another thunderbolt. This was an open admonitory letter to the city council and congregation at Frankfurt am Main. Reports, he said, had reached him from Frankfurt that they taught a Zwinglian interpretation of the Supper but in such a fashion as to give the false appearance of agreeing completely with the Lutherans. His open letter was to be a witness "before God and the world that if some among you were under the delusion that your preachers were united with us and taught in the same manner about the Holy Sacrament, they would learn from [the letter] that we are in no way united and that no one may rely on hearing our teaching from them."[49] Luther then proceeded to attack those who when they said that Christ's body and blood were present in the Sacrament meant by this that the true body and blood of Christ were indeed present but only spiritually and not bodily and were received only in the heart by faith rather than bodily by the mouth. This was satanic double-talk, he said. The simple person believed that these people were teaching the same as the Lutherans, and he went to the Supper but received only bread and wine, "for their teachers give nothing else and believe nothing else too."*

He urged the communicants not to be satisfied with vague formulas. They should demand to know what the minister was offering them with his hands. It was not enough for the minister to explain that it was the body "as Christ had in mind" and to urge the communicants not to inquire further. That was a hypocritical, deceptive answer. He advised that whoever knew from general knowledge that his minister taught in a Zwinglian manner should avoid that minister and do without the Sacrament all his life rather than receive it from that minister:

But if your minister is one of the double-talkers who says with his mouth that the body and blood of Christ are truly present in the Sacrament but it is suspected that he is being deceptive and believes something else than the words say, go to him . . . and ask him plainly what it is that he offers you with his hands and you receive with your mouth.

A vague, ambiguous answer will give him away as a satanic charlatan playing with God's Word.[50] This criticism came very close to hitting Bucer.†

Luther went to great pains to reject the assertion that he had ever taught in such a fashion himself.[51] He explained how he could trust the devil and his apostles to distort his words wherever they could and thereby to mislead people with his name, which they had done frequently in the past. It was necessary, he felt, to make his position clear and to warn against people who might misuse his name to mislead others, "although I should reasonably hope that no one could be so wanton and unconscionable as to strengthen and maintain his error with my name since my Confession is published and available to the world and my books conclusively testify with what great seriousness

---

* WA 30/3: 559. Luther once again seems to be tying Christ's presence to the intention of the officiating minister. See note 31 above.

† So close that Bucer anonymously composed the Frankfurt clergy's reply. See Walter Köhler, *Zwingli und Luther*, 2: 299–302.

I have fought against this error so that a fanatic should be heartily ashamed to turn or use a [single] letter of Luther's for his error."[52]

In August 1533 this question of responsibility figured prominently in Luther's letter to the Augsburg Council. He found it a truly troublesome matter that the Augsburg clergy taught in such an ambiguous fashion that people took part in the Supper with conflicting beliefs about what they were receiving and in fact received mere bread and wine:

And it is a hard burden for us that they pursue this under our name and appearance [of agreement with us], as if they could not mislead the people without us. It is for this reason I am requesting your Eminences diligently and amicably to have your preachers, for Christ's sake, refrain from this offense and cease boasting among the people that they teach and believe the same as we do. For we deny it straightaway and know all too well that they teach in a Zwinglian fashion. . . . If they wish to teach and lead the people, they should leave our name in peace and use their own or their master's [Zwingli's]. For we wish to be innocent in regard to their doctrine and all the souls who will be deceived by them.

He warned the Council that if they did not comply with his request, he would be forced to issue a public treatise testifying to his innocence in the matter.[53] When the Council responded with an explication and justification of their doctrine composed by the Augsburg clergy,[54] Luther sent a brusque reply:

I have received your letter together with your preachers' "Answer." Now I did not request that you should inform me of your preachers' doctrine, which I already knew about, but that they cease boasting of my name and doctrine. I am [now] excused and have done my part.[55]

This exchange, like the exchange with Frankfurt, was another setback to Bucer's efforts to reach a concord.[56]

As had happened in the past, it took the intervention of Landgraf Philipp to renew serious negotiations between the two parties. In mid-1534 the Landgraf had, by force of arms, reestablished Duke Ulrich in Württemberg, and Duke Ulrich had introduced the reformation into his land with an ambiguous Württemberg Concord which contained elements of both Zwinglianism and Lutheranism.[57] Friction soon developed between the Zwinglian and Lutheran ministers, and there was a threat of open conflict. This situation made the need for agreement between the Upper Germans and the Lutherans even more urgent. Late in the summer of 1534 at the Strasbourgers' suggestion, the Landgraf wrote to Melanchthon and suggested a theological conference. Melanchthon, who had already shown some interest in a negotiated agreement, was receptive to this suggestion.[58] The Landgraf also wrote to Luther in late September pointing out the dangers facing the Upper Germans from the papists and urging Luther to work for union and agreement in the matter of the Supper.[59] Luther responded favorably although cautiously on 17 October.[60] It was finally decided to invite Melanchthon and Bucer to Kassel in Hesse for intensive discussions.[61]

On 28 and 29 December 1534 Melanchthon and Bucer met in Kassel and discussed the issues dividing them. Melanchthon carried with him an "Instruction" from Luther drawn up on 17 December apparently at the request of Melanchthon, who, like Luther, was reluctant to bear full responsibility for the negotiations.[62] This "Instruction" contained seven points. First, Luther insisted that they must in no way allow it to be said that each side had previously misunderstood the other. Such a statement would not be believed by anyone and would only make matters worse than before. Second, since their opponents so far had insisted that the elements were a sign whereas they had insisted they were the body of Christ, he thought that nothing would be more useless than to establish some new, median position whereby their opponents would concede that Christ's body was truly present and they would concede that only bread was eaten. Such a position would encourage all sorts of speculation. "I would therefore prefer," he wrote, "that the disagreement between these two beliefs be allowed to slumber rather than that occasion be given for innumerable questions so that people would eventually not believe anything." Third, Luther believed that the text of the gospel, innumerable citations from the fathers, and the history of the church stood on their side. Points four to six dealt with citations from Augustine. The seventh point is worth citing at length:

Seven, if these points are preserved, I have nothing more to demand, etc. For (as Christ is my witness) I would have willingly redeemed this disagreement with my body and blood (even if I had more than one body). But what should I do? Perhaps they are in good conscience caught in another opinion, [and] we should therefore bear with them. If they are sincere, then the Lord Christ shall liberate them. I, on the other hand, am truly in good conscience caught in this opinion (unless I do not understand myself). They should also bear with me. If, however, they wish to hold to their opinion, namely, concerning the presence of Christ's body with the bread and demand that we nevertheless should tolerate each other, I shall gladly tolerate them in hopes of future fellowship. For in the meantime I cannot maintain fellowship with them in faith and feeling.

But Luther nevertheless saw no impediment to a political concord.[63] It is clear from these instructions that he harbored a strong distrust for the "median position" advocated by Bucer. And, as his contemporaneous letters to Jonas and the Landgraf show, he did not expect much to come from this conference.[64]

Contrary to Luther's expectations, the negotiations at Kassel bore fruit. Melanchthon returned with a formula for concord, a letter from Bucer replying point by point to Luther's "Instruction," and a flattering letter from the Landgraf reporting on the negotiations and expressing the hope that Luther would be favorably disposed to the concord.[65] At the Elector's request,[66] Luther conferred with Melanchthon and wrote out his opinion of the Kassel formula, which the Elector then sent to the Landgraf. Although Luther found nothing objectionable in the formula itself, he thought it best not to conclude the concord precipitously. Since the matter had been so widely and profoundly contested from the beginning of the controversy to the present, many Lutherans would for the time being scarcely believe that Bucer and the Upper Germans really believed this formula. It was therefore better to postpone concord and in the interim have the two parties maintain friendly relations. Time would determine whether the Upper Germans sincerely held the pure, correct position; suspicions among the Lutherans would abate; and, finally, a proper, enduring agreement could be reached. This would, of course, require further consultations and negotiations.[67]

Luther suggested orally to the electoral chancellor Gregory Brück and to the Elector that since Melanchthon had negotiated only with Bucer at Kassel, it would be necessary to determine what the other Upper Germans felt about this formula and whether or not they would be willing to commit themselves to it at some later conference. Other Lutheran theologians, also, should be polled for their opinion on the matter, and he wrote to the Landgraf directly to explain the need to proceed slowly and carefully toward agreement, and to reassure him that he would do all he could to bring about an eventual concord.[68] The Landgraf, although desirous of ending the division between the two parties as soon as possible, agreed to let matters rest for the time being.[69]

It was the city of Augsburg that got the negotiations going again in the summer of 1535. At the suggestion of one of Luther's table companions, Jodocus Neuheller, the tutor of the nephew of an Augsburg merchant, the Augsburg Council sent Gereon Sailer and the Lutheran preacher Kaspar Huber to Wittenberg with a friendly letter from the Augsburg clergy. They took with them also a confession of faith in ten articles penned by Bucer and signed by the Augsburg clergy, a treatise by Bucer, and a request that the Lutheran Urbanus Rhegius, who had helped introduce the reformation into Augsburg but who now was a preacher in Brunswick-Lüneburg, or someone else of Luther's choosing be sent to Augsburg as a minister.[70]

The envoys were given a friendly reception by Luther, who is said to have shed "tears of joy" at the prospect of concord.[71] In his letters to the Augsburg Council and the Augsburg clergy, he hailed the prospect of agreement:

For nothing has been a greater joy to me in the whole course of our gospel than after this sad disagreement finally to hope for or rather to see a sincere concord among us, for Dr. Gereon has spoken [and] your letters have resounded and urged in such a fashion that my wound, that is my suspicion, is completely healed and not even a scar remains.[72]

Now, with concord in the church, he could die in peace. Although he was unable to send Rhegius to Augsburg, he did arrange for their second choice, John Forster, a born Augsburger, to accept the call.[73]

Report of these developments quickly circulated among the Upper German cities.[74] On 19 August 1535 the Strasbourg clergy wrote Luther that Bucer was the author of the ten articles which the Augsburg clergy had signed and had sent to him, and that the clergy serving the imperial cities of Constance, Frankfurt, Ulm, Esslingen, Memmingen, Lindau, Kempten, Landau, Weissenburg, Biberach, and Isny had also signed them. They reported that these articles were also accepted by the Swiss, although for various reasons they had not signed them. Certain questions and expressions, which were not wrong in themselves, were avoided, they explained, "out of consideration for the weakness of the common people." The question of what the godless received in the Sacrament was in this category. Throughout the letter they addressed Luther in very deferential terms.[75] Several of the other Upper German cities also wrote expressing their joy at the news of the concord.[76] Sailer reported on the joyous reception that he and the news of his discussions with Luther had received in Augsburg, Strasbourg, and other Upper German cities.[77] John Forster sent his first impressions of Augsburg, where he found the ceremonies different from Wittenberg's but tolerable. As for the Supper, it was publicly confessed, although not as explicitly as in Wittenberg, that the body and blood of Christ were present. This was to be attributed to inexperience (*inscitiae*) rather than to wickedness, for they were zealously attempting to uphold the concord.[78] On 28 September Luther wrote the Elector that Augsburg, Ulm, Esslingen, and Strasbourg had written about the concord in unexpectedly friendly terms,[79] and on 5 October he wrote a series of letters to councils, friends, and acquaintances in the Upper German cities about the concord.[80] To the clergy in Strasbourg he wrote expressing his joy and assuring them that to establish the concord he would do all that was needful or demanded. He suggested that a conference should be called as soon as possible—in Hesse or Coburg if they wished him to be present, since it was likely that the Elector would not permit him to leave his lands—but he left the choice of time and place to the Strasbourgers.[81] The Strasbourgers apparently replied suggesting Easter as a good time but leaving the choice of place to Luther, and Luther in turn replied that he would suggest Eisenach, Gotha, or Weimar to the Elector.[82] On the same day he wrote Gerbel in Strasbourg that nothing more joyous could happen to him as he departed this world than to leave peace behind him.[83] The Elector decided that Eisenach was the most convenient location,[84] and on 25 March 1536 Luther wrote Bucer about the Elector's choice and suggested 14 May as the meeting date. He asked Bucer to inform the Swiss and Upper Germans of this date and place.[85]

Although unable to get the Swiss to participate, Bucer managed to round up representatives for the conference from Ulm, Augsburg, Constance, Frankfurt, Esslingen, Reutlingen, and Memmingen and from the Freiherr von Gemmingen.[86] On 13 May the Upper German party arrived in Eisenach to find that Luther was not yet there. Four days later Friedrich Myconius, the pastor and superintendent in Gotha, brought them a letter from Luther explaining that he could not come to Eisenach because of serious illness and suggesting that they move the conference to Grimma, where, if he could not meet them, he would at least be able to follow the negotiations by messenger.[87] The representatives decided, however, to travel to Wittenberg itself since it was only slightly more distant than Grimma. Bucer sent a letter ahead to Luther telling him that they expected to arrive in Wittenberg on the twenty-first of May.[88]

Myconius and another Lutheran, Justus Menius, rode with the party and carried on a long, detailed discussion on the Supper. Myconius reported that they soon reached complete agreement on the Lutheran understanding of the Supper, which Myconius had set down on paper to facilitate discussion.[89] They arrived in Wittenberg on Sunday, 21 May 1536.

Melanchthon and Cruciger met them in the afternoon and shared the bad tidings that a collection of Oecolampadius' and Zwingli's letters had recently been published with a preface by Bucer which conveyed the strong impression that he still supported their errors. This collection and preface had greatly troubled Luther and the Elector and made them seriously doubt that Bucer and the Upper Germans sincerely wished a concord. Moreover, Heinrich Bullinger, Zwingli's successor at Zurich, had just published in February Zwingli's last treatise, *A Short and Clear Exposition of Christian Faith* ..., in which Zwingli presented his old interpretation of the Supper and even asserted that certain pious pagans were among the elect. In his preface Bullinger had nothing but praise for the treatise.[90] Melanchthon, very depressed, had given up all hope of a concord, but his hopes were renewed by what Menius and Myconius told him of the discussions and the agreement reached on their journey to Wittenberg. At dinner that evening Menius and Myconius related to Luther the details of their discussion with the Upper Germans, sitting up until almost midnight, but Luther remained skeptical of the Upper Germans' sincerity.[91]

The next day at seven o'clock in the morning, Bucer and Capito met with Luther to discuss the procedures for the negotiations. They also delivered a number of letters and papers, including a letter from Forster full of complaints about the situation in Augsburg which did nothing to allay Luther's suspicions of the Upper Germans.[92]

At three o'clock that afternoon Bucer and Capito met in Luther's house with Luther, Bugenhagen, Jonas, Cruciger, Menius, Myconius, and two others. Bucer began the discussion with an extensive account of his efforts to reach a concord and of his desire for unity. Luther responded that he saw no use in discussing other points of Christian doctrine until they had reached agreement on the Supper. He told them that he had been encouraged by several of their treatises, especially Bucer's *Statement* (*Bericht*) to Münster, and by his own discussions with Gereon Sailer. He had received a letter, however, that gave him quite a different picture. He could only assume that the Upper Germans boasted that they agreed with the Lutherans and yet continued to teach that there was only bread and wine in the Supper, or if they did not teach it, they allowed the populace to persist in this error. If they did discuss the real presence of Christ, they did so in a word or two, and then went on to discuss the spiritual reception. In consequence, the populace still believed that there was nothing in the Supper but bread and wine and that Christ was present only in one's imagination.[93] If the ministers did this because they did not agree with the Lutherans on the doctrine of the presence of the body of Christ in the Supper or because they dared not say anything else on account of the unrest of the common people who had been misled by them, then they should wait. He thought it would be better in any case just to leave things as they were, for a fabricated concord would only make things worse. Posterity would not be fooled, and even if it were, God would not be.[94]

The ministers, Luther said, claimed and wrote that the disagreement over the Supper was only a battle over words. This he could not and would not tolerate: it was not the case and no one would believe that it was. Karlstadt and Zwingli had taught that Christ was not present, only bread and wine. Finally, he sternly reproached them because Bullinger had published and praised a book by Zwingli in which there were intolerable errors, and because Bucer had aided in the publication of Zwingli's letters and even provided a preface for this collection although in these letters Zwingli wrote most abominably about the Supper. The only conclusion he could draw was that they wished peace with him while persisting in their previous error. He could not nor did he wish to agree to this and thereby participate in others' sins; he had enough of his own.

Luther therefore set down two conditions: they must recant and condemn their previous teaching that there was nothing in the Supper but bread and wine, and they must inculcate in the people the realization that in the Supper the true body and blood of Christ are received with the mouth and by the godless as well as the pious. They should not devote all their time to the spiritual reception, for there was no controversy on that point. For his part, he was willing to admit that he had been too hard and sharp in his writings against Zwingli, Oecolampadius, and others. He did not wish to condemn their persons, for God could have saved them in some special fashion, but he could not give up his doctrine on the Supper.[95]

Bucer was shocked and upset by this speech and began a long, disjointed reply.[96] He complained about Luther's suspicions and said that if they had known that Luther harbored such thoughts about them, they could have saved themselves and their cities the time and money needed to come to Wittenberg. As for the two books, he explained that the collection of letters had been published not only without his knowledge but against his will, that the preface was a letter he had written years earlier with no idea that it would be published, and that Zwingli's book had been published before a meeting held in Basel at which the Strasbourgers had instructed the Swiss about the errors in Zwingli's way of speaking about the Supper, and about Luther's beliefs on the Supper which they had misunderstood. As far as a recantation was concerned, they were willing to recant everything in which they had previously erred, but they had never taught that only bread and wine were offered in the Supper. They acknowledged and were willing to acknowledge in the future that they had misunderstood Luther's position. But they could not recant a doctrine that they had never held. As for Luther's insistence that they should not say that it was only a battle over words and that each side had misunderstood the other, they could only say for themselves that they had misunderstood Luther and that Luther had misunderstood them and still did, since he continued to accuse them of denying the real presence. They were willing to say that it was an error to teach that only bread and wine were offered in the Supper, and they were willing to condemn this error as sharply as possible, but they could not condemn people who were free of this error.

Bucer then turned to the theological issues. He stated that he and all the preachers of the free imperial cities present taught that "through the institution and work of the Lord His true body and His true blood are truly, as the words of the Lord read, offered, given, and received with the visible signs." After dealing briefly with the question of the oral reception of Christ's body and blood, he set out their understanding of what the godless received. This was an issue that they did not usually mention to their congregations since they did not offer the sacrament to people known to be godless. When the subject had to be discussed, they taught that the completely godless who did not believe the words of the Sacrament did not receive anything but bread and wine, while those who believed the words of the Sacrament but still had some failing received the body and blood of the Lord but to their detriment.[97]

According to one report, Luther then repeated his two conditions with great earnestness, and explained that he and his colleagues were unable to do anything else but condemn Zwingli's and Oecolampadius' opinions on original sin and the Supper as found in their books. As he saw the course of the controversy, the Upper Germans had gradually approached the Lutheran position:

For first you had acknowledged that the bread in the Supper was not indeed the same as other bread or the wine the same as common wine, but rather it was a signification and memorial, a remembrance on the absent Christ, etc. Then they came even closer by acknowledging that the body of Christ and the blood of Christ were present, however in a spiritual fashion, that is, he sits at the right [hand] of God, but the mind [*Geist*] makes the body present with the bread and the blood with the wine through its speculation [*Speculiren*] and thinking, just as when one represents symbolically Hector by another person in a tragic play. Finally you came even closer to us ... because you freely confessed to me on the Coburg and now have written the same in several books that the bread is the true, natural, essential body of Christ, etc., and is received with the mouth of those to whom it is offered or given, but only if they are believers and apostles of Christ, for unbelievers receive no more than bread and wine. And therefore according to you it is the body of Christ, not by the power or strength of Christ who had so established and declared it, but rather by the power of our faith and according to our thoughts that bring it about that Christ, who is at the right of the Father, is present to our faith.

It was necessary, however, for them to say whether they taught that Christ was truly present by the power and institution of Christ, irrespective of the minister who offers it or of the worthiness or unworthiness of the recipient. At this point, because of Luther's illness, the conference had to be adjourned.[98]

Luther did not sleep that night, so on the following day the conference did not get under way until midafternoon. Luther began by repeating briefly his remarks of the preceding day and then restated the two central questions: were they willing to recant, each according to what he had taught and circulated against Christ, the Scriptures, and the teachings of the church; and were they willing to teach with the Lutherans the true presence steadfastly and unanimously? Since the other representatives were now present, Bucer repeated his confession of the day before and admitted that he previously had not understood several things sufficiently clearly and distinctly, and also had not taught sufficiently purely and properly. But as soon as he had learned better, he had corrected, recanted, and acknowledged his error as improper. He wished, moreover, to do so again so that he did not lead anyone into error.

Next Bucer discussed the reception by the godless. According to the Lutheran report, Bucer conceded that Christ was naturally present and received orally irrespective of the faith of the recipient as

long as the words of institution were not adulterated (*verfälscht*).[99]
According to the "protocol" later drawn up by the Upper Germans,
he confessed that those who believed the words of institution but
were in some way unworthy nevertheless were offered and received
the true body and blood of Christ. Those with no faith at all were
in fact offered the true body and blood through the institution of the
Lord, but received only bread and wine.[100]

After this statement, Luther asked each of the representatives in
turn whether or not he believed and taught what Bucer had just set
forth, and each assured him that he did. Then Luther and his colleagues departed to a neighboring room to discuss what should be
done next. No one voiced any objection to what the representatives
had said, assuming that they had meant it sincerely. The Lutherans
then returned to where the representatives were assembled, and Luther announced their decision:

> Honorable gentlemen and brothers, we have now heard your answer and
> confession that you believe and teach that in the Supper the true body and
> the true blood are given and received and not just bread and wine; also
> that this offering and reception takes place truly and not imaginarily.
> You take offense only on the matter of the godless, but nevertheless con-
> fess, as St. Paul says, that the unworthy receive the body of the Lord pro-
> vided the Lord's words of institution are not perverted; we do not want
> to quarrel over this. Because this is your belief, we are agreed and recog-
> nize and accept you as our dear brethren in the Lord as far as this article
> is concerned.[101]

Bucer and Capito began to cry for joy and all present thanked God
for this agreement.[102]

Melanchthon was entrusted with the task of drawing up articles
for all to sign. In the next several days, various other issues were discussed and resolved, both sides preached sermons, and, perhaps most
significant of all, they partook together of the Lord's Supper. The
representatives even agreed to submit themselves to the Augsburg
Confession and Apology.[103] On Monday, 29 May, the final articles
were signed and the representatives departed.[104] The Wittenberg
Concord was a reality.* Now it was up to the representatives, espe-

---

* Based, however, on a different interpretation by each party of the same formula.
See Köhler, 2: 453–55; Ernst Bizer, *Studien zur Geschichte des Abendmahlsstreits im
16. Jahrhundert* (Gütersloh, 1940; Darmstadt, 1962), pp. 117–30.

cially Bucer, to secure agreement to it from their cities and congregations. This was a lengthy and only partially successful task, but its history lies beyond the reach of this inquiry.[105]

Literally and figuratively, the Upper Germans had had to come to Luther to reach an agreement, and the agreement was made on Luther's terms. Luther saw all the concessions at Marburg and in the long negotiations leading to the Wittenberg Concord as being made solely by the other side. Until the Concord was reached, Luther had uncompromisingly denounced the Upper Germans as satanic hypocrites and charlatans, and had strenuously and self-righteously disclaimed any association with such opponents. In the Concord itself, the Upper Germans had to recant their previous error and agree that in the future they would teach the same as what the Lutherans taught. Whether the Upper Germans made their concessions out of political necessity or because they had sincerely come round to Luther's position, their actions had the effect of vindicating Luther's uncompromising stance during the years of dispute and confirming his judgment about the uncertainty, and hence the falsity, of his opponents' beliefs. Recognizing that there were real differences between his position and the Zwinglian, he never accepted Bucer's contention that the dispute had been a quarrel over words. For Luther it had been a quarrel between the true and false church, and with this Concord he felt the true church had won.

⁘ 7 ⁘

Against the Antinomians

The dispute between Luther and John Agricola over the proper use of the law is important to us for more than its theological significance. For one thing it served to confirm Luther's belief in a continuing struggle between the true and the false church. His conflict with Karlstadt and Müntzer had given rise to his convictions about false brethren, and his conflict with Agricola made him sure that these convictions were well founded. Agricola "proved" that there were false brethren who attempted to subvert the authority and teachings of the prophets and apostles and their latter day equivalents. This made it easier for Luther to ascribe the same falseness to all his evangelical opponents, some of whom perhaps scarcely deserved the attribution.

In the autumn of 1536 John Agricola, at that time a good friend of Luther's, was serving as pastor and schoolmaster for Count Albrecht of Mansfeld in Agricola's native town of Eisleben.[1] The relationship between prince and subject had begun as a comfortable one but had deteriorated. When with Luther's help Agricola finally left Eisleben to enter the Elector's service,* he wrote a bitter, tactless letter to the Count complaining that he had broken his promises of increased

* Agricola had been seeking an exit to Wittenberg for some time. Since Luther was more than willing to tout his friend to the Elector, the Elector finally requested Luther to invite Agricola to Wittenberg over the Christmas holidays, all expenses paid, to participate in theological discussions on the Schmalkaldic Articles, which Luther had drafted for the upcoming meeting of the Schmalkaldic League. Luther wrote Agricola on 15 December, informing him of the Elector's command. Agricola, immensely grateful, arrived in Wittenberg within two days with his wife and nine children. When suitable accommodations could not immediately be found, they moved in with the Luthers. The theological consultations were held as planned, and Agricola added his signature

support for Eisleben's pastor. The Count replied by accusing Agricola of having neglected his duties, of having overstepped his authority, of having had an overfondness for drink, and of having engaged in internecine disputes with his fellow evangelicals.[2]

It was probably early in January 1537 while away from Wittenberg that Luther received a letter from Count Albrecht charging that Agricola had established a sect in Eisleben opposed to the Wittenbergers, and describing Agricola as being potentially as dangerous as Müntzer, an improbable description.* At the time, Luther discounted the accusations against his good friend,[3] but if the dating of his table conversation can be trusted, by the twenty-first of March he was taking the accusations more seriously. Shown a set of theses attributed to Agricola that attacked the preaching of the law and the ten commandments before the preaching of grace and that cited a number of "pure" and "impure" passages on the law in Luther's own writings, Luther is reported to have exclaimed:

This is Agricola's opinion. He is driven by hatred and ambition. Oh, if we could [only] honor Master Philipp [Melanchthon] who teaches the use of the law most clearly and lucidly. Even I yield to him, although I dealt as clearly as I could with this matter in my Galatians commentary. Count Albrecht's prophecy will come true. He wrote to me: There is a Müntzer concealed there. For he who destroys the doctrine of the law politically, destroys the magistracy and home discipline; if he destroys [the law] ecclesiastically, then there is no knowledge of sin.[4]

To aggravate Luther's suspicions, reports soon reached him that Agricola had used a "new vocabulary" in his sermons before the evangelical princes' meeting at Zeitz. This vocabulary differed signifi-

---

to the Articles. Luther left for Schmalkalden on 3 January, consigning the care of his house, family, and preaching and teaching duties to his trusted friend Agricola. Obviously, Luther had no suspicion that Agricola differed with him in the slightest. See WABr 7: 586–87, 614, 616; Gustav Kawerau, *Johann Agricola von Eisleben* (Berlin, 1881), pp. 169–73; Joachim Rogge, *Johann Agricolas Lutherverständnis* (Berlin, 1960), pp. 132–35.

* I infer that this letter was received during this period because the table conversation of 21 March 1537 refers to this letter, but Luther had just returned to Wittenberg on 14 March, seven days earlier. Furthermore, Count Albrecht mentions both his letter to Luther and Luther's sickness in his letter to the Elector on 27 January. This letter may have included a copy of the Count's letter to Agricola of 27 December, as did the Count's letter to the Elector. The accusation that Agricola was potentially another

cantly from Luther's and that of the other Wittenbergers.[5] It is possible that Luther preached against these theses on 1 July, but without mentioning any names.[6] Bugenhagen, as he left for his long stay
in Denmark, expressly requested that Agricola not be allowed to substitute for him in his teaching or preaching duties, and Luther took
over the duties himself.[7] That July Agricola's *Three Sermons* also
appeared, published by the Wittenberg printer Hans Luft. Under
close inspection these sermons, too, raised serious doubts about Agricola's orthodoxy.[8] But it was another of his publications that really
got him into trouble. This was *A Short Summary of the Gospels*.

Agricola later claimed that he had shown a manuscript of this
treatise to Luther in May 1537, at which time Luther had said that
the treatise was not bad and had, tacitly at least, given it his approval.*
But in mid-November of the same year Luther halted the printing
of the treatise after six sheets had been run off, and he had all copies
destroyed except one which he annotated with critical comments.[9]
Moreover, he later accused Agricola of having gone behind his back
and of having misled Hans Luft into believing that Luther had read
and given his approval to the treatise.[10] The chronology of this affair,
although difficult to reconstruct with certainty, favors Luther's interpretation. As best we know, the events were as follows.

In late October Agricola and the Elector exchanged letters touching
on the *Short Summary*.[11] In his letter Agricola reported that he and
Luther had reached an understanding sometime after the Elector's
departure from Wittenberg in mid-October. Prior to this understanding he had been unable to get a hearing on his *Short Summary*, but
now, he reported, Luther no longer misunderstood him as he had

---

Müntzer may have been in this letter to Luther, or Luther may have learned of it from
the Count's letter to the Elector. See *D. Martin Luthers Werke. Tischreden* (Weimar,
1912–21), 5: 405 (hereafter cited as WATR); Carl Eduard Förstemann, *Neues Urkundenbuch zur Geschichte der evangelischen Kirchen-Reformation* (1842), 1: 291–96.

* WABr 8: 121–22. If Agricola in fact gave Luther this manuscript, then Luther certainly did not read it carefully, for it contained much he was later to object to. This
carelessness would be hard to explain in light of Luther's suspicions voiced about Agricola to his table companions in March. In addition, Agricola's claim that he showed
this treatise to Luther in May seems to conflict with his report to the Elector that he
previously had been unable to receive a hearing for his treatise. See Gustav Kawerau,
"Briefe und Urkunden zur Geschichte des antinomistischen Streites—I," *Zeitschrift für
Kirchengeschichte*, 4 (1880/81): 305–6.

previously and had come to realize that they were in substantive agreement. Agricola enclosed a summary of his doctrine (now lost), which apparently made reference to his *Short Summary*, and mentioned in the letter itself that the *Short Summary* was being printed.[12]

In his reply, the Elector greeted the news of reconciliation with approval but admonished Agricola to strive for unity in vocabulary as well as substance.[13] The Elector had noticed, quite rightly as it turned out, that there were still a number of differences between Agricola's doctrine and Luther's. He therefore instructed Chancellor Brück to verify Luther's approval of the publication of Agricola's treatise.[14] Apparently it was when alerted by this inquiry that Luther halted the printing and had the incomplete treatise confiscated.[15]

Among the papers collected by Agricola himself to document this controversy,[16] however, is a letter from him to Luther dated 2 September 1537 which suggests that Luther may have been informed much earlier than the Elector's inquiry that the treatise was in press. "I am not a little disturbed," Agricola wrote,

that you have now changed your mind about that treatise which is now being set in type by Hans Luft and about which you had said to me in church at Pentecost [20 May], after I had given it to you to read, that it was a good treatise. "That is not bad," [you said]. I have simply followed in the entire treatise this one doctrine [namely,] that a sermon on the death of our Lord Jesus Christ thoroughly frightens and depresses the minds and consciences of men, that is, it teaches repentance; but that a sermon on the resurrection of Christ encourages both consciences terrified by Christ's death and minds and consciences that are depressed, that is, it teaches remission of sins. This is the doctrine of all the apostles, especially Paul and Barnabas. . . . It is your doctrine as well.[17]

Note that this letter mentions a treatise "which is now being set in type by Hans Luft." As has been argued by the Weimar editors of Luther's works, it seems unlikely that this refers to Agricola's *Three Sermons*, which was published and in the hands of readers by July at the latest.[18] If, on the other hand, Agricola was referring to the *Short Summary*, then it is difficult to explain why Luther waited until mid-November to halt publication. To complicate matters, according to Agricola's own report to the Elector, he and Luther were reconciled only after the Elector had departed from Wittenberg in mid-October.* This is borne out by the fact that Luther preached against the antinomians on 30 September, although in a markedly restrained fashion.[19] But the dedication to the *Short Summary* is dated 24 September 1537,[20] three weeks after the 2 September letter indicating that Agricola was aware of Luther's objections to the treatise but some time before the reconciliation that Agricola reported to the Elector.†

It seems most probable to me that either Agricola's 2 September letter does not refer to the *Short Summary* or—and this seems even more likely—Luther either did not receive or did not read carefully this letter from Agricola.‡ Whatever the case, one thing seems clear: if Agricola's letter can be trusted and the dedication of the *Short Summary* was not postdated, then Agricola must have turned over part of the treatise to Luft before 2 September, the day he wrote to Luther, and then continued to work on the treatise, finishing the dedication on the twenty-fourth. During this entire period he knew that Luther objected to the treatise. In short, whether or not Agricola began publication believing he had Luther's approval, he did not halt publication after he definitely knew that Luther disapproved.§ Perhaps after the reconciliation in late October, Agricola thought that he had regained Luther's approval for the publication of the *Short Summary*, and that previously Luther had merely misunderstood his position.[21] If this was the case, then Agricola may have justified his continuing work on the *Short Summary* by his belief that he and Luther were in actual agreement and that only a misunderstanding divided them. The extent to which Agricola would have been de-

* Kawerau, "Briefe," p. 306. In his letter to the Elector, Agricola indicated that the *Short Summary* was presently in the press and implied that it only *now* had Luther's approval.

† The suggestion of the Weimar editors that the complicated legal procedure to halt publication may have taken several months fails to explain the date of the dedicatory epistle. See WABr 8: 122.

‡ Even if he received the letter, Luther may have refused to read it as he did with other letters of Agricola's (e.g. WABr 8: 342–43). It is possible, too, that Agricola's letter is misdated. If this letter was sent in November, then we would have no trouble with the chronology though it would still mean that Agricola continued to work on the treatise despite knowing that Luther objected.

§ Agricola's letter implies that at one time at least Agricola thought he had Luther's approval (WABr 8: 122). Luther later denied that he ever approved this treatise (WA 51: 431).

luding himself in this case becomes obvious when we examine Luther's annotations to the confiscated pages.

In his preface to the *Short Summary* Agricola argued that St. Paul distinguished between two aspects of revelation: the revelation of God's righteousness and the revelation of God's wrath from heaven. The first reveals the righteousness that counts before God and the second reveals the wrath that descends from heaven "upon those who are not obedient to the truth; who do not wish to believe, trust, or adhere to this revelation of God's righteousness; [and] also upon those who do not wish to improve or change themselves for the sake of the first revelation of God's righteousness, but rather remain as they were before." The revelation of God's righteousness brings and teaches forgiveness of sins, the revelation of God's wrath brings and teaches repentance. Luther annotated this passage with the comment: "Therefore repentance follows the remission of sins contrary to Christ's saying 'repentance and [then] remission of sins.' "

Next, Agricola argued that whenever either revelation takes place they both take place, prompting Luther to comment: "What's this? repentance/remission occur from both, that is, if you preach wrath or grace."[22] And when Agricola contended that in the New Testament and among Christians or in the gospel one should not preach the violating of the law but rather the violating of the Son, that is, that one recrucifies Christ who does not willingly for heaven's sake desist from what he should desist from and does not do what he should do, Luther underlined the passage and drew a hand in the margin pointing to it.[23]

All of Luther's annotations pointed like a hand to the fundamental disagreements between him and Agricola. Agricola argued that repentance followed the preaching of the remission of sins through Christ; Luther believed that repentance must be experienced before remission was preached. Agricola contended that the gospel revealed both wrath and grace; Luther believed that wrath was primarily revealed through the law, and grace primarily through the gospel. Agricola argued that people were sufficiently terrified by hearing of Christ's sacrifice for their sins and that the preaching of the law was unnecessary or even harmful; Luther argued that although the severity of Christ's sacrifice did demonstrate the enormity of man's sins, the law still needed to be preached forcefully and men still had to be convicted of their sin by the law.[24]

Whatever reconciliation had occurred in October was quite shattered by the confiscation of Agricola's treatise. Soon after the incident Luther was making the kind of remarks to his table companions that we are already familiar with. His friends were treading him underfoot and disturbing the gospel. "Oh, how it hurts to lose such a good friend," he exclaimed, "one who was loved so much. He sat at my table, laughed with me, and nevertheless was opposing me behind my back. I cannot tolerate that!" He was going to arrange a disputation to provoke him. Let him behave as humbly as he wished, he was not going to be satisfied by his deceit. On the contrary, he was intending to challenge him by name to defend his position. It was the crassest of errors to reject the law, for that undermined the church, the government, and the home. He had rebuked Agricola gently, he said, and had received a cunning response. Such scandalous arrogance was the mother of all heresies. Luther drew a parallel between Paul and himself: "That I must see them boasting and wanting to rule during my lifetime! As Paul said to the Corinthians: 'Would that they ruled without me.' The good Paul had to see and suffer the [same] thing." This suffering was spiritual suffering and worse than death. "I must suffer this, too, in these scandals and arrogance of my disciples, so that I would have preferred to suffer death."[25]

Luther decided to publish the antinomian theses that had been circulating about Wittenberg, adding a set of countertheses of his own. Warned by Melanchthon of Luther's intention, Agricola begged Luther not to carry out this plan, insisting that the theses were not his but would probably be attributed to him. He pledged his submission to Luther's authority.[26] He then approached Luther in church and gave his hand on the promise to remain true to Luther's teaching.[27] At this time he may also have given Luther an "incomplete book [*rhapsodia indigesta*]," which he followed with a letter the next day. This letter, as Agricola later described it, "set the Rhine afire."[28]

The letter began with a reference to the "incomplete book" that

Agricola had just given Luther. Then Agricola "most simply" explained that in Luther's writings he found two different ways of teaching repentance, one through both law and gospel, the other through the gospel alone. The latter way of teaching he found lucidly expressed in Luther's sermon on Christ's passion.[29] It should be determined, he wrote, which teaching was nearest that of the apostles. He thought this was a question worthy of being settled, since the church of their descendants might be at a loss if it saw two ways of teaching repentance. He closed the letter defensively: "As to doctrine, I appeal to all citizens of Eisleben to absolve me of having taught anything unworthy of the church."[30] Clearly, the contents of this letter, however "simply put," went to the very heart of the issue, and gave the strong impression that Agricola was not, after all, convinced of his error.

Luther published the "Theses Circulated Among Brethren" on the first of December.[31] Of the total of thirty-seven, eighteen were "antinomian" theses; there were also five "pure" and three "unpure" theses drawn from Luther's and Melanchthon's writings. These articles certainly were inspired by Agricola's teachings or can be found explicitly in his writings. The remaining eleven, divided into a group of three and a group of eight, probably derived in part from Agricola's students, in part from Agricola's opponents, in part from Luther himself, who wished to show the consequences of Agricola's position.[32] Agricola later objected most to two of these latter theses, which Luther acknowledged as not having been written by Agricola himself.[33] One read: "If you are a whore, a rascal, an adulterer, or otherwise a sinner, as long as you believe, you are on the road to salvation." And the other: "Although you are deeply stuck in sin [*mitten jnn der sunden stickest auffs hohest*], if you believe, you are in the middle of blessedness."[34]

Although Luther freely criticized Agricola at the dining table, he did not refer to him by name in the published theses. Rather, he explained that these "propositions" by an "uncertain author" had happened into his hands, and since he did not wish to give the appearance of approval by his silence, he had decided to publish them to indicate his abhorrence of their contents. Soon, God willing, he would hold a disputation over them.[35]

The disputation took place on 18 December.[36] Luther began with the observation that Satan never ceased persecuting "our savior and mediator Jesus Christ." With scandals, the persecution of tyrants, and the impious doctrine of heretics, Satan tried as best he could to upset within the church the pure and beneficial doctrine of justification. Luther emphasized the importance of transmitting pure doctrine to posterity, and warned against giving Satan the opportunity of invading the church and stirring up innumerable sects and scandals.[37] According to the report of the table talks, Luther then challenged a respondent to step forward, but Agricola, having failed to forestall the disputation, had decided to remain away.[38]

Agricola's absence prompted Luther to make numerous remarks to his table companions about Agricola's presumption and impenitence. If Agricola would not defend his position, then Luther would order him to preside over the next disputation. The rejection of Moses, that is, the law, was simply too gross. Agricola could not excuse himself by saying it was Cruciger and Rörer he had been reproaching and not Luther, for the catechism, the commandments, and the Augsburg Confession were his, not Cruciger's or Rörer's. If Agricola wished to preach repentance through the love of righteousness, then he would be preaching only the revelation of anger to the righteous, and to the impious nothing! In sum, Agricola wished to open the window to doctrines that would make everyone feel completely secure, for he wished to convert Luther's doctrine, which was a consolation to consciences, to a doctrine that encouraged fleshly licentiousness. "I had not expected such perfidy from him," Luther exclaimed. "He could have discussed his opinion with me at any time."[39] A few days later Luther explained that at the beginning of the reformation he had preached so strongly against the law because the many superstitions of the papacy had completely obscured the gospel of Christ. He had wished to liberate pious minds from torments of conscience caused by the papal overinsistence on the law, but he had never rejected the law.[40]

On the twenty-sixth of December Agricola wrote once more to Luther, this time pledging his faith and submission to Luther's authority.[41] It is said that Luther refused even to read this letter for several days after receiving it, and finally only skimmed it before he left for Torgau on the twenty-eighth. Agricola reports that Luther's wife, Käthie, and Justus Jonas (whom Agricola usually saw as the major villain in this drama) put in a good word for him and as a result of their intercession his relationship with Luther improved slightly—but only for a brief time.[42]

On 6 January 1538 Luther wrote Agricola a disdainful letter informing him that he was suspended from all his teaching and preaching duties. He accused Agricola of speaking against him "in corners." If Agricola wished to be reinstated, he should address his request to the University.[43] At this point Agricola was reduced to sending his wife, who was well liked by the Luthers, to ask what her husband should do to effect a reconciliation. Luther demanded that he take part in the next disputation, Agricola agreed, and the disputation took place on 12 January 1538.[44]

Agricola submitted two theses that he would defend so that he might be "instructed."[45] Luther acted as respondent. After Agricola was sufficiently "instructed," there was a public reconciliation, and Luther explained that Agricola had been under suspicion, but as a result of this confession he was now satisfied with him. The devil had caused enough external problems for the Lutherans without being permitted to add internal disputes for their enemies to rejoice over. He admonished all those present to remain in unity and harmony. They would still have more than enough to do, for the devil never rested.[46]

Luther now worked hard to reconcile Agricola with the Elector and his Wittenberg colleagues. He arranged for Agricola to resume preaching despite Bugenhagen's request that he not be allowed to do so and despite the suspicions of many that although Agricola confessed agreement in public he held his old opinions in private.[47] The Elector ordered Agricola to preach several sermons to prove the purity of his doctrine, and Luther said that he and others would examine these sermons with the greatest care.*

By late April Luther was once more disillusioned with Agricola,

* WATR 3: 572–73. In this same entry Luther explains that pride was the greatest pestilence to theology and that Zwingli and Agricola both suffered from this vice. He also complains about the agonies that this dispute had caused him: "I am no martyr sacrificing his blood, but God knows what temptations I have had in this affair. I almost died of anxiety before I published those theses."

perhaps because of the manner in which the sermons that had been ordered were performed.[48] He suspected Agricola of impenitence and deception, and he complained of how much he had done for him, excusing him to the Elector and allowing him to preach. "I have warned him sufficiently both publicly and privately," Luther stated, the issue of responsibility obviously in the forefront of his mind. "This can be repeated publicly and freely after my death."*

As noted in Chapter 5, in his preface to the 1538 edition of his Galatians Commentary Luther took the opportunity to add a denunciation of antinomianism. He admonished his readers that they should expect no peace in the church, "for the devil is not idle nor does he sleep." "Although I am nothing," he continued, "I have been in the ministry of Christ already twenty years. I can truly testify that I have been attacked by more than twenty sects, some of which have totally collapsed, others of which still quiver like parts of insects." But recently Satan had stirred up what Luther had least expected, namely, a sect which taught that the decalogue ought to be removed from the church, and that men ought not to be terrified by the law but ought to be warned sweetly through Christ's grace. The minister of Christ can be certain therefore that there will be heresies, Luther said:

> Let him hold fast to the consolation that there is no peace between Christ and Belial or between the seed of the serpent and the seed of the woman. Rather let him rejoice that he is enduring sects and those seditious spirits [that] perpetually follow after him, for our glory is this: the witness of our conscience that we find in standing and fighting on the side of the seed of the woman against the seed of the serpent.[49]

Agricola and the other "antinomians" were possessed by the same satanic spirit that motivated Luther's other evangelical opponents. The paradigm of the struggle between the true and false churches is again in evidence.

Sometime in September Luther held the third disputation against

---

* WATR 3: 660. This suspicion may have led Luther that summer or early autumn to request a printed revocation such as Agricola had already given orally in the second disputation. Reports of antinomian teachings from Lüneburg and elsewhere may also have spurred this request on. See E. Thiele, "Denkwürdigkeiten aus dem Leben des Johann Agricola von Eisleben," *Theologische Studien und Kritiken*, 80 (1907): 263; and cf. Melanchthon's report in Förstemanne, 1: 326, 335.

the antinomians, and Agricola had to begin once again the process of reconciliation.* Melanchthon later reported that about this time Agricola approached him with the draft of a revocation of his errors. Evidently not satisfied with it as presented, Melanchthon drew up a revised version for Agricola. But then, for reasons not entirely clear to historians, Agricola requested Luther to write a revocation for him.[50] Luther was happy to do so, but not in the manner Agricola expected. Agricola probably hoped that he would be moderate with him, Luther told his table companions, but he was going to seek Christ's honor, not Agricola's—quite the contrary, for he intended to use Agricola's own words to depict him as a cowardly, vain, and impious man who had greatly injured the church.[51] And that was what he did. The treatise was entitled *Against the Antinomians* and appeared in January 1539.[52] Agricola first read his recantation when it appeared on the open market.[53]

A central theme running throughout the treatise was Luther's disavowal of Agricola, and the dissociation of his name from Agricola's position. One would have thought, Luther wrote, that his disputations against the antinomians would have stilled any speculation that he and the antinomians agreed. But Satan, as always, wanted to implicate him in the matter: "I am afraid that if I had died at Schmalkalden, I would forever have been called the patron of such spirits, since they appeal to my books. In fact, they did all this behind my back, without my knowledge and against my will." Though Agricola was the originator and master of antinomianism, he had now backed down and wished to be in agreement with the Lutherans. Treatises continued to reach Wittenberg, however, that showed people believed

* The Weimar editors suggest, for lack of alternatives, that the third disputation against the antinomians must have occurred on 6 September at the doctoral disputation of Cyriacus Gerichius. True, Luther appears in the record of the disputation to be the only respondent. But the other possible date, 13 September, finds Luther in Lochau according to the normally reliable diary of Anthony Lauterbach (WA 39/1: 486–87). But what of Agricola's report in his "memoirs" that "on 6 September a peace was once again agreed upon between us that I testify by a public writing to that which I testified to in the disputation" (Thiele, p. 263)? Agricola is certainly referring here to the second disputation and not to the third, in which he took no part. But could the third disputation have occurred on the same day as this agreement? Perhaps, but it seems highly unlikely. Perhaps the disputation occurred on the 13th in the late afternoon after Luther returned from Lochau. Unfortunately, the evidence does not permit a conclusive answer.

or even boasted that Agricola and Luther agreed on the antinomian teaching. Therefore, Luther was forced to insist that Agricola issue a printed retraction, there being no other way to root out the poison in Eisleben and elsewhere.

Agricola, Luther explained, had agreed to issue a retraction but for fear that he might not be able to make the point forcefully enough, had empowered and requested Luther to write a retraction for him. Luther had agreed to this request, if for no other reason than that after his death neither Agricola nor anyone else could claim that he had not done anything about the matter and had permitted and approved everything.[54] He hoped that now that Agricola had mended his ways and recanted, the other antinomians who had got their antinomianism from him would do so as well.*

In his usual strong language, Luther rejected the antinomian teaching that the preaching of the law should not precede the preaching of the gospel and that repentance should be preached only from the gospel and not from both the law and the gospel.[55] He accused the antinomians of trying to throw out of the church both the law and the ten commandments, and characterized them all as vain, presumptuous men inventing something new in order to enhance their own reputations.[56]

In closing he told of attacks he had experienced in encounters with the devil, and he drew parallels from the past history of the church. He personally had endured more than twenty "storm winds and fanatics" which the devil had blown up against him. There was the papacy, then Müntzer and the rebellion, then Karlstadt, then the Anabaptists: "I had to learn from my own experience that the church, because of the precious word, ... cannot live in tranquillity, but must forever live in expectation of new gales from the devil. That is the way it has been from the beginning, as you read in the *Tripartite Ecclesiastical History* [of Cassiodorus] as well as in the books of the holy fathers."

Even if he lived another hundred years, Luther said, and could

---

* WA 50: 475 (LW 47: 115). But after this faint praise of Agricola's humility, Luther quickly added that if Agricola departed from this humility God could hurl him down once more. WA 50: 470 (LW 47: 108–9).

defeat not only the previous and present fanatics through God's grace but all future ones as well, he still saw clearly that his descendants would not have gained peace, because "the devil lives and rules." It was for the sake of the pious, he said, that he and others must live and preach, write, work, and suffer so many things. Otherwise when one regarded the devil and the false brethren, one might think it better to have done nothing, for they destroyed and blasphemed everything. "We cannot be any better," Luther said by way of consolation, "than the dear prophets and apostles who also had the same experience."[57]

Agricola, though he felt tremendously wronged by this treatise,[58] at least had retained his salary from the Elector and had been appointed to the newly formed, provisionary consistory.[59] He was scheduled to submit theses for disputation on 1 February to prove and ratify his return to the fold. But his theses only served to reignite the controversy.

The last eight of these seventeen theses were completely orthodox Lutheran. Theses one through nine, however, were strange allegorical utterances such as "(1.) John [the Baptist] did not sin in eating honey in the woods, and so he was rightly freed from punishment, (2.) but King Saul disturbed Israel when he forbade the people to eat honey." Luther glossed these theses in the most unfavorable way possible. John the Baptist was Agricola, eating honey was teaching grace, Saul was Luther the tyrant, and Israel was the church. The other seven theses suffered the same fate and even the eight orthodox theses were glossed by Luther to mean just the opposite of what they said.[60] Luther accused Agricola of stubbornly maintaining his old errors,[61] and he declared that he regretted having dealt so gently with him in his *Against the Antinomians*.[62]

In his treatise *On the Councils and the Church*, Luther added sharp attacks against the antinomians, accusing them of effectively rejecting Christ in their rejection of the law. He conceded that they preached well and seriously about Christ's grace and the forgiveness of sins, but he argued that they fled the consequent that law and sin must be preached as well. Now he attributed to them a composite of the two objectionable theses about being a whore and being stuck in sin, which he had printed in the "Theses Circulated Among Brethren" in preparation for the first disputation against the antinomians, and he accused them of using a Nestorian and Eutychian dialectic, of both teaching and denying Christ. They were fine Easter preachers but disgraceful Pentecost preachers, for they taught only redemption through Christ and not the sanctification through the Holy Spirit.[63] They rejected the ten commandments and strengthened those who remained in sin. They neither had Christ or the Holy Spirit nor understood them.[64]

Evidently some members of the University were not entirely sympathetic with Luther's attack, for word reached Luther that they were considering electing Agricola dean of the philosophical faculty. It is reported that he wrote a furious letter forbidding such an action "so that his vanity, presumption, and disobedience not be confirmed and strengthened."[65] He would have preferred to place the hypocrite Agricola under the ban.[66] Apparently, however, there was a brief time when he entertained more forgiving thoughts, for he reported to table companions that he had attempted to visit Agricola in early July in hopes of effecting a reconciliation. Agricola was not at home when Luther called, and later Luther expressed satisfaction at his failure, for there would have been no end to Agricola's conceit, he said, if he had found him at home.[67]

During the rest of the year 1539 Agricola collected material in his own defense, repeatedly lodged complaints with successive rectors of the University and with Bugenhagen and Melanchthon, and insisted that Luther had done him a manifest injustice. The theologians said later that many of Agricola's complaints eventually reached Luther, adding fuel to the fire.[68] Agricola's threat to file a legal complaint against Luther with the Elector, to appeal in writing to the preachers in Mansfeld and the city of Eisleben for exoneration, and even to publish an appeal addressed to the learned of Europe and all of Germany did not move Luther to change any of his accusations.[69]

Finally on 27 January 1540, Agricola sent off the threatened "Complaint" to the preachers in Mansfeld and the people of Eisleben.[70] On 7 April the Eisleben preacher Kaspar Güttel sent Luther a copy.[71] In the "Complaint," Agricola cited calumnies against his person in Luther's *Against the Antinomians* and *On the Councils and the*

Church, and in Luther's disputations and sermons.[72] There were three specific complaints. First, Luther had said that Agricola would not tolerate the teaching of the law. This, Agricola retorted, was a fallacious consequent: he had only said that the law should not be taught to make a person righteous or pious before God, or to rule the conscience, or to cause remorse in those who piously repent and turn to God; he had not rejected the law altogether. Second, Luther had said that Agricola taught that you may do murder, commit adultery, engage in all sorts of sins and scandals, and yet remain unharmed so long as you believe. Third, Luther had said that Agricola did not want to permit the catechism to be taught. Greatly excited about this third accusation, Agricola listed thirty-two consequences that would flow from the rejection of the catechism: one should not pray, say the Lord's prayer, honor God and parents, and so on.[73]

Agricola said that Luther must have been misled by others, especially Agricola's enemies. He pointed out that he had disputed twice on the matter, preached twice, lectured properly for more than two years, and had even sent a treatise on the matter to the preachers at Mansfeld, so that people should recognize that he had changed and improved his position on the law. But all this had been fruitless. He was, he said, deeply saddened that Luther, who had brought the pure teaching of the gospel once more to the light through God's miraculous grace and had comforted many souls and wretched consciences, should allow "poisonous slanderers and jealous defilers of God and men" to talk him into writing falsehoods about other people. Luther's treatment of him seemed grossly unjust:

I have allowed him to walk all over me for three years, and I have crept after him like a wretched dog. Three times the matter was reconciled with the shaking of hands and the promising of faithfulness. But each time it became worse until finally it has reached the point that there is no halt nor end to the libel and slander coming from the chancel.

He closed with sharp words directed against Luther, and an appeal to the people of Eisleben to testify in his behalf that never while their preacher and schoolmaster had he done or taught any of the listed errors.[74]

After a month had gone by Agricola sent a similar "Complaint" directly to the Elector, asking for his help in righting the injustices done to him.[75] Sometime during the next several months he also wrote a "Defense" of his "Complaint."[76] In the "Defense" he summarized his complaints in several sentences:

Now Eisleben [Agricola] says that the law is dangerously taught before or without the gospel because it is a servant of death, but fruitfully and wholly blessedly with or through the gospel and after the gospel, for the gospel reveals God's wrath.
It is attributed to him, however, that he does not want to permit [the teaching of] the law before, with, or after the gospel. He is complaining of this accusation, as if he gave everyone permission to sin freely, to abolish Christ and the Holy Spirit, and to be unrepentant. But his books, catechism, and his sermons at various imperial diets and elsewhere witness to the contrary.

To document these alleged calumnies Agricola cited extensive passages from Luther's *On the Councils and the Church* and shorter quotations from *Against the Antinomians*, *That Preachers Should Preach Against Usury* (1540), and the disputations against the antinomians. In one of these disputations, Agricola claimed, he had been accused of doing away with the catechism.[77]

Sometime after the writing of this "Defense" and probably after the end of April,[78] Luther composed a "Response" to Agricola's "Complaint" and "Defense."* He addressed it to Chancellor Brück, but it obviously was intended for the Elector's eyes as well.[79] Among the supporting documents sent with the "Response" was a letter from Wendelin Faber, a teacher in Eisleben, which deserves some attention.[80]

Faber wrote that he had "frequently" attended Agricola's lectures in Eisleben and had heard among other absurdities the following three arguments: that repentance, the knowledge of sin, and the fear of God should be taught not from the law but from the gospel; that for those living in the New Testament it was not a question of violating the law but solely of violating the son of God; that a particular syllogism should be followed in preaching. The major prem-

---

* WA 51: 429–44. All citations are from the manuscript rather than from the printed edition. The comparison of parallel passages in note 76 above shows that Luther was replying to both of Agricola's treatises.

ise of this syllogism was that the preacher should preach as best he could God's grace and mercy in Christ as presented in the Bible. The minor premise was that the preacher should exhort his hearers to examine themselves and discover how little faith they had shown in times of poverty, sickness, ignominy, fear of death, and the rest of human calamities. The conclusion followed that the people, now aware of their failings, would call on God for help in improving their lives. Faber declared unequivocally that if Agricola attempted to deny that he had taught such things, then the windows, chairs, benches, and so on, of the school in Eisleben would testify against him.

Agricola also taught, according to Faber, that when the minor premise was not preached with the major, then there was no gospel and Christ had become a Moses, that is, a lawgiver. And Agricola had labeled those who did not preach both the major and the minor premises "Witzelians" after his Catholic opponent in Eisleben, and also "law preachers," bacchants, and (scholastic) theologians. He had even established a sect in Eisleben that called itself the "minorists" after the minor premise, and some of his followers had announced that the major premise was properly preached in Wittenberg but not the minor. They also said (and Faber believed that they had it originally from Agricola) that Luther had become a "minorist" himself in his *A Simple Way to Pray, Written for a Friend,* and had learned this skill from Agricola. These followers were of the opinion that Luther was the Peter and Agricola the Paul of the reformation because Peter had to be rebuked by Paul for not teaching the gospel correctly.[81] Faber's letter, whatever its merits as an objective report, could not have been better calculated to confirm Luther's adverse judgments of Agricola. In his "Response" Luther repeated many of these disturbing charges and accused Agricola of a number of treacherous and deceitful deeds: he had established sects in Eisleben that were opposed to Luther and the Wittenberg theology; he had attempted to deceive the printer Hans Luft into printing his *Short Summary,* telling the poor man that Luther had read and approved it for printing, by which deceit he had hoped to lay the first stone against the Wittenbergers and their theology; he had attempted to spread his poison in sermons delivered at various imperial diets and during his 1535 trip to Vienna in the company of the Elector; and finally, he had played the friend to Luther, sat at Luther's table, joked with him, and all the while he had been working behind Luther's back to discredit him and his doctrine.[82]

Agricola was a treacherous liar, in Luther's opinion, consumed by vanity and the desire to be everything while Luther was nothing.[83] Whether Agricola realized it or not, he was ruled by a devil, who hoped to subvert the gospel through him.[84] Not only had Agricola deserved the criticism he had suffered so far, but he deserved even more, and Luther said that, given the opportunity after this legal process was over, he would see that he got it, for he thought he had been far too lenient with the man in the past.[85]

In answering Agricola's three specific complaints, Luther quoted repeatedly and with devastating effect, in such a way as to put him in the wrong, Agricola's own "Defense." "Now Eisleben [Agricola] says that the law is dangerously taught before or without the gospel because it is a servant of death."[86] If he conceded this, however, then he could not quibble with the consequences Luther drew from it, for "he who forbids the teaching of the law cannot teach about sin, and must allow people to live free and secure without knowledge of sin." This was Paul's conclusion, not Luther's. Also, where people have no knowledge of sin, there can be no understanding of forgiveness or grace. This, too, was a consequence drawn by Paul.[87] Luther concluded that Agricola stood condemned by his own admissions, and that Luther's own books and writings were thereby vindicated.[88]

A group of theologians, who were first consulted by the Elector and then by a commission established by the Elector to hear Agricola's complaint, sustained Luther completely.[89] They also said that Agricola had improperly interpreted all of Luther's critical remarks about antinomians as referring to him personally. Although they admitted that Luther's polemics were often harsh, they considered them justified by the seriousness of the error, and by the reports from Lüneburg, Pomerania, and elsewhere of antinomians hard at work. At one point the author of the theologians' report, probably Melanchthon, said that Agricola's intention to attack Luther in a treatise, or to force him into a retraction, showed that Agricola did not understand

Luther. He was a quite different man from what Agricola thought him to be. The theologians were surprised that Agricola did not realize that Luther was not a man like any other man.[90]

Agricola, sensing that events were taking a direction that he had not intended, attempted to withdraw his complaint. When he was unable to do so, he began looking for a way out and found it in an invitation by Joachim II of Brandenburg to come to Berlin as court chaplain. He requested permission to leave Wittenberg, waited a month without receiving a reply, and then, breaking his oath to remain in Wittenberg until the matter of his complaint had been resolved, departed.[91] During the next two years the controversy dragged on. It was never completely resolved. To his dying day, Luther never forgave Agricola, despite signs of his complete orthodoxy later on, and he even refused to allow him in his house when Agricola came visiting in 1545.[92]

In reviewing this controversy it is important to distinguish between what Agricola taught and what Luther saw as the necessary consequences of Agricola's teachings.* Luther maintained that Agricola opposed the preaching of the law before the preaching of grace, and wanted to preach remission of sins and repentance solely through the gospel. This charge was certainly justified. Agricola himself admitted to these teachings in his "Defense" and they can be found in his *Short Summary*. The practical consequences of Agricola's approach, Luther insisted, were the rejection of the law and the abandonment of all means of keeping non-Christians in even nominal obedience to the authorities of home, government, and church. These consequences were obvious to Luther, however much Agricola denied that they followed from his teachings.

There is some evidence in the "Theses Circulated Among Brethren," in the charges made by Count Albrecht of Mansfeld, and in Wendelin Faber's letter, that Agricola had advocated similar teachings in Eisleben. Perhaps his dispute with the Catholic preacher Witzel had led him to overemphasize his position and in so doing

---

* Melanchthon et al. in their two opinions either agreed with Luther's conclusions or pointed out that antinomians elsewhere (e.g. Lüneburg) had actually advocated such teachings. Förstemann, 1: 325–27, 334–36.

to establish unintentionally a school of thought that diverged from the Wittenberg school.[93] When he originally advocated to his students the preaching of remission and repentance through the preaching of the gospel and rejected the preaching of the law (at least before the preaching of the gospel),* he may sincerely have believed that he and Luther agreed. At the very least, he may have felt that though sometimes misled by theologians like Melanchthon,† Luther did advocate the preaching of repentance through the preaching of the gospel and that he, Agricola, was emphasizing the soundest and most essential part of Luther's doctrine. But the fact remains that, whatever the extenuating circumstances, and however unfair Luther's judgment of Agricola's motives, Agricola *had* founded a "sect" in Eisleben opposed to the Wittenberg doctrine, and Luther was justified in charging that he had.

It is possible, too, that Agricola himself never made any invidious comparisons between himself and Luther, but it seems clear from the "Theses Circulated Among Brethren" and from Faber's letter that some of his students did.‡ Such comparisons could not but inflame Luther and convince him that Agricola was seeking glory and fame by inventing novelties and "correcting" Luther.

Agricola had perhaps his most serious clash with Luther over the publication of the *Short Summary*. There are difficulties with the chronology and therefore with the exact interpretation of this affair, but one conclusion seems inescapable: Agricola may have initiated publication on the strength of an assumed approval, but he knowingly continued publication without it. Under these circumstances, Luther is scarcely at fault for being incensed by Agricola's presumption and behavior.

---

* Luther maintained that this qualification was a feeble attempt to clean up his original teaching. WA 51: 436.
† There was an earlier dispute between Agricola and Melanchthon in 1527 over the visitation articles. See Kawerau, *Agricola*, pp. 140–42; Rogge, pp. 98ff.
‡ Faber believed that Agricola's students had these comments and ideas originally from Agricola (Förstemann, 1: 333). It seems likely that Agricola had at least some hand in drawing up the list of pure and impure teachings in Luther's work, which then appeared in the "Theses Circulated Among Brethren" (WA 39/1: 343–44). He certainly was able on other occasions to cite sections of Luther's work that he thought favored his position.

Agricola increased his difficulties by denying all responsibility for the "Theses Circulated Among Brethren." True, he may not himself have written the first series and the list of pure and impure passages, but they did reflect accurately his own teachings as found, for instance, in the *Short Summary*. The second series was not his, and he could justifiably point this out. By rejecting both series out of hand, however, he simply confirmed Luther's belief that he was acting deceitfully and hypocritically.

Much of the later dispute followed the pattern established in the beginning. Agricola seems to have taken a tremendously long time to realize what was at issue. Repeatedly he raised the same specific "antinomian" teaching with which he had begun. First it was the 1537 *Short Summary*, then the 1538 letter "which set the Rhine afire," then his 1 February 1539 disputation, and then, incredibly, his 1540 "Defense." He seems to have been unable to shake the conviction that Luther merely misunderstood him. Again and again he tried to show that he was simply following Luther's own teachings, and though each time he made this claim he got a furious (and justified) reaction from Luther, he stubbornly kept on trying. At first, because he could find isolated citations from Luther that supported his position, he may have been unable to accept the fact that he had misunderstood Luther's teachings. But after being forced to admit his error, he still tried to fend off any accusation of bad faith and to minimize such error as he had admitted. To Luther this was bound to seem more an attempt to justify himself and preserve his reputation than an admission of his error and an expression of his desire for correction.

Agricola may well have been sincere when he claimed that he had committed an honest mistake, but by the time he made this claim it was too late to convince Luther of his sincerity. This was mostly his own fault. His repeated return to the inflammatory issue, his repeated insistence that Luther also had advocated this teaching, and his repeated attempts to deny complicity or to minimize differences had destroyed his credibility. As Agricola himself acknowledged in his "Complaint," there were at least three reconciliations,[94] but after each one Agricola by carelessness or disingenuousness or perhaps plain stupidity reignited the Rhine. To be sure, the Rhine became more inflammable after each blaze, but Agricola did his part to re-kindle the fire. With each flare-up, Luther himself became more harsh in his condemnations and more extreme in his accusations. This, of course, added to Agricola's sense of being wronged. Agricola himself, however, must bear most of the blame for his own suffering. Perhaps as Melanchthon and the other theologians suggested, he should have known what sort of man he was dealing with.

Luther's biblical paradigm is much in evidence in his dispute with Agricola. On repeated occasions he linked the dispute to the con-tinuing and unavoidable struggle between the true and the false church that began with Cain and Abel and that would end only at the last judgment.[95] The devil's role is explicitly recognized. It is he who is ruling Agricola.[96] It is he who benefits from the dispute.[97] It is he who is attempting to subvert Luther's name and authority.[98] Luther could compare the antinomians with the false brethren of the Bible and with the heretics of the patristic period, and see himself in the same position as Paul and the other apostles and prophets fighting the false brethren.[99]

Agricola is "found" to display the typical attributes of the false brother. He is vain, seeking to please the crowd through the intro-duction of novelties.[100] He is deceitful, hypocritical, and a liar, claim-ing that he is now in agreement with Luther while secretly harbor-ing his old opinions.[101] He is cowardly and avoids persecution by re-fusing to defend his error or to admit his mistake.[102] He is just wait-ing for Luther's death to spread his poison.[103] He tries to use Luther's name and authority to support his own heretical teachings.[104] In short, the only common sign of the false brother that Luther does not claim to find in Agricola is teaching without a call.

Also, Luther's behavior is consistent with his biblical model. He describes at length (and truthfully, we may assume) the temptation, pain, and distress the dispute caused him.[105] He recognized that it was his lot to suffer as it had been Paul's.[106] But since the contro-versy was over doctrine, he recognized only God's honor. He con-demned his onetime friend ruthlessly, since respect of persons is su-perseded by respect for God.[107] It was his responsibility to dissociate himself from false doctrine, to give it no comfort, and after several warnings to condemn and shun it as commanded.[108] He was determined to leave a clear testament that could not be misrepresented after his death.[109]

Luther, it seems, occupied a special status in the eyes of his colleagues. The "Opinion" rendered by Melanchthon and the other theologians says that Luther was not a man like other men, as Agricola himself recognized when he criticized him for failings that could occur to "great people."[110] After Luther's death Agricola, notwithstanding certain harsh feelings, found it expedient to list him in the line of the prophets and apostles, as the Elijah of his time.[111]

❧I 8 I❧

The Last Testament

Since my death is now imminent, I want to take this testimony and this honor along with me before my dear Lord and Savior Jesus Christ's judgment seat, that I have earnestly condemned and rejected the fanatics and enemies of the sacrament—Karlstadt, Zwingli, Oecolampadius, Schwenckfeld, and their disciples at Zurich and wherever they are—according to his command, Titus 3: "A heretic should be warned once, and once again; after that have done with him recognizing that a man of that sort has a distorted mind and stands self-condemned in his sins."[1]

As Luther entered the 1540's he was more than ever gripped by the conviction that he was participating in the continuing struggle between the church of Christ and the synagogue of Satan. In one of his sermons he discussed this struggle in terms of the battle between Michael and the dragon. Michael was Jesus Christ, Luther said, and the dragon was Satan. In this case the battle was not among angels but within the church, where one found the Anabaptists and sacramentarians. A continuous battle was raging between the true and false teachers, between the true church and the Anabaptists, sacramentarians, and the mighty dragon the pope. The battle was waged over baptism, the Word, and faith. "We are fighting," he explained, "against the pope, the Anabaptists, and the Turks with the objective of keeping this faith pure." Just as Christ had angels and true teachers, the devil had false teachers, bishops, and heretics. "They have as their lord the old dragon, just as Christ is our leader."[2]

Luther believed that this struggle began when Cain slew Abel for the title of "church": "From the beginning those who truly were the people of God suffered persecutions from those who were not."[3] From the beginning the true church had been persecuted for faith in Christ, the promised blessed seed. This faith had been shared by all the saints including Adam and Eve, Noah, Abraham and Isaac, and all the patriarchs, prophets, apostles, and martyrs.[4]

The struggle had been going on since the beginning of the world, Luther believed, but as he grew older he had a strong premonition that the end of this struggle was near. He saw events as pointing to the last judgment, for which he frequently and ardently prayed.[5] He believed that the natural world had deteriorated markedly since paradise and even in his own lifetime.[6] Morality, too, had taken a downward course. The final battle was near. And in these last days he felt compelled to issue repeated warnings to his Wittenberg congregation, to the German princes, and to the German people.

Luther decried the reestablishment of brothels, once removed in the cleansing tide of the reformation.[7] He issued printed warnings and sermons against the syphilitic whores sent by the devil to Wittenberg to mislead students and discredit the reformation.[8] He was greatly offended, too, by the predatory behavior of various young girls, and announced to the Elector that many a student was being trapped into immorality or marriage. "And I have heard," he wrote, "that many parents have ordered home their children and still do so. They say that when they send their children to us for studies, we hang wives around their necks and rob them of their children, which is giving this fine school a bad name."[9]

Repeatedly he condemned the German nobility for pursuing desires of the flesh. Drunkenness was one of their most common vices, he contended, and one shared by most Germans.[10] They also refused to support the ministry properly, although in papal times the money had flowed like water.[11] And they conspired with farmers to withhold grain supplies in order to raise prices while people died of starvation in the towns.[12] Usury was rampant, he charged, and openly practiced in evangelical towns.[13] Servants were disobedient and disrespectful.[14]

Luther also maintained that Satan's maneuvers in these days signaled the final battle. The papacy with its frequently postponed council seemed more obviously than ever to be the beast of Daniel.[15] To

Luther, papal hypocrisy was transparent, but he feared that simple souls might be duped by even the promise of a council.[16] Even the Jews, those old enemies of Christendom, now seemed bent on converting Christians to their ancient error; he heard rumors and reports of their activities.[17]

Satan was also active within the evangelical fold, stirring up false brethren and using Luther's name and authority to subvert the gospel. Reports reached him of a former student of his preaching sacramentarian doctrine in Bohemia.[18] The antinomians, especially Agricola, were using his writings to support their error. Kaspar Schwenckfeld adorned his treatises with rich citations from Luther's works. The Zurichers republished Zwingli's works and praised a book in which Zwingli listed pagan saints. Even within Wittenberg the jurists continued to murmur about the validity of priestly marriages[19] and to support the un-Christian practice of secret engagements.[20] Evangelical princes, cousins even, came close to shedding each other's blood.[21] Philipp of Hesse entered into a bigamous marriage after obtaining a qualified approval from Luther through misrepresentation, and then tracts appeared justifying the act.[22] But of all these many signs of deterioration that Luther found, the worst in his eyes was the ingratitude and contempt with which the gospel was being received.[23] Surely the end must be near. And looking about he saw another sign: the scourge of God approached.

This scourge was the Turk, who was blessed with success despite the prayers and efforts of Germany.[24] The German princes were divided among themselves, and Luther charged that some of them even diverted taxes intended to arm Germany against the Turks into their own pockets and gathered armies to use against the evangelicals rather than against the common enemy.[25] Luther was sure that as a prelude to the end Germany would feel the Turkish hand, and he was not certain whether he ought to bewail their fate or take grim satisfaction in God's vengeance.[26] He realized, too, that his own end was near. He was often unwell and frequently prayed for release.[27] But before he departed he felt that he must make his final testament against the enemies of God: the Antichrist, the Jews, the false brethren.

Luther in the 1540's saw himself as one of God's champions, girded for the last battle of his life and of the world. He had to defend the Word against the devil's frantic last attack, he had to repudiate the false brethren, and he had to condemn all those who misused his name. His last testament must be plain. His conscience must be clear before he met his Lord face to face. We find continued in the final battle of Luther's life many of the themes that have run through the preceding chapters. Luther's last testament was the culmination of all that had gone before.

During the late 1530's and the early 1540's Luther was fairly restrained in his public dealings with the sacramentarians. As a result of the Wittenberg Concord of 1536, a number of the Swiss and southern German cities had moved from the enemy camp into the ranks of friends, and Luther wrote to several evangelical communities in Italy that he felt the preachers of these subscribing cities were now following the true gospel, although the old leaven was not entirely removed from among their congregations.[28] The unrepentant, among whom Luther numbered the Zurichers, Karlstadt at Basel, and the roaming Kaspar Schwenckfeld, were subjected during this period to only a few passing swipes. True, these swipes could wound, and we shall later consider some of the reactions of those who were struck. Before going on, however, we should consider an important side incident: Luther's reaction to Karlstadt's death.

On Christmas Eve 1541 Luther's old opponent Andreas Bodenstein von Karlstadt died of the plague in Basel, where he was a member of the theological faculty. He left behind a wife and children.* A report of his death soon reached Luther with accounts of strange circumstances surrounding his departure from this world. On 16 February Luther wrote Justus Jonas that he wanted to know if Karlstadt had died repentant, and he related a story from a friend in Basel who claimed that a ghost was wandering near Karlstadt's grave and in his house, causing an uproar by throwing stones and rubbish.[29] We do not know who this friend in Basel was, but we do have the account sent from Basel on 17 March by the Basel preacher Oswald Myconius,

---

* Luther and Melanchthon later wrote to the Basel Council asking it to look after Karlstadt's widow and children. They did this at the request of Christoph von Mochau, the widow's uncle. WABr 10: 71–72.

no friend of Karlstadt's.[30] Myconius reported that Karlstadt had been bothered for some time by a demon, and that this demon had vexed him while he was preaching the day before coming down with the plague. It was reported that the demon continued to vex Karlstadt during his illness.[31]

On 26 March Luther wrote to Jacob Propst in Bremen about the ghost that had troubled Karlstadt during his sickness and had caused disturbances in Karlstadt's house after his death. He told Propst that he always had wished and still wished that Karlstadt would be saved, but said that he could not like or approve of Karlstadt's not having repented before he died.[32] It seems that Luther had now answered for himself the question he had put to Jonas, and had decided that Karlstadt had died impenitent.

A few days later Veit Dietrich sent even more dreadful details about poor Karlstadt's last days. Dietrich stated flatly that Karlstadt had been killed by the devil. He supported his assertion with reports from Basel churchmen. They had written that a large man had entered the church while Karlstadt was preaching, and visible to Karlstadt and to many others, had taken an empty seat next to one of the magistrates, and had then departed. This man had next entered Karlstadt's house and, finding Karlstadt's young son there alone, had lifted him up as if he were going to hurl him to the ground. Instead, he had released the boy unhurt and had commanded him to tell his father that he would return in three days and carry him off—which, they affirmed, he in fact did. Dietrich reported that the Basel churchmen had also said that after Karlstadt had finished his sermon, he had inquired from the citizen next to whom the large man had sat who he was, but the citizen had not seen anyone.[33] Dietrich concluded that Karlstadt had not died from the plague but had succumbed in fright of his impending death.[34]

Luther passed on this account almost word for word to Amsdorf.[35] A week later he wrote again to assure Amsdorf that the account was perfectly true and added: "But you know the nature of the man so that it is no wonder [to you] if he finally found the just reward for his deeds which were tolerated so long in God's patience."[36] Luther was by no means alone in accepting this improbable story. A Basel student reported that it was given general credence in Wittenberg.[37] But the account held special significance for Luther, for it proved what he had long claimed: that Karlstadt was possessed by the devil and was a member of Satan's false church.

The first serious controversy of this last period of Luther's life was over a Bible. With no doubt the best of intentions but with perhaps less than the best judgment, the Zurich printer Christoph Froschauer sent Luther a copy of the Latin Bible produced by the Zurich ministers. Luther was not pleased by the gift, and on 31 August 1543 he wrote a letter to Froschauer that set off a flurry of correspondence among Bucer, Melanchthon, and the Zurichers, and prompted the Zurichers to reissue Zwingli's works in order to respond to Luther's accusations.[38]

In Luther's letter to Froschauer he thanked him for his consideration but made it quite clear what he thought of such a gift. It was a work of the Zurich ministers, with whom Luther, as a member of the church of God, could have no communion. Therefore he expressed his sorrow that the Zurich ministers had worked so diligently for nothing, and that they should also be lost souls. They had been sufficiently admonished to desist from their error, and to cease leading the poor people to hell along with themselves. Since no admonition had helped, Luther had to conclude that they would have to be abandoned to their fate. So he asked Froschauer in the future not to send him as a gift any work of theirs. "I do not wish to be a party to condemned and blasphemous teaching," Luther wrote, "but rather [I wish] to know that I am innocent and to pray and to teach against them until my death." He informed Froschauer that he still prayed that God might convert some of the Zurich ministers and might also "help the poor church finally to become free of such false, seductive preachers." Although they laughed now, Luther was sure that they would eventually cry when they found the same divine judgment as had Zwingli, whom they followed.[39]

Not at all surprisingly, the Zurichers were greatly offended by Luther's letter, and it fell to Bucer and Melanchthon to apologize and try to calm their anger. The letters exchanged among Bullinger, Bucer, and Melanchthon provide an interesting insight into their feelings about Luther and into the difference between their attitude toward polemics and Luther's.[40] Most interesting for our purposes are Bucer's remarks in Luther's defense. These were written in response to a letter from Bullinger which severely condemned Luther's polemics and revealed Bullinger's deep concern for decorum and "appropriate" behavior and his fear of offending "pious Christians."[41]

Although Bucer readily acknowledged the justice of many of Bullinger's criticisms and complaints, he came out strongly in Luther's favor. It was true, he said, that Luther was impetuous and reportedly did not allow himself to be restrained by coercion or pleas, but that was the way God was using Luther in the preaching of His gospel, in explaining the power of faith and good works, and in casting down the Antichrist. God had granted him such trust and authority in so many churches that there was no one truly zealous for Christ who had heard him publicly and was not yet corrupted by bad doctrine who thought he should be opposed, much less removed from his ministry. Bucer acknowledged that Luther was extolled by many who were not his followers, and that many admired and sought to imitate Luther's faults rather than his virtues; nevertheless, there was still a multitude of saintly men who honored him as the highest apostle of Christ.

Bucer said further that when he put to one side the matters under contention and considered matters concerning the interpretation of Scripture, the main doctrinal points of Christianity, and exhortation to duty, he was forced to take the side of those who yielded preeminence in sacred matters to Luther. To be sure, Luther's humanity showed through. But who, Bucer asked, could produce only divine works? Luther was such a man that all pious and learned men who knew him held him to be a marvelous instrument of God who was awakened for the welfare of God's people. They also knew that he could not be dissuaded from his method of disputation and that even to try to dissuade him might cause even greater scandals in the church. So they put up with it, since they could not correct it.[42]

The dust had hardly settled on the matter of the Zurich Bible when Luther issued his *Short Confession on the Lord's Supper*. He made this treatise the occasion to dissociate himself publicly once more—

and actually for the last time—from all sacramentarians. He wished to quell rumors that he and the sacramentarians in any way agreed. And knowing that he would die soon, he wished to leave behind a clear and final testament against these false brethren. This was necessary to fulfill his duty to the true church and to clear his conscience before God. The immediate provocation for the writing of the treatise (in addition to a report that a former Wittenberg student was espousing sacramentarian teachings) was the activity of the Silesian nobleman Kaspar Schwenckfeld.[43]

Luther had long seen a serious misuse of his name and authority in the writings of Kaspar Schwenckfeld. In 1526 Luther had met briefly with the man and had later admonished him by letter to desist from his errors concerning the Lord's Supper.[44] Evidently the admonition had had some effect, for Schwenckfeld on several occasions expressed a feeling of gratitude and indebtedness to Luther for leading him toward the truth.[45]

Needless to say, Luther was not pleased with being given credit for leading anyone to Schwenckfeld's brand of truth. But certainly more serious in Luther's eyes was Schwenckfeld's frequent use of Luther's writings to defend his own position. He had taken such liberties in his replies to the Swiss, especially Joachim Vadian, the St. Gallen humanist, and in his response when he was condemned in March 1540 by Melanchthon and the other evangelical theologians at the meeting in Schmalkalden. He had also made particular use of Luther's writings, especially the early works, in his *Confession and Explanation of the Knowledge of Christ and of His Divine Glory* of 1541.[46] To add insult to injury, Schwenckfeld had accused Luther along with Melanchthon and Brenz of condemning him for teachings that they themselves had once espoused.[47] As we have seen, it was just such a claim made by Agricola that fueled Luther's ire in the antinomian dispute. Schwenckfeld even had the temerity to send a copy of this *Confession* to Melanchthon with the request that he share it with Luther.[48] He asked for comments, though it seems more likely that he was asking for trouble.

Luther had previously attacked Schwenckfeld, though without naming him, in his *Concerning the Last Words of David* (1543), where he lumped him together with "Jews, heretics, and Mohammedans" under the thinly veiled epithet "Blindfeld."[49] He also had attacked him by name in a quarterly disputation held on 28 February 1540, which was later published.[50]

Schwenckfeld thought that he had been wronged in these two writings and that Luther obviously misunderstood him, and he felt obliged on this account to write Luther a personal letter explaining his position.[51] With the letter he sent a collection of citations from Vadian's works, which he felt demonstrated Vadian's errors; a collection of citations from Luther and Bugenhagen, which he felt supported his own position; a copy of Vadian's *Thorough Report and Excerpt from the Books by Dr. Joachim von Watt ... Whether or Not Christ the Lord Even in His Glory Is a Creature According to His Assumed Flesh*; and two other works of his own. About Vadian's treatise he wrote to Luther, "I can in no way believe that if you had read it or knew what was in it, you could remain silent."[52]

In the letter Schwenckfeld once again expressed his gratitude to Luther for his earlier help, although he said that he could not now agree with Luther on every point.[53] He claimed that Luther's previous teachings had been no different from his, for which reason he had adduced Luther's writings to support his position in his *Confession*. He drew particular attention to Luther's *On the Councils and the Church* and his 1522 postil on Heb. 1:1–12 for Christmas day.[54] He repeated his contention that it was the Swiss who were in error, and that although the Swiss claimed Luther for their side, their error was not shared by Luther except in his most recent writings. He felt it necessary to draw the matter to Luther's attention, since Luther seemed unaware of all that was going on, and also to clear his own name from the charge of Eutychian heresy or other error.[55]

Such a list of claims had a predictable effect on Luther: he was enraged. He fired off a sharp condemnatory note which he left unsealed, and in order not to honor Schwenckfeld's name, he addressed the note to the messenger who had delivered Schwenckfeld's letter and documents rather than to Schwenckfeld himself.[56] Evidently Schwenckfeld circulated copies of this note from Luther, and a friend of the reformer intercepted a copy and sent it on to Luther. It was to this unknown friend that the *Short Confession* was dedicated.[57]

Luther's *Short Confession* was more than anything else a matter of conscience. He began it by feigning indifference to the attacks of Schwenckfeld or any of the other sacramentarians. "It makes no more difference to me," he wrote, "if he [Schwenckfeld] or his accursed swarm of fanatics, Zwinglians, and the like praise or scold me than if Jews, Turks, pope, and actually all devils scold or praise me."[58] He only wished to be able to testify before the Lord's throne that he had condemned and shunned the fanatics and enemies of the Sacrament as commanded in Titus 3: "A heretic should be warned once, and once again; after that, have done with him, recognizing that a man of that sort has a distorted mind and stands self-condemned in his sins."[59] Among these enemies he listed Karlstadt, Zwingli, Oecolampadius, Schwenckfeld (whom he called "Stenckfeld," that is, "Stinkfield"), and "their disciples at Zurich or wherever they are." "They have been admonished often enough and also earnestly enough by me and others," he said: "The books are extant."[60]

Luther remarked on how strange it seemed to him that Schwenckfeld had become so bold as to approach him with letters and books, for he knew or should have known that he was Luther's unreconciled enemy. Instead of realizing this, he thought that Luther would welcome books and letters from him, which would give rise to the "insane" notion that Luther was in complete agreement with Schwenckfeld and the fanatics and had recanted everything. "Indeed, I have been often told previously," Luther explained, "that the fanatics boasted that I agreed with them, which I did not want to believe, since no one would want such things written publicly of himself."[61]

Luther argued that by circulating the note he had written him, Schwenckfeld wished to be seen as a great martyr, just as the fanatics made big talk about Christian love and rebuked Luther for being proud, hard, and without charity, and for dividing the church on account of a single, unnecessary or insignificant article concerning the Lord's Supper. "In fact," Luther contended, "whatever they did to me, they claimed that I had done to them; whatever I had to suffer at their hands, they boasted that they had to suffer at mine."[62] In short, Schwenckfeld and the other fanatics were running true to form.

In these introductory remarks about Schwenckfeld, Luther had already firmly established the central goal of the treatise: to testify to the world before his death and judgment that he had condemned, was condemning, and always would condemn the sacramentarians and their false teachings. Now he turned to the Swiss, first giving his version of the recent history of the dispute with them.

Fifteen years ago he, Zwingli, Oecolampadius, and others had met in Marburg and agreed on a number of Christian articles, reaching an impasse only on the article on the Supper. Luther believed that it was solely the sacramentarians who had given ground: "For at Marburg, too, we did not agree with them in a single article of faith, but they joined us in assenting to all articles with the exception of the article on the sacrament." They even improved their position on the Supper and admitted "that it was not mere bread and wine in the Lord's Supper, as they had most vehemently contended until then, but that the body and blood were also in it though not bodily, only spiritually," and then only for true believers. "Because Zwingli and his followers yielded in so many important articles of faith, I was quite hopeful," Luther wrote, "that in time the one remaining article would also be agreed upon."[63]

This hope had proved false. Luther related how their partial accord had collapsed. First, Zwingli had been cut down by the papists on the field of battle, and Oecolampadius had died of grief soon thereafter. Luther considered these deaths to be divine warnings against the sacramentarians.[64] Then in 1536 Zwingli's *A Short and Clear Exposition of Christian Faith* had been published posthumously by his Zurich followers. This book completely dashed Luther's hopes, for in it Zwingli "not only remains an enemy of the Holy Sacrament but also becomes a full-blown heathen," since he lists among the saved in heaven a number of pagans.[65] Luther, greatly shocked, was forced to some hard conclusions:

For, because he was able to write this after our agreement at Marburg, it is certain that in every respect he dealt with us with a false heart and tongue at Marburg. Therefore I had to despair (as I still must) of the salvation of his soul, if he died with such a disposition.

But Zwingli's salvation was not the only one put in question. If the Zurich ministers could publish such a book and so praise and honor it, Luther had to conclude that they, too, were past hope:

Because Zwingli not only repudiated the Marburg Agreement in this book (in fact, did not take the agreement seriously), but did what was worse and became a heathen, and yet his comrades, the fanatics, praise and honor this book (which also contains many other abominations), therefore, I have abandoned all my hope for their improvement. In fact I have ignored them to the extent that I did not want to write against this book nor pray for them any more, because I had seen that all my previous writings and admonitions, in addition to my Christian love and fidelity demonstrated at Marburg, were so badly received and would thus necessarily be shamefully lost.

So Luther begged anyone who might have heard of this agreement at Marburg not to make the error of believing that Luther agreed with the fanatics: "I would much rather let myself be torn apart or burned a hundred times before I would be of one mind or will with Schwenckfeld, Zwingli, Karlstadt, Oecolampadius, and whoever else they might be, these loathsome fanatics, or before I would acknowledge their teaching."[66] Although the *Short Confession* is filled with many similar disavowals and denunciations,[67] one disavowal in particular may be cited, for it summarizes much of Luther's motivation: "For because I am sure that they are wrong and blaspheme God, and because their own conscience must testify against them, I shall and can cheerfully say in the presence of my dear Lord Jesus Christ on the day of judgment: Lord Jesus, I have faithfully warned and admonished them of that which their own conscience convicts them; this they will have to confess before you, you know this, dear Lord."[68]

Luther cited a number of warnings the Swiss had had. He had admonished them himself in his writings, and his admonition was not to be despised, for he was a servant of Christ, as much as, if not more than, they, and had worked in Christ's church before they had.[69] In addition to the warnings of men, the Swiss had also received warnings from God. There were Zwingli's and Oecolampadius' early deaths, and Zwingli's by the sword at that.[70] It should have been a warning to them, too, that among themselves they could not agree on an exposition of Scripture—Luther noted some seven different interpretations of the words of institution for the Supper (recalling the seven-headed beast of *Revelations*). Yet all these warnings, Luther wrote, had been in vain. The Swiss had persisted in their error, and therefore, following Paul's injunction, he had to shun them and have no association with them: "For I would have to condemn myself into the abyss of hell together with them if I should make common cause with them or have fellowship with them or should be silent about it when I notice or hear that they presumed to be or boasted about being in fellowship with me."[71]

Luther was particularly incensed that the sacramentarians had called the Lutherans' God a "baked" or "bread" or "wine" God, and had called the Lutherans "flesh-gobblers" and "blood-guzzlers." With these epithets they were doing both the Lutherans and the Lord an intentional wrong and fabricating slanderous lies. "This," Luther said, "was a sure sign that there was no benevolent spirit dwelling in them." They knew that the Lutherans had never taught or believed any such thing, but wishing to enhance their own reputation at the expense of the Lutherans, they spread among the rabble the notion that the Lutherans believed in a local presence and that Christ was eaten piecemeal as a wolf gobbles up a sheep, and that Christ's blood was drunk as a cow guzzles water. Such shameless accusations and lies came from the devil. Not even the papists taught such a thing, as the fanatics well knew. Yet they even attempted to injure the Lutherans by calling them "papists." To demonstrate Christian love, the Lutherans had not brought these things up at Marburg: "For (God knows), how we were obliged to hear that we possessed no Christian love, that we despised the ministers of Christ, that we grieved and confused the church, etc. There were no sinners on earth except us alone, and there were no saints in heaven except the fanatics alone."

Even if it were true that mere bread and wine were present, should the Swiss use such terms as "baked God" or "bread God"? Luther, obviously wrought up by his own rhetorical question, went on to call the sacramentarians by their "proper names." Not only were they "bread-gobblers" and "wine-guzzlers," they were "soul-gobblers" and "soul-murderers" and possessed of "a bedeviled, thoroughly bedeviled, hyper-bedeviled heart and lying mouth." These epithets were completely appropriate, Luther said, "because it cannot be denied that with their blasphemies they shamelessly lied against their own consciences, and they still have not repented but rather rejoice in their wickedness."[72]

This last charge explained and justified Luther's condemnations of the sacramentarians. He had been asked whether God would be so vehement and so horribly strict that He would want to condemn men on account of one article if they faithfully adhered to and believed all the other articles. This question, Luther declared, was the refuge of all heretics, and he answered it unequivocally. "It is certain," he wrote, "that whoever does not believe or does not want properly to believe one article (after he is warned and instructed) certainly believes no article with seriousness and good faith." The Holy Spirit did not allow itself to be divided or split.[73]

So Luther admonished his readers not to believe any of the sacramentarians' claims, not even that they believed in Christ as both man and God: "They are certainly lying about everything that they say about this. True, they confess it with their mouths (as the devil even called the Lord, God's son), 'But their heart is far from it [Matt. 15].'" For anyone who dares to give the lie to God in one of His words intentionally and after being warned and instructed dares (and also certainly does) give the lie to God in all His words.[74] The sacramentarians did this, treating God's Word as if it were man's word (or a fool's word) to be changed according to their own opinions. In the same way, all their pretense of morality and Christian love was a sham, and their arguments about the spiritual eating and drinking of the Supper were fig leaves to hide their poison.[75] Repeatedly Luther stated that the sacramentarians were controlled by the devil.[76]

For some time Luther had felt that there should perhaps be a public explanation of why the Wittenbergers had discontinued the elevation of the host. When the practice of elevating the Sacrament was discontinued in the Wittenberg Parish Church on 25 June 1542, worried inquiries quickly followed.* Did this action signify a change in Luther's understanding of the Sacrament in the direction of the sacramentarian position? Did Luther and the Wittenbergers no longer hold to the real presence of Christ in the elements?[77] The very next day he had to reassure an anxious Prince George of Anhalt that such

---

* It is unclear what responsibility Luther had for this change in the service. On several occasions he ascribed responsibility to Bugenhagen. But letters by Philipp of Hesse and Melanchthon seem to indicate that Luther was at least in some part responsible. See WABr 10: 86 n. 3, for a discussion of this question.

ceremonies were not articles of faith.[78] The following 10 November he complained to Spalatin that he was still being annoyed by questions about the abolition of the elevation,[79] and in January of the next year he wrote to Brück that "the ceremonies that have nothing to do with salvation are giving us more to do than the great necessary articles, as they have always done from the very beginning." He had not yet decided whether he should publish something on the matter. Uniformity in ceremonial procedure seemed impossible, and he concluded significantly that "so it went with the apostles themselves with the ceremonies of Moses; they had to allow everyone to be free to eat, dress, and behave as he wished."[80] Finally, in mid-1544, Luther felt constrained to publish something on the elevation, and having disposed of the sacramentarians he added a section to the *Short Confession.*[81]

The essence of Luther's argument was that since ceremonies were not articles of faith, they should in no way be allowed to become snares to conscience, as Satan would have them be. Man was their master and not their servant.[82] Again and again he explained that he had retained the elevation only to spite the devil, who, through Karlstadt, had tried to make the elevation a matter of conscience and a sin; were it not for the devil, he might have discontinued the use long before instead of waiting for Karlstadt's death. And if the need ever arose to reestablish the elevation to combat some heresy, Luther said that he would not hesitate to do so.[83]

Luther saw the devil's hand in the whole business. He wrote one correspondent that since Satan realized that Luther could not be conquered publicly, he thought to bring him into ill-repute through snake-like and secret hissings in corners, and to distort the Word of truth under the title of Luther's name.[84] In his *Short Confession* Luther stated:

Therefore the enemies of the Sacrament have no cause to boast that we allowed the elevation to be abolished for their sake or to please them. And no one should draw the conclusion that we wish by this action to draw closer to their blasphemous error much less give way to it.[85]

In 1545 Heinrich Bullinger, speaking for the Zurich ministers, responded to Luther's *Short Confession* with the *True Confession.*[86] This treatise included the Zurich version of the Marburg Colloquy;

a list of Luther's subsequent and, to Bullinger's notion, unjustified attacks on the Zurichers; an explanation of the Zurichers' dogmatic position on the Supper, along with counterarguments to Luther's; and, at the end, a thorough and provocative criticism of Luther's polemical style, similar to that in Bullinger's 1543 letter to Bucer mentioned earlier.[87]

In the course of the treatise Bullinger touched on and rejected nearly all of Luther's charges and characterizations. He said that in spite of Luther's accusations to the contrary, they had no intention of remaining silent until after Luther's death before advocating their teachings. This the *True Confession* itself showed.[88] They had not boasted of agreement with Luther or attempted to support their own teachings with Luther's name.[89] Bullinger took strong exception to Luther's labeling the Zurichers "revealed liars," and he totally rejected Luther's charge that they were ruled by the devil.[90] To Luther's characterization of the sacramentarians as "vain spirits," Bullinger countered that the real "vain spirit" was Luther: "He boasts of being the German prophet and apostle who need learn from no one, but from whom all others learn." He accused Luther of trying to be the final authority that allowed of no contradiction: "If someone does not say what he says or if someone wishes to say more than he says, then he is banished and condemned as a heretic." Luther wanted credit for everything despite the contributions made by others.[91]

Bullinger was willing to concede gladly and freely that God had accomplished many great things through Luther for the benefit of believers and for the destruction of the papacy. The Zurichers had always granted him his due honor. But no modest believer, Bullinger argued, could be happy that Luther thought so highly of himself, that he was unnecessarily contentious, and that some people praised him so excessively (much as the Franciscans did, for example, with their Francis) and thus made him more arrogant.[92]

Bullinger's evaluation of the differences between Luther's polemics and those of the prophets and apostles raises some fascinating questions. Bullinger argued that the servants of God—the prophets, John the Baptist, the apostles, and Jesus Christ himself—sometimes used sharp, almost coarse, language. They had kept within the bounds of moderation, however, and their rebukes had been accompanied with good arguments which powerfully attracted the people to them. In contrast, Luther observed no moderation and presented few arguments, and when God provided him with a good argument, he obscured it with evil and disgusting language. While the servants of God rebuked bravely (*dapffer*) and without frivolity, Luther's rebuking was much too frivolous and showed little bravery (*dapfferkeit*). The servants of God sought God's honor, not their own; they did not promote their own quarrels or seek to increase their own reputations; they sought only the salvation of sinners. And therefore, although their words were pungent and sharply spoken, still they had a fatherly spirit. But Luther pushed his own affairs and quarrels, made a great show, and immediately committed to the devil all those who did not yield to him. So there was much hostile spirit in all his rebuking and little fatherly spirit. The servants of God sharpened or softened their chastisement according to the size and number of the misdeeds. But Luther, with his argument that error on one article made worthless the adherence to all others, threw the baby out with the bath. The servants of God rebuked only those deserving of rebuke. Luther, on the other hand, raged against the innocent and the guilty alike and reviled the innocent no less furiously than the most malicious rascals. Therefore, Bullinger concluded, the manner in which God's holy prophets and apostles delivered their rebukes did not justify Luther's polemics at all.[93]

For some time Luther considered whether or not he should respond to this treatise. Finally he decided to include a short response in his *Against the Asses of Paris and Louvaine* and his *Thirty-Nine Articles*, but he died before these treatises were finished.[94] For our purposes the *Short Confession* was the culmination of Luther's dispute with the sacramentarians. It was Luther's last testament against the false brethren.

Conclusion

From 1522 to his death in 1546 Luther clashed with a succession of major evangelical opponents. First there was Karlstadt, then Müntzer, then Zwingli, Oecolampadius, Bucer, and the other sacramentarians, then John Agricola, and finally Kaspar Schwenckfeld and once again the Swiss sacramentarians. For the most part, these opponents accepted the central reformation principles and assumptions that differentiated evangelicals from Catholics.* At the same time, they came to conclusions different from Luther's on issues such as acceptable ceremonial practice, the real presence in the Lord's Supper, the separation of secular and spiritual authority, and the relation between law and gospel. As it happened, they were able to convince a large number of evangelicals to accept their positions, and, consequently, they posed a major challenge to Luther's version of the gospel message and to his authority within the reformation movement.

There are several ways in which controversies between evangelicals and Catholics differed strikingly from controversies among evangelicals. In controversies between evangelicals and Catholics, Luther usually made an effort not to attach his name to the beliefs he espoused; when challenged by other evangelicals, he occasionally supplemented his theological arguments with claims about himself and his special role in the reformation movement. In controversies between evangelicals and Catholics, each side accused the other of satanic motivation and exchanged the vilest personal abuse; in controversies among evangelicals, the accusations of demonic possession and the *ad hominem* abuse tended to come more from Luther than from his oppo-

* This is less true of Müntzer and Schwenckfeld than of the others.

nents.* Again and again Luther accused Zwingli, Oecolampadius, Bucer, Agricola, Bullinger, and Schwenckfeld of being false brethren and lying hypocrites, but these men generally acknowledged that Luther was a fellow Christian even though he erred. And although Catholic and evangelical opponents alike attacked Luther's authority, whereas the Catholics attempted to discredit it entirely, the evangelical opponents rarely asserted that Luther had no legitimate authority, insisting only that Luther, like any other man, could be in error.

As a practical matter if nothing else, Luther needed to see that his teachings and movement were distinguished in the public mind from those of his evangelical opponents. To begin with, he needed to make it easier for "simple people" to choose between his teachings and those of his opponents. In the major controversies among evangelicals a substantial number of the evangelicals did not understand either the reasons for the disagreement or its significance, and as a consequence they were distressed and confused. This is evident in the contentions, especially by Bucer and his faction, that the disagreement between them and Luther did not separate the true church from the false, that it was only a battle over words, and that it involved only issues that did not pertain to salvation. It is also evident in the frequently heard pleas for moderation, charity, and fraternal toleration. It was necessary for Luther to help those who were confused to see that the disagreement was significant and real, and to make it as likely as possible that they would choose to support his side of the controversy.

This need was much less compelling in controversies with Catholics, since Catholics and evangelicals agreed that there was a fundamental difference in their understanding of the Christian message. Since they based their arguments on different authorities, the reasons for their disagreement were apparent, and each was certain that he was right and his opponent wrong. The members of the reformation movement, however, were generally in agreement on the central principles that differentiated their belief from Catholicism, and most of them accepted the Scripture as the only authority and source of doctrine. They might, as they did at the Colloquy of Marburg, agree on every article of doctrine but one; yet despite their common use of Scripture as the sole basis for their position, each side was unable to

* Müntzer is again an exception.

convince the other of its error. With the wisdom of hindsight and after years of debate, we can see that profound differences in assumptions underlay the two positions. But in the initial stages of the dispute, these differences either were not clear or seemed to many insignificant. It was this confusion that had to be overcome.

Luther also needed to disclaim any responsibility for his evangelical opponents. Because he and these opponents shared many beliefs, and because prior association often linked their names in the public mind, especially if his opponents still professed agreement with Luther, it was possible for Catholics and even evangelicals to hold Luther and his movement responsible for the deeds, and especially the misdeeds, of his opponents. Therefore, the more clearly Luther could distinguish his position from that of his opponents, the more he could argue with seeming justice that he and his movement were not responsible for the men who opposed him or for their actions.

This essay has focused on two ways in which Luther sharpened the differences between himself and his evangelical opponents. One was by his claiming special authority, and on this basis attempting to get those who were unsure or who did not fully understand the disagreement or its significance to accept his position. The second way was by maligning his evangelical opponents, and thus raising doubts about the validity of doctrine espoused by such evil men. On the basis of the material offered him by Scripture and the history of the Church, he developed a world view that not only supported his claim of special authority but also explained the division among evangelicals, sustained his position theologically and psychologically, and justified to both himself and his followers his unrestrained attack on other evangelicals. This world view posited an unchanging struggle between the true church and the false. Beginning with Cain and Abel, it had continued through the Old and New Testament histories, and had reached its apocalyptic climax in Luther's day. The human contestants in this struggle were the true and the false prophets. Within this schema, Luther was a true prophet, his evangelical opponents false prophets.

Luther might have advanced special claims about himself in the early years of the reformation, but he did not do so. When Catholics accused him of claiming to be a prophet, he denied the accusation and rejected the role. His claim to a special role was made when he was challenged by other evangelicals. It was at this point, perhaps because conventional arguments were not persuasive enough for those evangelicals who did not understand the disagreement, that Luther resorted to a claim of personal authority as well.

It was with the intention of testing his evangelical opponents that Luther had defined the characteristics of the true prophet. At that time he had not applied the definition to himself, although many of his followers had maintained long before that he was no ordinary man.[1] Gradually, however, he came to see himself as occupying in his time the role occupied by the true prophets and apostles in biblical times. He possessed the proper characteristics as he had defined them, and he had consistently acted as a prophet was supposed to.

By the 1530's he was drawing explicit parallels between St. Paul's experiences and his own, and using these parallels to justify his actions. Both St. Paul and he suffered tremendous doubts and temptations; they both had been forcibly rescued from a perverted faith; they both had received their authority and message from God, not from men; and they both had their false apostles—their fanatics who attacked their names, attempted to subvert their doctrine, accused them of violating the requirements of Christian charity, and sought to deprive them and their followers of the title of Church. These tribulations, suffered by them both, were the characteristics, the distinguishing marks, the "stigmata" of God's true spokesmen.

Almost from the first encounter with his evangelical opponents Luther accused them of being false brethren, much like the false prophets and apostles in the biblical accounts. He charged that they were all possessed by Satan's spirit and were bent on destroying the true church. This characterization of his opponents was embedded in an elaborate system that was extremely difficult for them to invalidate or attack, and that frequently placed them in a double bind. Because, as Luther asserted, they were ruled by the satanic spirit, he directed his attack more against this spirit than against the men it occupied, and attributed to them not only what they had allegedly done but what, because of the satanic spirit, they were allegedly *capable* of doing. When his opponents objected to being classified as though they were all of one mind and pointed to the fact that there were differences among them, Luther replied that the differences were only on the surface, that the satanic spirit was a spirit of discord, and that the very fact that they disagreed among themselves showed that they were possessed by Satan.

If they resisted Luther's admonitions and his arguments, he said that they thereby demonstrated their satanic perversity, obduracy, and vanity. If, on the other hand, they requested a concord or expressed a willingness to be instructed if they had erred, Luther said they thereby showed their uncertainty. This proved that they could not possess the Holy Spirit, which bestowed certainty of faith. If they appeared to yield to any of his arguments or to abandon a previous position (even a position that only some of them had espoused), Luther saw this as a tacit admission that all their beliefs were false, for the Holy Spirit did not allow true believers to err in any matter of faith. Lacking the Holy Spirit, they were of necessity slaves of Satan, all their avowals of Christian belief were a sham, and all evidence to the contrary could be dismissed as deception and works-righteousness.

It was fateful for the course of Luther's controversies with other evangelicals that his first opponents were men like Karlstadt, the Zwickau prophets, and Müntzer. Each of these men did indeed possess many of the characteristics of the false prophet: they lacked a proper call, they boasted of special revelation, they confused the worldly and divine kingdoms, they were legalistic, they were involved in inciting mob action, they were vain, they resisted a fraternal admonition, and so on. And once Luther had built up his stereotype of the false prophet from the accounts of Scripture and his encounters with these men, and had found it confirmed in Orlamünde and in the Peasants' War, he tended to find the same characteristics in other evangelical opponents and to ignore, misperceive, or rationalize away characteristics and actions inconsistent with the stereotype.* Luther acted on this stereotyping of his evangelical opponents by sharply rebuking them and refusing to have any fellowship with them. This

---

* There is nothing necessarily hypocritical about this, since the individual is normally not aware of this sort of psychological process. See Albert H. Hastorf, David J. Schneider, and Judith Polefka, *Person Perception* (Menlo Park, Calif., 1970), pp. 48–59.

treatment provoked the very "hot, fanatical replies" that his stereotype had led him to expect.

The *ad hominem* attack was used more extensively and more successfully by Luther than by his evangelical opponents. Certainly the opponents attacked Luther's arguments, complained bitterly about his characterizations of them, and accused him of slighting the requirements of Christian charity, modesty, and decorum; nonetheless, most of them paid some honor to Luther and his accomplishments, arguing only that he, too, could err and require correction. Several explanations can be advanced for this striking difference between Luther's attacks on his evangelical opponents and their responses. For one thing, their responses may have been largely tactical. If they wished to recruit followers from within the movement, they had to combat indirectly, if not directly, the authority and esteem that Luther enjoyed among evangelicals. They had to get Luther's followers to listen to them and to accept the possibility that Luther's *Imprimatur* did not certify a doctrine as gospel truth. Their way of going about this was to acknowledge, at least in public, Luther's importance and the debt that they and the movement owed him. Then they would argue that Luther had erred only on certain issues, and that evangelicals should follow Luther where Luther was correct, but follow them where Luther needed correction. Obviously, it would be very difficult for these opponents, once they had acknowledged some debt to Luther, to reciprocate his unrestrained polemics, especially if they were only attempting to "correct" him.

Another reason for their restraint may be found in the humanist training that many of these men shared. Their humanist concern for modesty and temperance, and their preoccupation with the effects as well as the substance of polemics, may have foreclosed the possibility of unrestrained counterattack. Concern of this kind is prominent, for example, in Bullinger's letter to Bucer over the affair of the Zurich Bible. After briefly discussing Luther's letter to Froschauer, Bullinger characterized Luther's efforts in his *Against Hanswurst* (1541)[2] as unbecoming, completely immodest, entirely scurrilous, and frivolous. In *Against the Jews and Their Lies* (1543)[3] Luther's foul language and scurrility, unbefitting anyone and especially an aged theologian, rendered his profitable and plausible arguments useless and unfit. Modesty, prudence, piety, and gravity were what suited such a theologian as Luther. The example of Luther's audacious raillery, Bullinger said, had spread and captured many ministers who then troubled true piety. Moreover, it had strengthened and hardened the kingdom of the Antichrist, whose worshipers clamored that evangelical ministers were not heralds of the gospel but satiric and abusive buffoons. They should all be at pains, Bullinger advised, to take the church and modesty into account, to recall the example of the prophets and apostles, and to prevent the occurrence, on account of jealousy and arrogance, of something more severe.[4] With these precepts in mind, Bullinger was not apt to unleash a blast at Luther in the same vein as Luther's attack on him.

A third possibility, and one that I believe accounts for much of the behavior of men such as Zwingli, Oecolampadius, Bucer, and Bullinger, is that their qualified deference to Luther was sincere. These men paid honor to Luther and his accomplishments because they sincerely agreed with a large part of what he had taught and done. As Zwingli admitted, Luther had been the first to challenge the papacy:

You confronted the enemy so comfortingly that all those who had previously been fearful how the abominable Antichrist would be endured were strengthened and they sprang to your aid. For this reason we should justly thank God that He had awakened you when no one dared [to attack the Antichrist].[5]

Oecolampadius confessed to Luther: "I do not willingly oppose you whom I recognize as a worthy and cherished servant of the gospel through whom God has opened the eyes of many to recognize the true path of truth."[6] And Bucer admonished his readers that they should not reject everything Luther taught just because he had erred on some points.[7] Of course these men felt that Luther, like any other man, had his weaknesses and could and did err. But for the sake of what Luther with divine aid had accomplished, they were willing to bear with his faults and to correct his errors fraternally.

Although Luther remained throughout his life a professor of theology at Wittenberg, his advice and counsel were sought by theologians, princes, and magistrates from all parts of Europe. I believe that these people sought Luther's advice and counsel primarily because they, too, sincerely agreed with much of what he had taught and done. But did people follow Luther for the further reason that they shared his vision of the special role that he was playing in the divine plan? Although this is not a question that can be answered categorically, there are many indications that the vision was shared.

It appears that some of Luther's opponents at least were convinced that many people thought too highly of him. In 1524 the Strasbourg ministers remarked on how many thousands of souls hung on the words from Luther's mouth because they were persuaded that it was the mouth of the Lord.[8] And in 1527 Bucer commented sarcastically that many were so beguiled by the brilliance of Luther's name that they regarded as true without scrutiny everything that Luther believed, reasoning that since Luther had been the first to restore the gospel and had not erred in great matters, he could not be mistaken in anything.[9] Also in 1527, Zwingli complained that Luther indulged in abuse so that simple people, influenced by his authority or name, in which they had much faith, would come to hate his opponents.[10] In 1543 Bullinger remarked that the arrogance of human nature was revealed when all the priests and ministers indiscriminately adored Luther's writings as oracles, and when they praised his spirit as if apostolic and from whose fullness they had received all things.[11] Two years later Bullinger complained that some people praised Luther so excessively that he had become increasingly arrogant.[12]

When we turn to Luther's supporters we find evidence of a belief that God had sent Luther for the renewal and preservation of the gospel. One of the most striking expressions of this belief occurs in a passage from Melanchthon's oration at Luther's funeral in 1546:

The Son of God, as Paul observes, sits at the right hand of the Eternal Father and gives gifts unto men, namely, the gospel and the Holy Spirit. That He might bestow these He raises up prophets, apostles, teachers, and pastors, and selects from our midst those who study, hear, and delight in the writings of the prophets and apostles.

Then after listing the patriarchs, prophets, apostles, and church fathers, Melanchthon concluded:

To that splendid list of most illustrious men raised up by God to gather and establish the Church, and recognized as the chief glory of the human race, must be added the name of Martin Luther. Solon, Themistocles, Scipio, Augustus, and others who established or ruled over vast empires were great men indeed; but far inferior were they to our leaders, Isaiah, John the Baptist, Paul, Augustin, and Luther.[13]

Even allowing for the nature of the occasion and for the exaggeration common to the age, it would seem from this passage that at least some Lutherans believed Luther to have been a special instrument in God's hands. Such a conviction could well be a further reason why Luther's opponents deferred to him and why men followed him. And if the conviction was widely held, as the complaints of Luther's opponents suggest, it could have been one source of Luther's enormous authority.

The face that Luther turned toward his evangelical opponents was not a pretty one. With a monumental sense of certainty and self-righteousness, he abused and condemned men who, to all appearances, were sincerely searching for the truth and ardently desired to find agreement with the Saxon reformer. But his followers accepted and supported Luther despite his intemperance and severity; they accepted his faults and excused them. Melanchthon's words spoken at Luther's funeral probably summed up the feelings of these evangelicals who, though they winced at Luther's unrestrained attacks, nonetheless followed and defended him through the long years of controversy:

Some by no means evil-minded persons have complained that Luther displayed too much severity. I will not deny this. But I answer in the language of Erasmus: "Because of the magnitude of the disorders God gave this age a violent physician." When God raised up this instrument against the proud and impudent enemies of the truth, He spoke as He did to Jeremiah: "Behold I place My words in thy mouth; destroy and build." Over against these enemies God set this mighty destroyer. In vain do they find fault with God.[14]

Notes

Notes

ABBREVIATIONS

ARG Archiv für Reformationsgeschichte.
CR *Corpus Reformatorum.* Halle/Saale, 1835–60; 1905– .
C.Schw. *Corpus Schwenckfeldianorum.* Hartford, Conn., 1907– .
KK Köstlin, Julius. *Martin Luther: Sein Leben und seine Schriften.* 5th ed. rev., continued after the author's death by Gustav Kawerau. 2 vols. Berlin, 1903.
LW *Luther's Works.* American Edition. 55 vols. Philadelphia and St. Louis, 1955– .
LWZ *The Latin Works of Huldreich Zwingli.* Translated and edited by Samuel M. Jackson, et al. New York, 1912; Philadelphia, 1922, 1929.
S–J *Luther's Correspondence and Other Contemporary Letters.* Translated and edited by Preserved Smith and Charles M. Jacobs. Vol. 2. Philadelphia, 1918.
St.L *D. Martin Luthers sämmtliche Schriften.* Edited by Johann Georg Walch, 2nd ed. published in modern German. 23 vols. St. Louis, 1880–1910.
WA *D. Martin Luthers Werke. Kritische Gesamtausgabe.* 58 vols. Weimar, 1883– .
WABr *D. Martin Luthers Werke. Briefwechsel.* 13 vols. Weimar, 1930– .
WATR *D. Martin Luthers Werke. Tischreden.* 6 vols. Weimar, 1912–21.
ZKG Zeitschrift für Kirchengeschichte.

INTRODUCTION

1. See Friedrich Beisser, *Claritas scripturae bei Martin Luther* (Göttingen, 1966), and Ernst-Wilhelm Kohls, "Luthers Aussagen über die Mitte, Klarheit und Selbstätigkeit der Heiligen Schrift," *Luther-Jahrbuch* 40 (1973): 46–75.
2. Müntzer came close to matching Luther's abuse. See e.g. Günther Franz, ed., *Thomas Müntzer: Schriften und Briefe* (Gütersloh, 1968), pp. 322–43.
3. Heinrich Bornkamm, "Probleme der Lutherbiographie," in *Lutherforschung Heute,* ed. Vilmos Vajta (Berlin, 1958), pp. 19–20.
4. Since Luther was never engaged in a major controversy with Anabaptists, I decided not to treat Luther's relations with these particular false brethren.

For those interested in this topic, see John S. Oyer, *Lutheran Reformers Against Anabaptists: Luther, Melanchthon and Menius and the Anabaptists of Central Europe* (The Hague, 1964).

5. See e.g. Erich Seeberg, "Der Gegensatz zwischen Zwingli, Schwenckfeld und Luther" in *Reinhold Seeberg Festschrift* (Leipzig, 1929); Ernst Sommerlath, *Der Sinn des Abendmahls nach Luthers Gedanken über das Abendmahl 1527–1529* (Leipzig, 1930); Wilhelm Maurer, *Luther und die Schwärmer* (Berlin, 1952); Hans Grass, *Die Abendmahlslehre bei Luther und Calvin*, 2nd. ed. (Gütersloh, 1954); Karl G. Steck, *Luther und die Schwärmer* (Zurich, 1955); two works by Rudolf Hermann: *Zum Streit um die Überwindung des Gesetzes. Erörterung zu Luthers Antinomerthesen* (Weimar, 1958), and "Zur Bedeutung der lex ihres Unvermögens und dennoch Bleibens nach Luthers Antinomerthesen," in *Gott und die Götter. Festgabe für Erich Fascher* (Berlin, 1958); Hayo Gerdes, *Luthers Streit mit den Schwärmern um das rechte Verständnis des Gesetzes Mose* (Göttingen, 1955); Albrecht Peters, *Realpräsenz: Luthers Zeugnis von Christi Gegenwart im Abendmahl* (Berlin, 1960); Wilhelm Neuser, *Die Abendmahlslehre Melanchthons in ihrer geschichtlichen Entwicklung (1519–1530)* (Neukirchen-Vluyn, 1968); Ronald J. Sider, *Andreas Bodenstein von Karlstadt: The Development of His Thought, 1517–1525.* Studies in Medieval and Reformation Thought, vol. 11 (Leiden, 1974).

6. My preliminary thinking and research on Luther's relations with evangelical opponents was guided by the psychological theories of cognitive dissonance, person perception, observational learning, and roles. For an introduction to these theories, see Salvatore R. Maddi, *Personality Theories: A Comparative Analysis*, rev. ed. (Homewood, Ill., 1972); Albert H. Hastorf, David J. Schneider, and Judith Polefka, *Person Perception* (Menlo Park, Calif., 1970); two works by Albert Bandura: *Psychological Modeling: Conflicting Theories* (Chicago, 1971), and *Social Learning Theory* (New York, 1971); and Michael Banton, *Roles: An Introduction to the Study of Social Relations* (New York, 1965). My research forced me to the conclusion that although a historian with the aid of psychological theory can develop a plausible explanation for past human behavior, it is almost impossible for the explanation to meet the standards of proof that a modern psychologist insists on (see e.g. Walter Mischel, *Personality and Assessment* [New York, 1968]). For an excellent discussion of some of the problems, see Robert F. Berkhofer, Jr., *A Behavioral Approach to Historical Analysis* (New York, 1969). Those interested in how these theories may be applied to Luther's relations with evangelical opponents should consult my dissertation, "Luther and the False Brethren" (Ph.D. diss., Stanford University, 1974).

CHAPTER ONE

1. Gustav Kawerau started the debate in *Deutsche Literatur Zeitung* 14 (1893): 1584–86. Then followed Friedrich von Bezold, "Luthers Rückkehr von der Wartburg," *ZKG* 20 (1900): 186–233; Gustav Kawerau, *Luthers Rückkehr von der Wartburg* (Halle, 1902); Hermann Barge, *Andreas Bodenstein von Karlstadt* (Leipzig, 1905; Nieuwkoop, 1968), 1: 398ff.; Karl Müller, *Luther und Karlstadt, Stücke aus ihrem Gegenseit* (Tübingen, 1907), pp. 88–103; Her-

mann Barge, "Luther und Karlstadt in Wittenberg," *Historische Zeitschrift* 99 (1907): 256–324; *Idem, Frühprotestantisches Gemeindechristentum in Wittenberg und Orlamünde* (Leipzig, 1909), pp. 156–83; Walter Köhler, *Göttingische gelehrte Anzeigen* 174 (1912): 505–50; Hermann Barge, "Zur Genesis der frühreformatorischen Vorgänge in Wittenberg," *Historische Vierteljahrschrift* (1914): 1–33.

2. Since I originally wrote this chapter, James S. Preus published a thorough study of the Wittenberg Movement: James S. Preus, *Carlstadt's "Ordinaciones" and Luther's Liberty*, Harvard Theological Studies, vol. 26 (Cambridge, 1974). Two other recent works that deal in part with the Wittenberg Movement are Ronald J. Sider, *Andreas Bodenstein von Karlstadt: The Development of His Thought, 1517–1525*, pp. 153ff, and Wilhelm Neuser, *Die Abendmahlslehre Melanchthon in ihrer geschichtlichen Entwicklung (1519–1530)*, pp. 114–213 (cited in Sider, p. 153 n. 22). Neuser and Preus reach a number of similar conclusions in their analyses of Luther's return to Wittenberg.

3. Nikolaus Müller, ed., *Die Wittenberg Bewegung 1521 und 1522* (Leipzig, 1911), no. 4.

4. *Ibid.*, nos. 4, 5, 8, 9, 10.
5. *Ibid.*, no. 15; see also no. 10.
6. *Ibid.*, nos. 15, 18.
7. *Ibid.*, no. 16.
8. *Ibid.*, no. 25.
9. *Ibid.*, nos. 28, 29, 80.
10. *Ibid.*, no. 28.
11. *Ibid.*, nos. 32, 36, 68.
12. *Ibid.*, nos. 32, 33, 38, 53, 68.
13. *Ibid.*, nos. 68, 73.
14. WABr 2: 409–10 (LW 48: 351).
15. WA 8: 676–87 (LW 45: 57–74).
16. N. Müller, no. 43.
17. *Ibid.*, no. 54.
18. *Ibid.*, nos. 54, 68.
19. *Ibid.*, nos. 57, 68.
20. *Ibid.*, no. 57.
21. *Ibid.*, no. 61.
22. *Ibid.*, nos. 58, 61, 62, 68, 69, 73.
23. *Ibid.*, no. 68.
24. *Ibid.*, nos. 61, 62, 63, 68, 69, 73.
25. *Ibid.*, nos. 65, 66, 68.
26. *Ibid.*, nos. 59, 60, 62, 63, 64, 68.
27. *Ibid.*, no. 59; see also nos. 60, 62, 64, 68.
28. WABr 2: 443–44 (LW 48: 380–81). See also WABr 2: 422–23, 424–27 (LW 48: 360–64, 365–72).
29. N. Müller, nos. 63, 64.
30. *Ibid.*, no. 69.
31. *Ibid.*, nos. 68, 73.
32. *Ibid.*, no. 67.
33. *Ibid.*, no. 72.
34. See Hans Lietzmann, ed., *Die Wittenberger und Leisniger Kastenordnung* (Bonn, 1907), pp. 1–6. Cf. N. Müller, no. 75.
35. N. Müller, no. 75.
36. E.g. WABr 2: 423 (LW 48: 363).
37. WA 8: 323–25, 573–669 (LW 44: 251–400); WABr 2: 397, 404–5, 415 (LW 48: 321, 337–38, 358–59).
38. E.g. WABr 2: 372–73 (LW 48: 281); WA 8: 411–76, 482–563. See also WABr 2: 399–401, 402–5 (LW 48: 324–28), for the transmittal of these treatises.
39. WABr 2: 409–10 (LW 48: 351).
40. N. Müller, nos. 32, 36, 37, 68.
41. WABr 2: 331–32, 337, 367 (LW 48: 214, 223–24, 273).
42. WABr 2: 402–3 (LW 48: 327).

43. WABr 2: 462 (LW 48: 399). See also note 41 above.
44. WA 8: 676–87 (LW 45: 57–74).
45. WABr 2: 409–10 (LW 48: 351).
46. N. Müller, nos. 81, 82, 84.
47. On 5 February 1522 Melanchthon wrote Einsiedel that he had discussed the need for moderation with both men, but that he could not stem the tide. Still he hoped that such errors would be avoided in the future. Then he commented, "If we have a reformation here, may God grant that it be to His honor" [Es ist eyn reformatio vorhanden, gott gebe, das sie zu seyner ehre reyche] (N. Müller, no. 84). As Preus notes (p. 42), this is an ambiguous evaluation of the movement. See also Ulscenius' 24 January report that Melanchthon was so disturbed by certain "outrages" that he considered leaving the city for a time (N. Müller, no. 74). Cf. Preus, pp. 33–34, and K. Müller, pp. 62–63.
48. N. Müller, no. 97.
49. *Ibid.*, no. 95.
50. *Ibid.*, nos. 95, 96, 97, 99.
51. WABr 2: 371–72, 373–75, 377–78, 380, 390 (LW 48: 279–82, 283–88, 290, 293–94, 311).
52. WABr 2: 423 (LW 48: 363).
53. See K. Müller, esp. pp. 1–28, 56–58; Barge, *Gemeindechristentum,* esp. pp. 37–47, 76–94.
54. E.g. WABr 2: 448–49, 456 (LW 48: 387–88, 392).
55. WABr 2: 412 (LW 48: 354–55).
56. WABr 2: 409–10, 412 (LW 48: 350–51, 353).
57. WABr 2: 449–53 (S–J 2: 90–93).
58. WABr 2: 427 (LW 48: 372).
59. See note 29 above.
60. WABr 2: 448–49 (LW 48: 387–88). Luther's decision to return to Wittenberg, and also the apparent change in his evaluation of the events there, may have been prompted by a letter from the Wittenberg congregation (WABr 2: 460 [LW 48: 395]) and perhaps also by a letter from the Wittenberg City Council. See WA 10/3: 10 (LW 51: 73). Cf. E. L. Enders, ed., *Luthers Briefwechsel* (Stuttgart, 1891), 3: 298 n. 1, cited by Preus, p. 61 n. 44.
61. See Karl Pallas, ed., "Briefe und Akten zur Visitationsreise des Bischofs Johannes VII. von Meissen im Kurfürstentum Sachsen 1522," *ARG* 5 (1907/8): 217–312.
62. WABr 2: 449–53 (S–J 2: 90–93).
63. See N. Müller, nos. 58, 61, 62, 63, 65, 66, 68, 69, 73, etc., for an indication of Karlstadt's and Zwilling's highly visible roles in the reforms. For some of the correspondence on the attempt to silence or restrain the two men, see *ibid.,* nos. 81, 82, 83, 84.
64. *Ibid.*, no. 89.
65. *Ibid.*, no. 56.
66. "Auff die annderung der Mess wollet vns auch berichten, warumb jr diese Newerung furgenomen, wie es auch damit gehalten werden, was jr auch hierjnn fur Cristlich vnnd gut ansehet" (*ibid.*, no. 92, p. 192). The Elector di-

rected this question especially to changes in the elevation of the host and in the words of consecration.

67. *Ibid.*, no. 93.

68. *Ibid.*, nos. 95, 96, 97.

69. *Ibid.*, no. 99.

70. See especially Karlstadt's *Ob man gemach fahren und des Argernisses des Schwachen verschonen soll*, in Erich Hertzsch, ed., *Karlstadts Schriften aus den Jahren 1523–25* (Halle, 1956), 1: 74ff.

71. N. Müller, no. 93; cf. *ibid.*, nos. 16, 43, 75.

72. WA 15: 337, 16–18.   73. See N. Müller, nos. 81, 82, 84.

74. See note 60 above.   75. WABr 2: 454 (LW 48: 389–90).

76. WABr 2: 455–56 (LW 48: 391).   77. WABr 2: 456 (LW 48: 392).

78. WABr 2: 457–59 (LW 48: 394).   79. WABr 2: 465–73.

80. WABr 2: 459–62 (LW 48: 394–98). This is from the first draft of the letter.

81. WABr 2: 462 (LW 48: 398–99).

82. WA 8: 680 lines 20–21 (LW 45: 63).

83. WA 8: 680 (LW 45: 63).

84. E.g. WA 8: 681, 683 (LW 45: 64, 68).

85. WA 8: 681, 683 (LW 45: 65, 68).

86. Luther's Invocavit sermons contain a detailed elaboration of these points; see WA 10/3: 1–64 (LW 51: 70–100). For a more acerbic evaluation of Luther's position, see Preus, pp. 63–73, 78–88.

87. Barge interprets the epithet to refer directly to Karlstadt. See *Gemeindechristentum*, p. 163.

88. WABr 2: 478 line 5.

89. WABr 2: 491.

90. N. Müller, no. 93.

91. *Ibid.*, nos. 92, 93. Cf. Barge, *Karlstadt*, 1: 398ff.

92. N. Müller, no. 61.

93. WABr 2: 454 (LW 48: 389–90).

94. WABr 2: 424–25 (LW 48: 366).

95. WABr 2: 424–25 (LW 48: 365–67).

96. WABr 2: 425 lines 39–40. The translation in LW 48: 367 runs: "Therefore examine [them] and do not even listen if they speak of the glorified Jesus, unless you have first heard of the crucified Jesus." The Latin reads: "Tenta ergo et ne Ihesum quidem audias gloriosum, nisi prius videris crucifixum."

97. WABr 2: 424 (LW 48: 366).

98. See Karlstadt's *Von abtuhung der Bylder, Und das keyn Betdler unther den Christen seyn soll*, ed. Hans Lietzmann (Bonn, 1911).

99. Barge, *Karlstadt*, 1: 290, 359–60.

100. WABr 2: 491.

101. WABr 2: 491 lines 15–16 and n. 1. An alternate reading: "he wished to become suddenly a new teacher and to set up his ordinances among the people while reducing my [Luther's] authority." This alternate reading might indicate a more selfish motive on Luther's part. Cf. Preus, p. 66.

214] *Notes to Pages 24–29*

102. See Barge, *Karlstadt*, 2: 563–65, for excerpts from the confiscated treatise.
103. WABr 2: 509 (S–J 2: 121).
104. Barge, *Karlstadt*, 2: 562–65.
105. WABr 2: 509 (S–J 2: 121).
106. E.g. WABr 2: 427, 448–49, 460, 471, 478, 491, 493 (LW 48: 371–72, 387–88, 395–96; S–J 2: 102, 112).
107. WABr 2: 471, 509.   108. KK 1: 509–10.
109. WABr 2: 493 lines 17–30.   110. WABr 2: 495 lines 41–45.
111. WATR 2, no. 2060; 3, nos. 2837a, 2837b.
112. WATR 3, nos. 2837a, 2837b.   113. See note 111 above.
114. WABr 2: 472 (S–J 2: 102).   115. WABr 2: 478 (S–J 2: 112).
116. WABr 2: 502–9, 517–24, 538–42, 545–47, 551–53, 575–76, 580–81, etc.
117. See Gordon Rupp, *Patterns of Reformation* (London, 1969), pp. 52–53; N. Müller, no. 68.
118. See Paul Wappler, *Thomas Müntzer in Zwickau und die "Zwickauer Propheten"* (Gütersloh, 1966), esp. pp. 56–79.
119. WA 10/3: 8 (LW 51: 72–73).
120. WABr 2: 460 (LW 48: 395).
121. WA 10/3: 18–19 (LW 51: 77–78).
122. See Karl Holl, "Martin Luther on Luther," trans. H. C. Erik Midelfort, in *Interpreters of Luther*, ed. Jaroslav Pelikan (Philadelphia, 1968), pp. 9–34; two works by Hans Preuss: *Martin Luther. Der Prophet* (Gütersloh, 1933), and *Martin Luther. Der Deutsche* (Gütersloh, 1934); Hans von Campenhausen, "Reformatorisches Selbstbewusstsein und reformatorisches Geschichtsbewusstsein bei Luther, 1517–1522," *ARG* 37 (1940): 128–49; Wolfgang Günter, "Die geschichtstheologischen Voraussetzungen von Luthers Selbstverständnis," in *Von Konstanz nach Trient. Beiträge zur Kirchengeschichte von den Reformkonzilien bis zum Tridentinum. Festgabe für August Franzen*, ed. R. Bäumer (Paderborn, 1972), pp. 379–94. See also Wolfgang Höhne, *Luthers Anschauungen über die Kontinuität der Kirche* (Berlin/Hamburg, 1963), pp. 124–56; and Ulrich Asendorf, *Eschatologie bei Luther* (Göttingen, 1967), pp. 214–21.
123. E.g. Preuss, *Luther. Der Prophet*, and Bruno Markgraf, *Die Junge Luther als Genie* (Leipzig, 1929).
124. Von Campenhausen, esp. p. 134.
125. WABr 2: 182.
126. WA 7: 311–15 (LW 32: 8–10); WA 10/2: 58 (LW 43: 68).
127. See Hermann Steinlein, *Luthers Doktorat* (Leipzig, 1912), esp. pp. 36–46.
128. Von Campenhausen, p. 142.
129. Cf. Erwin Iserloh, *The Theses Were Not Posted. Luther Between Reform and Reformation*, trans. Jared Wicks (Boston, 1968); Franz Lau, "Die gegenwärtige Diskussion um Luthers Thesenanschlag," *Luther-Jahrbuch* 34 (1967): 11–59; and Bernhard Lohse, "Die Lutherforschung im deutschen Sprachbereich seit 1966," *Luther-Jahrbuch* 38 (1971), esp. pp. 100–102.
130. WABr 1: 112 (LW 48: 49).
131. WABr 2: 254–55 (LW 48: 196–97).
132. See Wilhelm Borth, *Die Luthersache (Causa Lutheri), 1517–1524: Die Anfänge der Reformation als Frage von Politik und Recht* (Lübeck, 1970).

133. E.g. WABr 1: 170. See Rupp, *Patterns of Reformation*, p. 67; and Karl Bauer, *Die Wittenberger Universitätstheologie und die Anfänge der deutschen Reformation* (Tübingen, 1928).

134. WA 10/3: 18–19 (LW 51: 77).

135. WABr 1: 191–92 (LW 48: 76–79). Cf. Gustav Mix, "Luther und Melanchthon in ihrer gegenseitigen Beurteilung," *Theologische Studien und Kritiken* 74 (1901): 458–521; and Wilhelm Pauck, "Luther und Melanchthon," in *Luther und Melanchthon*, ed. Vilmos Vajta (Göttingen, 1961), pp. 11–31.

136. WABr 1: 513.

137. Mix, pp. 476–78.

138. WABr 2: 348 lines 48–49 (LW 48: 232). Cf. WABr 2: 167 lines 7–9: "Forte ego praecursor sum Philippi, cui exemplo Heliae viam parem in spiritu et virtute."

139. WABr 2: 356 (LW 48: 257).

140. WABr 2: 388 (LW 48: 308–9).

141. *Ibid.* Cf. WABr 2: 390–91 (LW 48: 311–12).

142. N. Müller, no. 59.

143. *Ibid.*, no. 60. Cf. no. 64.

144. WABr 2: 424 lines 9–10 (LW 48: 365–66).

145. N. Müller, no. 84.

146. CR 1: 566.

147. E.g. CR 1, nos. 215, 216, 235. See also Mix, pp. 483–86.

148. WABr 3: 258–59.

149. WA 10/2: 309–10; 12: 56–57.

150. See notes 140 and 141 above, and Mix, pp. 482–86.

151. E.g. Mix, pp. 483–86, 493–97.

152. WA 10/3: 8 (LW 51: 72–73).

153. WABr 2: 462–65.

154. WABr 2: 472 lines 11–20 (S–J 2: 102).

155. N. Müller, no. 102 (S–J 2: 115).

156. See J. M. Kittelson, "Wolfgang Capito, Humanist and Reformer" (Ph.D. diss., Stanford University, 1969).

CHAPTER TWO

1. See Hermann Barge, *Andreas Bodenstein von Karlstadt*, 2: 95ff. For the account that follows see also Karl Müller, *Luther und Karlstadt. Stücke aus ihrem Gegenseit*, pp. 137ff; Hermann Barge, "Der Streit über die Grundlagen der religiosen Erneuerung in der Kontroverse zwischen Luther und Karlstadt 1524/25," in *Studium Lipsiense* (Berlin, 1909); Gordon Rupp, *Patterns of Reformation*, pp. 111ff.

2. The most important of these are collected in Erich Hertzsch, ed., *Karlstadts Schriften aus den Jahren 1523–25*. St.L. also contains several treatises not found in Hertzsch. For an analysis of Karlstadt's theological position, see Ronald J. Sider, *Andreas Bodenstein von Karlstadt: The Development of His Thought, 1517–1525*, pp. 202ff.

3. WABr 3: 233. Cf. WABr 3: 234 (LW 49: 70–71).

4. WABr 3: 231, 255 n. 3. Cf. Barge, *Karlstadt*, 2: 101ff.

5. WABr 3: 256.
6. WABr 3: 254 (LW 49: 72-73).
7. WABr 3: 256.
8. WABr 3: 307.
9. Barge, *Karlstadt*, 2: 106-12.
10. For the following section I have used Paul Wappler, *Thomas Müntzer in Zwickau und die "Zwickauer Propheten,"* and Carl Hinrichs, *Luther und Müntzer* (Berlin, 1952). Max Steinmetz, *Das Müntzerbild von Martin Luther bis Friedrich Engels* (Berlin, 1971), surveys the different interpretations of Müntzer in western thought.
11. WABr 3: 104-7.
12. Rupp, p. 187, suggests this. Luther did attempt to have Müntzer confer with the Wittenbergers about his teachings; see WABr 3: 120 (S-J 2: 193).
13. WABr 3: 307-8.
14. WABr 3: 310.
15. Günther Franz, ed., *Thomas Müntzer: Schriften und Briefe*, pp. 242-63. George H. Williams, ed., *Spiritual and Anabaptist Writers* (Philadelphia, 1957), pp. 47-70, gives an English translation of the sermon.
16. WA 15: 210 (LW 40: 49).
17. WA 15: 211 (LW 40: 50).
18. WA 15: 212 (LW 40: 51).
19. WA 15: 214 (LW 40: 53).
20. WA 15: 219 (LW 40: 57).
21. For what follows, see Rupp, pp. 206-8; Hinrichs, pp. 75-136.
22. See WA 15: 238-40.
23. WA 15: 239.
24. WABr 3: 354, 356, 361.
25. WA 15: 336, 339.
26. WA 15: 336. For a discussion of this letter, see Barge, *Karlstadt*, 2: 112ff.
27. E.g. WA 15: 335-36.
28. WA 15: 340.
29. WA 15: 339.
30. WA 15: 336.
31. WA 15: 337.
32. WA 15: 337-39.
33. WA 15: 343.
34. WA 15: 342.
35. "Ir habt ewern abschidt zu Ihen erlanngt, darumb mügt ir wol hynaussgeen." WA 15: 344.
36. "Seyt ir doch mein fürst nicht, das ir mir zugebiettenn habt, wue er aber des fürstlichen bevelch hette, möchte er denselben fürlegen." *Ibid.*
37. WA 18: 89-90 (LW 40: 107).
38. WA 15: 345.
39. WA 15: 346.
40. WA 18: 84 (LW 40: 100-101).
41. WA 15: 395 (LW 40: 69).
42. Referred to in WABr 3: 353.
43. Cf. WABr 3: 353.
44. Barge thinks that this suggestion was not made until 22 September and then only at the instigation of Kaspar Glatz; see Barge, *Karlstadt*, 2: 138; also Barge, *Frühprotestantisches Gemeindechristentum in Wittenberg und Orlamünde*, p. 274. Karl Müller, on the other hand, argues that this suggestion was made orally at this time; see his *Luther und Karlstadt. Stücke aus ihrem Gegenseit*, pp. 175-76.
45. WABr 3: 344.
46. WABr 3: 346.
47. I have accepted the older dating of this letter rather than the dating suggested by WABr 3: 342, WABr 3: 343 lines 5-8 ("Ihr habt, ehe Ihr uns ersuchet,

die Sach angefangen und den Gulden von Dr. Martin empfangen. Was ist's nu, dass Ihr uns zuletzt, wann Ihr zuvor getan habt, was Euch gelust, umb Gnad oder Gunst ersucht?") compel me to assume that the letter to which this is a response must have been written by Karlstadt after his confrontation with Luther, else why would Luther suggest that Karlstadt be criticized for accepting the challenge before asking permission of his prince?

48. Hertzsch, *Karlstadts Schriften*, 2: 53.
49. *Ibid.*, 2: 54. Cf. Barge, *Karlstadt*, 2: 137.
50. WABr 3: 343 (LW 49: 84–85).   51. WABr 3: 353.
52. Hertzsch, 2: 55–56.   53. Barge, *Karlstadt*, 2: 141.
54. WABr 3: 381–87.   55. WABr 3: 382–84.
56. WABr 3: 387.   57. WABr 3: 399.
58. WABr 3: 379.   59. WABr 3: 378–80.
60. WABr 3: 404–5 (S–J 2: 273–74).   61. WA 15: 392 (LW 40: 66).
62. WA 15: 393 (LW 40: 67).   63. WA 15: 394 (LW 40: 68).
64. WA 15: 394–95 (LW 40: 68–69).   65. WA 15: 395 (LW 40: 69).
66. WA 15: 396–97 (LW 40: 70–71).
67. WA 18: 125 (LW 40: 143). For a detailed consideration of Luther's arguments, see Hayo Gerdes, *Luthers Streit mit den Schwärmern um das rechte Verständnis des Gesetzes Mose*; Rupp, pp. 141–48; Barge, *Karlstadt*, 2: 271–75; C. F. Jäger, *Andreas Bodenstein von Carlstadt* (Stuttgart, 1856).
68. E.g. WA 18: 139 lines 8–12 (LW 40: 149).
69. WA 18: 62 (LW 40: 79). Cf. WA 18: 136 (LW 40: 146).
70. WA 18: 72 (LW 40: 89).   71. WA 18: 88 (LW 40: 105–6).
72. WA 18: 64 (LW 40: 81–82).   73. WA 18: 66 (LW 40: 84).
74. See e.g. Gerdes, pp. 42ff.   75. WA 18: 95–96 (LW 40: 112).
76. WA 18: 94 (LW 40: 111).   77. WA 18: 96 (LW 40: 112–13).
78. WA 18: 97 (LW 40: 113–14).   79. WA 18: 98–99 (LW 40: 115).
80. WA 18: 85–86, 99 (LW 40: 103, 115).
81. WA 18: 86 (LW 40: 103).   82. WA 18: 90 (LW 40: 107).
83. WA 18: 88–90 (LW 40: 106–7).   84. WA 18: 93 (LW 40: 110).
85. WA 18: 88 (LW 40: 107).   86. WA 18: 99 (LW 40: 115–16).
87. WA 18: 111 (LW 40: 128).   88. WA 18: 116 (LW 40: 133–34).
89. WA 18: 142 (LW 40: 152).   90. WA 18: 147 (LW 40: 157).
91. WA 18: 144–51 (LW 40: 154–61).
92. WA 18: 149–82 (LW 40: 159–92).
93. WA 18: 182–212 (LW 40: 192–22).
94. E.g. WA 18: 147, 191, 201, *passim* (LW 40: 156–57, 201, 211, *passim*).
95. E.g. WA 18: 190–91, 201, 207 (LW 40: 200–201, 211, 217).
96. WA 18: 191 (LW 40: 200–201).
97. WA 18: 202 (LW 40: 212).
98. WABr 3: 379.
99. See WA 15: 210, 392 (LW 40: 49, 66).

CHAPTER THREE

1. Günther Franz, *Der deutsche Bauernkrieg* (Darmstadt, 1956), pp. 174–79 (LW 46: 8–16). For a valuable analysis of the peasants' grievances, see Hans J.

Hillerbrand, "The German Reformation and the Peasants' War," in *The Social History of the Reformation*, ed. L. P. Buck and J. W. Zophy (Columbus, Ohio, 1972), pp. 106–36.
2. See Hubert Kirchner, *Luther and the Peasants' War*, trans. by D. Jodock (Philadelphia, 1972), pp. 8–10, for a discussion of Luther's sources.
3. See Hillerbrand, pp. 123–26, for some examples and a discussion of this charge.
4. Heinrich Boehmer, ed., *Urkunden zur Geschichte des Bauernkrieges und der Wiedertäufer*, Kleine Texte für theologische und philologische Vorlesungen und Übungen (Bonn, 1910; Berlin, 1933), 50/51: 22–24.
5. WA 18: 291–92 (LW 46: 17).
6. WA 18: 293 (LW 46: 18–19). Cf. WA 18: 294, 334.
7. WA 18: 295–96 (LW 46: 20–21).   8. WA 18: 304 (LW 46: 25).
9. E.g. WA 18: 308, 310, 311.   10. WA 18: 313 (LW 46: 31).
11. WA 18: 314 (LW 46: 31–32).   12. WA 18: 317–18 (LW 46: 33).
13. WA 18: 329 (LW 46: 40–41).   14. WA 18: 331 (LW 46: 42).
15. WA 18: 333 (LW 46: 43).   16. WA 18: 334 (LW 46: 43).
17. WA 18: 336.   18. WA 18: 342.
19. WA 18: 336–43.   20. See WA 17/1: xxxii.
21. WA 17/1: xxxi–xxxii; WATR 5, no. 6429.
22. See Kurt Aland, " 'Auch wider die reuberischen und mörderischen rotten der anderen bawren,' Eine Anmerkung zu Luthers Haltung im Bauernkrieg," *Theologische Literaturzeitung* 74 (1949): 299–303.
23. WA 18: 357–58 (LW 46: 49–51).
24. WA 18: 359 (LW 46: 52).   25. WA 18: 360 (LW 46: 53–54).
26. WA 18: 360–61 (LW 46: 54).   27. WA 18: 358 (LW 46: 50).
28. WA 18: 361 (LW 46: 54).   29. WA 18: 359 (LW 46: 51–52).
30. WA 18: 361 (LW 46: 55).
31. Rühel in his letter of 21 May assumes that Luther knows about these recent events. WABr 3: 504–5.
32. WABr 3: 504–6. For the prophecy see WA 18: 332 (LW 46: 42).
33. WABr 3: 507–8 (S–J 2: 317–18).
34. WA 18: 367.
35. Translated in Gordon Rupp, *Patterns of Reformation*, pp. 239–40.
36. WA 18: 373.   37. WABr 3: 510–11.
38. WABr 3: 515–16 (S–J 2: 320).   39. WABr 3: 517–18 (LW 49: 113).
40. WA 17/1: 265–67.   41. WABr 3: 536–37 (S–J 2: 327–28).
42. WA 18: 384–86 (LW 46: 63–65).   43. WA 18: 388 (LW 46: 68).
44. WA 18: 388–89 (LW 46: 69).   45. WA 18: 390 (LW 46: 70).
46. WA 18: 390–91 (LW 46: 71).
47. WA 18: 392 (LW 46: 73). Cf. WA 18: 399–401 (LW 46: 82–84).
48. WA 18: 393 (LW 46: 74).
49. WA 18: 393 (LW 46: 75).
50. WA 18: 400–401 (LW 46: 84). Cf. WA 18: 399 (LW 46: 82).
51. WA 18: 395 (LW 46: 77).
52. WABr 3: 409.
53. So contends Hermann Barge in opposition to Karl Müller. See Barge,

Andreas Bodenstein von Karlstadt, 2: 265–66, 312–15; K. Müller, *Luther und Karlstadt. Stücke aus ihrem Gegenseit,* pp. 180–85; and Barge, *Frühprotestantisches Gemeindechristentum in Wittenberg und Orlamünde,* pp. 336–40.

54. WABr 3: 418.
55. WABr 3: 420–21.
56. WABr 3: 424 (S–J 2: 292).
57. WABr 3: 424–25 (S–J 2: 292–93; the translation is incomplete).
58. E.g. WABr 3: 430 (S–J 2: 293).
59. WABr 3: 430, 452, 437, 438.
60. WABr 3: 441–42. Cf. Barge, *Karlstadt,* 2: 312–13.
61. CR 1: 726–27.   62. WABr 3: 450.
63. WABr 3: 449–50.   64. WABr 3: 456.
65. WABr 3: 457.   66. WA 18: 439 lines 1–6.
67. Compare Barge, *Karlstadt,* 2: 364–66, and K. Müller, *Luther und Karlstadt,* pp. 187–89. See also Barge, *Gemeindechristentum,* pp. 347–48.
68. WA 18: 439.
69. WA 18: 438–45.
70. WA 18: 436–38.
71. See the Instructions to Spalatin, WABr 3: 573–74.
72. WA 18: 457.   73. WA 18: 455, 456.
74. WA 18: 458.   75. WA 18: 459.
76. WA 18: 459–60.   77. WABr 3: 544.
78. WABr 3: 555 (LW 49: 122–23).   79. WABr 3: 565–66.
80. WABr 3: 572–74.   81. WA 18: 454.
82. See Martin Greschat, "Luthers Haltung im Bauernkrieg," *ARG* 56 (1965): 31–47, for an elaboration on this. Hartmut Lehmann, "Luther und der Bauernkrieg," *Geschichte in Wissenschaft und Unterricht* 20 (1969): 126–39, argues that Greschat overstresses Luther's apocalyptic fears (pp. 135–36).

CHAPTER FOUR

1. WABr 3: 373 (LW 49: 88–90); WABr 3: 397. The definitive study of these controversies is Walter Köhler, *Zwingli und Luther. Ihr Streit über das Abendmahl nach seinen politischen und religiösen Beziehungen,* 2 vols. (Leipzig, 1924; Gütersloh, 1953). A highly partisan but nonetheless useful English account is Hermann Sasse, *This Is My Body: Luther's Contention for the Real Presence in the Sacrament of the Altar* (Minneapolis, Minn., 1959). The reader is referred to Köhler's massive study for a much fuller and detailed account of the history and theological issues discussed in this chapter. For a discussion of Luther's characterization of Zwingli, see Oskar Farner, *Das Zwinglibild Luthers* (Tübingen, 1931). Kurt Guggisberg, *Das Zwinglibild des Protestantismus im Wandel der Zeiten* (Leipzig, 1934), surveys the views of Zwingli in Protestant thought.

2. WABr 3: 422, 437.
3. See Köhler, 1: 178–84.
4. WABr 3: 331. This is an excerpt from a longer description.
5. WABr 3: 373 (LW 49: 88–90). Cf. WABr 3: 397.
6. WABr 3: 422 (S–J 2: 282).

7. WABr 3: 437.
8. WABr 3: 358–60, 461. CR 90: 335–54.
9. CR 90: 343–45.   10. CR 90: 335–36.
11. CR 90: 628–912.   12. CR 90: 792–93 (LWZ 3: 221).
13. WABr 3: 544.   14. WABr 3: 555 (LW 49: 122).
15. See Köhler, 1: 61–117 and 137–282, for a detailed exposition of Zwingli's position and publications in this period as well as a picture of the general situation prior to the outbreak of the dispute between Luther and Zwingli.
16. See *ibid.*, 1: 117–37.
17. CR 90: 779 (LWZ 3: 204–5).
18. The theological arguments have been treated in detail elsewhere. Köhler summarizes each of Zwingli's treatises during these years of controversy and presents a thorough exposition of Zwingli's position. See especially Köhler, vol. 1, chap. 10. See also Erich Seeberg, "Der Gegensatz zwischen Zwingli, Schwenckfeld, und Luther," in *Reinhold Seeberg Festschrift* (Leipzig, 1929), pp. 43–80.
19. See WABr 3: 599.
20. See St.L 20: 500–505 and 522–75.
21. CR 91: 546–76; St.L 20: 599–635.
22. See James Kittelson, "Martin Bucer and the Sacramentarian Controversy: The Origins of His Policy of Concord," *ARG* 64 (1973): 166–83.
23. WABr 3: 586–87 (S–J 2: 338–39). See also WABr 3: 608–11.
24. WABr 3: 586 (S–J 2: 338–39).
25. See e.g. Köhler, 1: 152–54, 310–14, for a discussion of this two-front battle and its implications.
26. WABr 3: 593.
27. WABr 3: 608–11 and 604–6 (S–J 2: 346–50). See also Luther's brief letter to the Strasbourgers (WABr 3: 602 [S–J 2: 345–46]).
28. From Casel's report, WABr 3: 608–11. I give only a brief summary.
29. WABr 3: 605 (S–J 2: 348).
30. WABr 3: 653 (LW 49: 141).
31. WA 19: 118–25.
32. WA 19: 457–61, 529–30. See also WABr 4: 19 (S–J 2: 363), and especially WABr 4: 42 (LW 49: 146–47).
33. See St.L 20: 582–635.   34. St.L 20: 582.
35. St.L 20: 589–90.   36. St.L 20: 599.
37. Köhler, 1: 360. Leo Jud also claimed Bugenhagen's support in his pseudonymous treatise (see note 39 below) by citing one of the interpolated passages (WA 19: 464).
38. See Köhler, 1: 370–76.
39. *Des Hochgelerten Erasmi von Roterdam, vnnd D. M. Luthers maynung vom Nachtmahl* (1526). Foundation for Reformation Research microfilm no. s16.109a Dr. 13. See also WA 19: 464.
40. WA 19: 471–73 (S–J 2: 377–81).
41. WA 19: 473 (S–J 2: 380–81).
42. *Oratio Joannis Bugenhagii Pomerani, quod ipsius non sit opinio illa de eucharista, quae in psalterio sub nomine eius Germanice translato legitur* (1526). See Köhler, 1: 360.

43. WA 19: 482–523 (LW 36: 329–61).
44. St.L 17: 1584–1605.   45. St.L 17: 1585.
46. St.L 17: 1593.   47. St.L 17: 1595.
48. St.L 17: 1604.
49. WA 23: 64–283 (LW 37: 13–150). I cite the printed version.
50. WA 23: 69 (LW 37: 15–16).
51. WA 23: 71 (LW 37: 18).
52. WA 23: 79 (LW 37: 23).
53. WA 23: 73–75 (LW 37: 19–21).
54. E.g. WA 23: 77–81 (LW 37: 21–24).
55. WA 23: 83–85 (LW 37: 26). Cf. WA 23: 253 (LW 37: 130–31).
56. WA 23: 85–87 (LW 37: 27).
57. WA 23: 133 (LW 37: 57).
58. WA 23: 151 (LW 37: 68).
59. WA 23: 189 (LW 37: 92). The italicized words are in Latin in the original.
60. WA 23: 193 (LW 37: 95).   61. WA 23: 191 (LW 37: 93).
62. WA 23: 261 (LW 37: 135).   63. WA 23: 279–81 (LW 37: 147–48).
64. WA 23: 281–83 (LW 37: 150).   65. E.g. CR 92: 772–73.
66. CR 92: 805–977.   67. WA 23: 69 (LW 37: 15–16).
68. CR 92: 815–18.   69. CR 92: 818.
70. CR 92: 819–24. See Köhler, 1: 550–51, for a judgment on the validity of these charges.
71. CR 92: 824.   72. CR 92: 848–49.
73. *Ibid.*   74. E.g. CR 92: 830–31.
75. E.g. CR 92: 840ff.   76. CR 92: 974–76.
77. See Köhler, 1: 546–58, for a summary discussion.
78. WA 26: 261–509 (LW 37: 161–372).
79. WA 26: 261 (LW 37: 162).
80. WA 26: 262 (LW 37: 163).
81. Cf. WA 26: 499–500, 509 (LW 37: 360–61, 372).
82. WA 26: 401–2 (LW 37: 270).
83. WA 26: 317 (LW 37: 206–7).
84. WA 26: 342 (LW 37: 231).
85. For a detailed treatment of this important treatise, see Köhler, 1: 622–43.
86. WA 26: 379 (LW 37: 252).
87. WA 26: 433–45 (LW 37: 288–303).
88. CR 93/2: 22–248.   89. CR 97: 108–9 (S–J 2: 473–74).
90. CR 97: 117–18.   91. See KK 2: 111–14.
92. WABr 5: 76–77 (LW 49: 226).   93. See WABr 5: 101 (LW 49: 229).
94. WABr 5: 103.
95. WABr 5: 103–5. The letter in the form actually sent is given in WABr 5: 101–2 (LW 49: 229–31).
96. WABr 5: 125 (S–J 2: 488–89).   97. WABr 5: 141 (S–J 2: 493–94).
98. *Ibid.*; CR 1: 1066 (S–J 2: 477). 99. See Köhler, 2: 23–66.
100. *Ibid.*, 2: 57–58, 65–66. Hermann Barge, *Andreas Bodenstein von Karlstadt,* 2: 376–408.
101. The most thorough of these reconstructions is Walter Köhler, *Das Marburger Religionsgespräch 1529: Versuch eine Rekonstruktion* (Leipzig, 1929).

Sasse, *This Is My Body*, pp. 223–72, reconstructs the colloquy in English. For the texts, see WA 30/3: 110–71 (LW 38: 15–89). See also Köhler, *Zwingli und Luther*, 2: 66–163.

102. CR 1: 1099. Sasse, pp. 223–25. See also Köhler, *Religionsgespräch*, pp. 48–49.
103. Köhler, *Religionsgespräch*, p. 48.
104. For what follows, see Sasse, pp. 229–58; Köhler, *Religionsgespräch*, pp. 7–31.
105. For the second day's session see Sasse, pp. 258–66; Köhler, *Religionsgespräch*, pp. 31–38.
106. WA 30/3: 149 (LW 38: 70); Köhler, *Religionsgespräch*, p. 38.
107. WA 30/3: 150 (LW 38: 70–71); Köhler, *Religionsgespräch*, p. 38.
108. WA 30/3: 160–61 (LW 38: 85–89).
109. WABr 5: 155 (S–J 2: 495–96). Cf. WABr 5: 154 (LW 49: 236–37).
110. See Köhler, *Zwingli und Luther*, 2: 139–42.
111. WABr 5: 160–61 (S–J 2: 501). Cf. WABr 5: 170 (S–J 2: 503–4).
112. See *ibid.*, e.g. More on this will be said in Chapter 5.
113. CR 1: 1098 (S–J 2: 500).
114. WABr 5: 170 (S–J 2: 503–4).
115. WATR 4, nos. 4719, 5006; 5, no. 5469. Cited by Köhler, *Zwingli und Luther*, 2: 143.
116. See Köhler, *Zwingli und Luther*, 2: 139–58, for an exposition of the victory declarations on both sides.

CHAPTER FIVE

1. See Hermann Steinlein, *Luthers Doktorat*, pp. 67–87, for Luther's comments on his doctorate during the 1530's.
2. WA 40/1: 15–32, 33–688; 40/2: 1–184 (LW 26 and 27). Gerhard Schulze, "Die Vorlesung Luthers über den Galaterbrief von 1531 und der gedruckte Kommentar von 1535," *Theologische Studien und Kritiken* 98/99 (1926): 18–82, has shown that the printed version cannot always be trusted as an exact record of what Luther said. For this reason, all citations in the text are from Rörer's notes of the lectures unless otherwise indicated. The prefaces of 1535 and 1538 were written by Luther and should therefore be reliable.
3. For more on this see Oswald Bayer, *Promissio: Eine Untersuchung zum Wortverständnis beim fruhen Luther* (Göttingen, 1971); Heinrich Bornkamm, *Luther and the Old Testament*, ed. Victor I. Gruhn, trans. Eric W. and Ruth C. Gritsch (Philadelphia, 1969); two articles by Gerhard Ebeling: "The New Hermeneutics and the Young Luther," *Theology Today* 21 (1964): 34–46, and "Die Anfänge von Luthers Hermeneutik," *Zeitschrift für Theologie und Kirche* 48 (1951): 172–229; James S. Preus, *From Shadow to Promise: Old Testament Interpretation from Augustine to the Young Luther* (Cambridge, Mass., 1969).
4. See Jaroslav Pelikan, *Luther the Expositor* (St. Louis, 1959), chap. 5: "The History of the People of God."
5. WA 40/1: 36. 6. WA 40/1: 36.
7. WA 40/1: 34 (LW 27: 145–46). 8. WA 40/1: 53.
9. WA 40/1: 680–83; 40/2: 58–59, 74–76.

10. WA 40/1: 66–67.
11. WA 40/1: 37.
12. WA 40/1: 52–53.
13. WA 40/2: 58–59. Cf. WA 40/1: 645–47.
14. WA 40/1: 646–47. Cf. WA 40/2: 53–54, 58–59.
15. WA 40/1: 37. Cf. WA 40/1: 67; 40/2: 74–76.
16. WA 43: 38 (LW 3: 227). Luther's commentary can only be used with caution, however. See Peter Meinhold, *Die Genesisvorlesung Luthers und ihre Herausgeber* (Stuttgart, 1936).
17. WA 42: 79 (LW 1: 103).
18. WA 42: 142 (LW 1: 190).
19. WA 44: 635 (LW 8: 76).
20. WA 42: 567 (LW 3: 26).
21. See e.g. WA 42: 187, 215, 229, 269 (LW 1: 252–53, 291, 311; 2: 10).
22. WA 42: 188 (LW 1: 254).
23. Cf. WA 42: 117–18 (LW 1: 156).
24. WA 43: 3 (LW 3: 179).
25. WA 42: 560 (LW 3: 17).
26. WA 43: 90 (LW 3: 301).
27. WA 42: 188 (LW 1: 254).
28. WA 42: 188 (LW 1: 253).
29. WA 40/1: 134.
30. WA 40/1: 136–38.
31. WA 40/1: 145.
32. WA 40/2: 182–83.
33. WA 40/1: 681.
34. WA 40/1: 644.
35. WA 40/1: 474–75.
36. WA 40/1: 626.
37. WA 40/1: 640.
38. WA 40/1: 628–29.
39. WA 40/1: 626, note to line 4.
40. WA 40/1: 125.
41. WA 40/2: 169.
42. WA 40/2: 52–53.
43. WA 40/1: 54–55.
44. WA 40/1: 203 lines 4–11, 206 lines 5–11.
45. WA 40/1: 109.
46. WA 40/1: 118.
47. WA 40/2: 44–45.
48. WA 40/2: 137.
49. WA 40/2: 45–46.
50. WA 40/1: 319.
51. E.g. WA 40/1: 317, 319–20, 322–23.
52. WA 40/1: 319–20.
53. WA 40/1: 322–24. Cf. WA 40/1: 317.
54. Oskar Farner, *Das Zwinglibild Luthers*, discusses this accusation in Zwingli's case.
55. WA 40/2: 127–28. See WA 40/2: 150, for other critical remarks about Karlstadt's pride. For Zwingli, see WA 40/2: 154–55; 40/1: 589–90. For Oecolampadius, see WA 40/2: 152, where Zwingli is also mentioned.
56. WA 40/2: 152.
57. WA 40/2: 134.
58. WA 40/1: 356. Cf. WA 40/1: 352–59.
59. WA 40/2: 134.
60. WA 40/1: 66–67.
61. WA 40/1: 192–93.
62. WA 40/1: 192, note to line 11 in Cruciger's hand.
63. WA 40/1: 187–88.
64. WA 40/1: 180–81. "Das Thema dieses einfachen, unreflektierten 'Rühmens' im Sinne von Danken führt weiter in die tiefere Schicht des reflektierten, paradoxen 'Sichrühmens' in Zusammenhang der von Gott gestellten Aufgabe. Das Vorbild dafür war für Luther der Apostel Paulus und sein 'törichtes' und

doch in der gegebenen Situation notwendiges Rühmen (2. Kor. 11, 16ff.). Luther sieht sich in seinem Kampf gegen die 'Schwärmer' und 'Rottengeister' in der gleichen Situation wie Paulus gegenüber seinen korinthischen Gegnern und macht darum vom seinem Beispiel, wo es nötig ist, Gebrauch, vor allem gegenüber Müntzer (Ein Brief an die Fürsten zu Sachsen von dem aufrührerischen Geist, 1524. 15; 215, 28ff.). Aber solches 'Rühmen' mündet zuletzt wie bei Paulus in das Rühmen seiner 'Schwachheit,' d.h. seiner geistlichen Anfechtungen, die wie der spitze, grüne Stecken, an dem die Gänse aufgehängt werden, ihm 'durch Leib und Leben' gehen. Für die Art, wie er sich aus der Erfahrung des Paulus und Paulus aus seiner versteht, ist die Predigt über 2. Kor. 11, 19ff. (1536. 41, 512 ff.; Zitat 515, 32ff.) sehr aufschlussreich. Nicht weniger, wie er die scharfe Ironie des Paulus imitieren in trotzigen Humor transponieren kann (Sendbrief vom Dolmetschen, 1530. 30 II; 635, 8ff.)." Heinrich Bornkamm, "Luther als Schriftsteller," *Sitzungsberichte der Heidelberger Academie der Wissenschaften, Phil.-Hist. Klasse*, no. 1 (1965), p. 11, n. 16.

65. WA 40/2: 45–49. Cf. WA 40/2: 50–52, 136–37, 183.
66. WA 40/2: 52.
67. See Roland Bainton, "Luther's Use of Direct Discourse," in *Luther Today* (Decorah, Iowa, 1957), pp. 13–25.

68. WA 40/1: 122–23.
69. WA 40/2: 165.
70. WA 40/1: 572–73.
71. WA 40/1: 351.
72. WA 40/1: 630.
73. WA 40/2: 56–57.
74. WA 40/1: 618.
75. WA 40/1: 168–69.
76. WA 40/1: 177–78.
77. WA 40/2: 61–62.
78. WA 40/1: 111–12.
79. WA 42: 416 (LW 2: 219).
80. WA 40/1: 611–12, 504–5.
81. WA 40/1: 634. The printed version reads in part: "If we were not being disciplined by the power and wiles of tyrants and heretics, as well as by terrors of heart and the flaming darts of Satan (Eph. 6:16), Paul would be as obscure and unknown to us as he was to the whole world in past centuries and still is today to our opponents, the papists and the fanatics. Therefore it is the gift of prophecy and our own effort, together with inward and outward trials, that opens to us the meaning of Paul and of all the Scriptures." (*Ibid.* [LW 26: 418].)

CHAPTER SIX

1. Walter Köhler, *Zwingli und Luther. Ihr Streit über das Abendmahl nach seinen politischen und religiösen Beziehungen*, 2: 45–49, 164ff. Köhler provides the most detailed consideration of the history of the negotiations leading up to and including the Wittenberg Concord. See also Ernst Bizer, *Studien zur Geschichte des Abendmahlsstreits im 16. Jahrhundert* (Gütersloh, 1940; Darmstadt, 1962); and Hastings Eells, *Martin Bucer* (New Haven, 1931).

2. Köhler, 2: 166–68.
3. WABr 5: 183 (LW 49: 249–50).
4. Köhler, 2: 168–77.
5. *Ibid.*, pp. 177–80.
6. WABr 5: 237 (LW 49: 264–67).
7. WABr 5: 246. See Hermann Barge, *Andreas Bodenstein von Karlstadt*, 2: 416ff.

8. WABr 5: 298.
9. KK 2: 192–95.
10. WABr 5: 305.
11. See WABr 5: 328–29, for a discussion of the dating of this letter and the probable stimulus for its composition. Melanchthon repeatedly urged Luther to write Philipp, apparently unaware that Luther had already done so. WABr 5: 336, 365, 387.
12. WABr 5: 330–31 (LW 49: 300–303).
13. WABr 5: 331–32 (LW 49: 303–4). Cf. WABr 5: 333.
14. WABr 5: 340.
15. E.g. WABr 5: 357–58, 362, 365, 387, 474.
16. WABr 5: 475–76. See Köhler, 2: 201–3.
17. WABr 5: 490.
18. WABr 5: 496.
19. See Köhler, 2: 220–36, for a detailed account of these negotiations.
20. WABr 5: 562.   21. WABr 5: 568–69.
22. See Köhler, 2: 224–25.   23. WABr 5: 568.
24. WABr 5: 617.
25. For the account that follows, see Köhler, 2: 233–36.
26. See Hans Virck, ed., *Politische Correspondenz der Stadt Strassburg im Zeitalter der Reformation* (Strasbourg, 1882), 1: 512–13; Johann W. Baum, *Capito und Butzer* (Elberfeld, 1860), pp. 473–75.
27. WABr 5: 678.
28. For a detailed consideration of the following, see Köhler, 2: 243–47.
29. *Ibid.*, pp. 243–47.
30. WABr 6: 20–21.
31. See Köhler, 2: 258 n. 4, 298. Cf. WABr 6: 28 lines 8–15.
32. WABr 6: 25–26.
33. WABr 6: 28–29.
34. WABr 6: 23, 27.
35. WABr 6: 38. Cf. the joint opinion on Bucer's 5 February letter to the Landgraf issued by Luther, Jonas, and Melanchthon. This opinion stresses as the primary issue Christ's true presence in the signs of bread and wine. WABr 6: 49–51.
36. WABr 6: 30–33; Köhler, 2: 259–60.
37. WABr 6: 61.   38. WABr 6: 60. Cf. WABr 6: 173.
39. Köhler, vol. 2, chap. 6.   40. WABr 6: 236.
41. WABr 6: 243.   42. WABr 6: 246. Cf. WABr 6: 244.
43. WA 38: 204.   44. WABr 6: 244–45.
45. Köhler, 2: 281.
46. See WA 30/3: 547–53, for the account that follows.
47. WA 30/3: 550.   48. Köhler, 2: 292–96.
49. WA 30/3: 558.   50. WA 30/3: 561.
51. WA 30/3: 563–64.   52. WA 30/3: 564.
53. WABr 6: 510–11.   54. WABr 6: 540; St.L 17: 2035–46.
55. WABr 6: 548.

56. See Köhler, 2: 276–84, for a detailed consideration of the controversies in Augsburg.

57. See *ibid.*, chap. 8. 58. CR 2: 788–89.
59. WABr 7: 103. 60. WABr 7: 110.
61. See Köhler, vol. 2, chap. 9.
62. WABr 7: 127. Cf. CR 2: 822; WA 38: 297.
63. WA 38: 298–99.
64. WABr 7: 127, 128. 65. CR 2: 807–8; WABr 7: 144–45.
66. WABr 7: 149–50. 67. WA 38: 300.
68. WABr 7: 156–58. 69. WABr 7: 159–60.
70. WABr 7: 196–98, 200. 71. Cited by Bizer, p. 85 n. 1.
72. WABr 7: 213. 73. WABr 7: 211–12, 220–21.
74. See Köhler, 2: 389ff. 75. WABr 7: 234–36.
76. See WABr 7: 242–43, 248, 252–53, 272–73.
77. WABr 7: 258–63.
78. WABr 7: 254–55.
79. WABr 7: 278.
80. WABr 7: 286–87, 288–89, 290, 291–92, 293, 294, 296, 297.
81. WABr 7: 286–87.
82. WABr 7: 328. Cf. WABr 7: 354. The letter from the Strasbourgers is lost.
83. WABr 7: 328.
84. WABr 7: 355.
85. WABr 7: 379.
86. The account that follows is a composite from several reports. See St.L 17: 2090–118; Köhler, vol. 2, chap. 11, esp. pp. 442–55; Bizer, pp. 93–117.
87. WABr 7: 410.
88. WABr 7: 413–14.
89. St.L 17: 2091–92.
90. See M. Schuler and J. Schulthess, eds., *Huldreich Zwinglis Werke* (Zurich, 1928–42), 4: 42–78 (LWZ 2: 235–93).
91. St.L 17: 2092.
92. See WABr 7: 460, for Luther's comments.
93. St.L 17: 2103. 94. St.L 17: 2093.
95. St.L 17: 2013–14. 96. St.L 17: 2094.
97. St.L 17: 2107–8. 98. St.L 17: 2095–96.
99. St.L 17: 2096–97. 100. St.L 17: 2109–10.
101. St.L 17: 2111. 102. St.L 17: 2098.
103. Köhler, 2: 449–53; Bizer, pp. 108–16.
104. Eells, *Martin Bucer*, pp. 202–3, gives a translation of the three articles on the Supper.
105. The full details of these negotiations may be found in Köhler, vol. 2, chap. 12.

CHAPTER SEVEN

1. The major secondary sources for much of what follows are Gustav Kawerau, *Johann Agricola von Eisleben* (Berlin, 1881), and Joachim Rogge, *Johann Agricolas Lutherverständnis* (Berlin, 1960). The three primary sources used

most frequently are Carl Eduard Förstemann, *Neues Urkundenbuch zur Geschichte der evangelische Kirchen-Reformation* (1842), 1: 291–356; Gustav Kawerau, "Briefe und Urkunden zur Geschichte des antinomistischen Streites —I," *ZKG* 4 (1880/81): 299–324; and E. Thiele, ed., "Denkwürdigkeiten aus dem Leben des Johann Agricola von Eisleben," *Theologische Studien und Kritiken*, 80 (1907): 246–70.

2. Kawerau, *Agricola*, pp. 168–69; Rogge, pp. 133–34. Agricola's letter to the Count is contained in the Count's reply (Förstemann, 1: 291–95). See also the Count's letter to the Elector (*ibid.*, 1: 295–96).

3. WA 51: 429–30.

4. WATR 5: 405 (no. 3554).

5. Kawerau, *Agricola*, p. 173.

6. Kawerau, *Agricola*, pp. 175–76, suggests that this sermon might be a portion of Postil 262 (according to Aland's numbering) (WA 22: 86–88). WA 45: xxv points out that if this sermon occurred on this day then the 1 Peter sermon (WA 45: 102–4) must have been held in the afternoon. The editors concede that this is possible, but not likely since Luther also preached the next afternoon. The editors also note that it would be quite remarkable that Rörer's notebooks did not contain this afternoon sermon.

7. CR 3: 397. Kawerau, *Agricola*, p. 176.

8. Kawerau, *Agricola*, p. 174; Rogge, pp. 140–41.

9. CR 3: 454; Förstemann, 1: 296–311.

10. WA 51: 431.

11. Kawerau, "Briefe," pp. 305–6; Förstemann, 1: 311–12.

12. Kawerau, "Briefe," p. 306. I am accepting the argument of the Weimar editors (WA 50: 463 n. 5) that this summary was not the same as the one Agricola sent Luther. Kawerau, "Briefe," pp. 304–5.

13. Förstemann, 1: 311–12.

14. *Ibid.*, p. 313.

15. So argues Kawerau, *Agricola*, p. 181.

16. In his own account of the dispute, Agricola at one point refers the reader to the letter collection. Thiele draws the conclusion that this collection is that found by Kawerau (Kawerau, "Briefe"). See Thiele, p. 263 n. 2.

17. WABr 8: 122. Agricola included with this letter a summary of his doctrine; see Kawerau, "Briefe," pp. 304–5.

18. WABr 8: 121–22.

19. WA 45: 145–56.

20. Förstemann, 1: 298.

21. Kawerau, "Briefe," p. 306. See also note 16 above.

22. Förstemann, 1: 299. In the original, the words "repentance" and "remission" are written one above the other.

23. *Ibid.*, 303.

24. See Kawerau, *Agricola*, pp. 183–92; Rogge, pp. 156–62.

25. WATR 3: 480–82.

26. WABr 8: 159; Thiele, p. 258. In the following section I am accepting Rogge's arguments for the redating of this letter and WA 8, no. 3254, p. 279; see Rogge, pp. 165–68.

27. Thiele, p. 258.
29. WA 2: 136–42.
31. WA 39/1: 342–45.
32. Kawerau, *Agricola*, pp. 181–82. Cf. Rogge, pp. 145–56.
33. Förstemann, 1: 314.
35. WA 39/1: 342.
37. WA 39/1: 360.
38. See Kawerau, *Agricola*, p. 193; CR 3: 461; WATR 3: 483.
39. WATR 3: 483.
40. WATR 3: 484.
41. WABr 8: 343. Cf. Kawerau, *Agricola*, p. 197 n. 3.
42. See Thiele, p. 259.
44. Thiele, p. 259.
46. Kawerau, "Briefe," p. 309.
48. Kawerau, *Agricola*, p. 195. Cf. Rogge, pp. 183–85.
49. WA 40/1: 36–37. This addition to the preface was probably written between August 28 and early September. See WA 40/1: 3.
50. Förstemann, 1: 326; WA 50: 469; Thiele, p. 263.
51. Thiele, p. 263; Förstemann, 1: 326; WA 50: 469; WATR 4: 88.
52. WA 50: 468–77 (LW 47: 107–19).
53. Förstemann, 1: 319.
54. WA 50: 469 (LW 47: 107–8).
55. WA 50: 471–72 (LW 47: 110–12).
56. WA 50: 468, 474 (LW 47: 107, 115).
57. See WA 50: 474–76 (LW 47: 114–17).
58. E.g. Thiele, p. 265.
59. Kawerau, *Agricola*, pp. 196–97.
60. Kawerau, "Briefe," pp. 313–14.
61. Kawerau, *Agricola*, pp. 200–201; Rogge, pp. 198–200.
62. WABr 8: 362.
63. WA 50: 599.
64. WA 50: 627.
65. WATR 4: 360.
66. WATR 4: 390.
67. WATR 4: 433–34. This citation contains a number of other interesting comments.
68. Kawerau, *Agricola*, pp. 201–2; Förstemann, 1: 336; Thiele, p. 267.
69. WABr 9: 86.
70. Förstemann, 1: 315, 317–20.
71. WABr 9: 86–88.
72. Förstemann, 1: 317.
73. *Ibid.*, pp. 317–18. I have been unable to find this third accusation in any of Luther's writings. Agricola claimed in his "memoirs" that Luther made this accusation in *Against the Antinomians*; see Thiele, p. 265.
74. Förstemann, 1: 319–20, 315.
75. *Ibid.*, pp. 317–20.
76. *Ibid.*, pp. 337–39. Agricola's "Defense" was dated by Förstemann and accepted by the Weimar editors as written sometime shortly before 8 June, when the theologians wrote their second opinion (Förstemann, 1: 334–36). Luther's *Wider den Eisleben* is set by the Weimar editors in the last third of April 1540. But in this treatise Luther cites not only from Agricola's "Complaint" but also from his "Defense" (e.g. WA 51: 436 lines 18–19, 438 lines 8–10, 439 lines 11–12, 434 lines 4–7). For example:

AGRICOLA

Nhun sagt Eyssleben, das das Gesetze fur odder ohn das Euangelium
fehrlich gelert wird, denn es ist Ministerium mortis, aber fruchtbarlich vnd
gantz seligklich mit ader durchs Euangelium vnd nach dem Euangelio.
Denn das Euangelium offenbart Gottes zorn.
Es wirdt Ihm aber auffgelegt, Ehr
wolle kein Gesetze leyden widder fur,
nach mit, noch nach dem Euangelio.
Das ist seine beschwerung, daruber
ehr clagtt, alss sollt ehr vrlaub geben
haben Jederman, frey zu sundigen,
Cristum vnd den heyligen geyst auff-
zuheben vnd keine busse zu thun, so
doch seyne Buecher, Catechismus vnd
seyne predigen, die ehr auff etlichen
Reichstegen vnd sunsten gethan, das
widderspiel zeugen. . . .
(Förstemann, 1: 337)

LUTHER

Er spricht nocht itzt vnuerschampt
ynn der klage Das gesetz on Euan-
gelion werde ferlich gepredigt. Denn
es ist ein ministerium Mortis.
(WA 51: 439 lines 11–12; WA 51:
439 n. 4 comments that this passage
is nowhere to be found in the "Complaint." This is because it is in the
"Defense"!)
Und hilfft yhn nichts sein gaucken,
de lege, post vel cum Euangelio, wie
hernach.
(WA 51: 438 lines 8–9)
Er klagt das ich yhm auff gelegt, Er
wolle kein gesetz leiden vnd vrlaug
geben frey zu sundigen, Christum vnd
den heiligen geist auffheben vnd keine
busse thun u. So doch dagen Seine
bucher predigt u. das wider spiel zeugen u.
(WA 51: 434 lines 4–7)

This comparison shows that Luther must have had a copy of Agricola's "Defense" when he wrote his "Response" to Chancellor Brück and, indirectly, to
the Elector. Therefore either Agricola wrote this "Defense" earlier than has
previously been supposed or Luther wrote his letter to Brück later than has been
supposed.

There also remains the question of how Luther managed to obtain a copy of
the "Defense." Did Agricola send him one through the intermediary of Sebas-
tian Fröschel, whom Luther had sent to Agricola to inquire about his plans
(WABr 9: 86–87)? Or could Luther's letter to Brück have been written after 15
June, when the commission was formed, and after Brück or some other member
of the commission had provided him with a copy of Agricola's "Defense"? Incidentally, this opens the question whether Luther was first informed of Agricola's "Complaint" by Güttel or by the source which also provided him with
the "Defense." We do know that the Elector did not want Luther to be informed
of the "Complaint" for fear of his reaction, but this same reluctance need not
apply to Brück or even Agricola himself. See Förstemann, 1: 331–32.

77. Förstemann, 1: 337–38. Agricola used the printer's marks to identify the
relevant passages.

78. If, as the Weimar editors suggest, the letter from Faber is that of 24 and
26 April to Güttel, then Luther was not likely to have received it until very late
April or early May (WA 51: 429 n. 3; Förstemann, 1: 332–34). For the dating
of Faber's letter, see Kawerau, *Agricola*, p. 166 n. 1.

79. WA 51: 427.

80. Luther enclosed with his "Response" Agricola's "propositions," Agricola's unfinished *Short Summary*, which Luther had confiscated in November 1538, and a letter each from Kaspar Güttel and Wendelin Faber testifying to Agricola's efforts in Eisleben against Luther and Luther's doctrine (WA 51: 429). The Weimar editors (WA 51: 427 and 429 n. 1) state without substantiating their claim that the "propositions" referred to are Agricola's theses for debate on 1 February 1539 (Kawerau, "Briefe," pp. 313–15). When Jonas et al. (Förstemann, 1: 334–36, esp. 334 col. 2 to 335 col. 1) discuss Agricola's complaint they refer to the *"propositiones,"* by which they mean the "Theses Circulated Among Brethren." Furthermore, Luther's own discussion in his "Response" seems clearly to refer to the "Theses Circulated Among Brethren" rather than to the 1 February 1539 theses. The two letters are probably Güttel's letter to Luther of 7 April and Faber's (two-part?) letter to Güttel of 24 and 26 April (WA 51: 429 n. 3; cf. Kawerau, *Agricola*, p. 166 n. 1).

81. Förstemann, 1: 332–34; WA 38: 358–75.

82. WA 51: 429–32.
83. E.g. WA 51: 432, 435.
84. WA 51: 441.
85. WA 51: 434.
86. Cf. Förstemann, 1: 337.
87. WA 51: 437–38.
88. WA 51: 440.

89. Förstemann, 1: 325–27, 334–36. Förstemann suggests that Melanchthon was the primary author although his signature is not present.

90. *Ibid.*, pp. 326–27, 335–36.

91. Kawerau, *Agricola*, pp. 205–7; Rogge, pp. 209–10.

92. Kawerau, *Agricola*, pp. 211–22, 242–43; Rogge, pp. 211–32; WABr 11: 81–83.

93. See Kawerau, *Agricola*, pp. 152–67.

94. Förstemann, 1: 319.

95. E.g. WA 50: 475–76 (LW 47: 117); WA 40/1: 36–37.

96. WA 51: 441.

97. E.g. WA 39/1: 360; 50: 473–74 (LW 47: 113–14). See also Kawerau, "Briefe," p. 309.

98. E.g. WA 50: 469 (LW 47: 107–8).

99. E.g. WATR 4: 355–56, and 3: 482; WA 50: 473–74 (LW 47: 113–14).

100. E.g. WA 50: 474 (LW 47: 114); WA 51: 432, 435; WATR 3: 572–73, and 4: 88.

101. Luther's "Response" is filled with such accusations; see WA 51: 429–43.

102. E.g. WA 51: 432.

103. WA 50: 469 (LW 47: 107–8); WATR 4: 390; Kawerau, "Briefe," p. 314. Cf. Thiele, p. 263.

104. E.g. WA 50: 469 (LW 47: 107–8); WA 51: 431–32.

105. E.g. WATR 3: 481, 572–73.

106. E.g. WATR 3: 482; Cf. WA 50: 474 (LW 47: 114).

107. E.g. WATR 3: 480–81; 4: 88.

108. E.g. WATR 3: 660.

109. WA 50: 469 (LW 47: 107–8); WATR 3: 660.

110. Förstemann, 1: 327; and Thiele, pp. 258 and 265, e.g.

111. Kawerau, *Agricola*, pp. 243–45; Rogge, pp. 233–35.

CHAPTER EIGHT

1. WA 54: 141 (LW 38: 287–88).   2. WA 49: 570–87.
3. WA 49: 109 lines 15–29.   4. WA 49: 368.
5. E.g. WABr 9: 68, 559; 10: 23–24, 284, 309, 370, 442–43, 467–68. Luther even calculated the probable end of the world as part of his 1541 Chronology; see WA 53: 22–184.
6. "The world is deteriorating from day to day. There are clear indications that these misfortunes were brought upon Adam as a warning to the first world to maintain stricter order. But gradually, at the time of Noah, this maintenance of order weakened. . . . Accordingly, when the entire earth had been laid waste by the Deluge, and every living thing on earth, with the exception of a few human beings, had been destroyed, the age which followed the time of Noah undoubtedly lived in the fear of God. But as the years advanced, they, too, were corrupted and depraved by Satan. . . . The period when the gospel first became known among us was rather respectable. Now there is almost no fear of God, our shortcomings grow daily, and false prophets are even making their appearance. What else can we hope for except that when our iniquities have become full, either everything will be destroyed, or Germany will pay the penalties for its sins in some other way?" (WA 42: 154 [LW 1: 206–7]). "Thus farmers testify that nature is gradually growing old, that 30 or 40 years ago trees, whether they were in forests or in gardens, grew up more quickly than they do now, and that the growth of six or seven years on the trees of these times barely equals a year's increase of the earlier age" (WA 44: 628 [LW 8: 67]). See also WA 42: 154ff, 161, 249, 270, 304ff, 425 [LW 1: 206ff, 216, 336; 2: 12, 60ff, 231]). Cf. many of the comments in the letters cited in note 5 above.
7. E.g. WABr 12: 295–98; 9: 228–29; 10: 396 lines 2–9.
8. WA 49: 278–79.
9. WABr 10: 500 lines 12–15.
10. E.g. WA 47: 757–71, which was delivered in 1539 and published in 1542, probably at Luther's initiative.
11. E.g. WA 49: 35–40, 562–69. See Susan K. Boles, "The Economic Position of Lutheran Pastors in Ernestine Thuringia 1521–1555," *ARG* 63 (1972): 94–125.
12. E.g. WA 51: 332, 339, 414ff.
13. E.g. WA 51: 331–424; 49: 30–35.
14. E.g. WA 49: 488–91, 716–23. Cf. WABr 9: 547–48.
15. See *On the Councils and the Church* (WA 50: 509–653 [LW 41: 9–178]) and *Against the Papacy at Rome Instituted by the Devil* (WA 54: 206–99 [LW 41: 263–376]).
16. WA 50: 509–14 (LW 41: 9–14).
17. See *Against the Sabbatarians: Letter to a Good Friend* (WA 50: 312–37 [LW 47: 65–98]).
18. Luther's response is in WABr 10: 555–56.
19. KK 2: 469–71.
20. See e.g. WABr 10: 498–503, 504–9, 523; WA 49: 297–307, 318–19.
21. The Elector John Frederick and Duke Moritz came close to war over Wurzen. KK 2: 566–67; WABr 10: 31–36. Cf. WABr 10: 48–49.

22. KK 2: 524ff. Cf. William Walker Rockwell, *Die Doppelehe des Landgrafen Philipp von Hessen* (Marburg, 1904). For Luther's response see WA 53: 190–201.

23. E.g. WA 49: 40–45, 62–66, 708–15.

24. KK 2: 402, 563; WA 51: 585–625; WA 50: 485–87.

25. Cf. WA 50: 485–87; 53: 211–12, 558–60; 51: 585–625.

26. E.g. WABr 9: 559–62. Sermons: WA 49: 325–43, 488–91, 708–23. See also note 25.

27. KK 2: 597; also, e.g., WABr 9: 370, 384, and 10: 23–24, 55, 98, 277, 284, 314, 320, 328, 335.

28. WABr 10: 330–31.

29. WABr 9: 621, 622.

30. See Hermann Barge, *Andreas Bodenstein von Karlstadt*, 2: 471ff, 484ff.

31. WABr 10: 14.

32. WABr 10: 24.

33. The alternate version seems to indicate that Karlstadt questioned the magistrate. See WABr 10: 27 n. 2.

34. WABr 10: 27.   35. WABr 10: 29, 30.

36. WABr 10: 49.   37. WABr 10: 12–13.

38. Bullinger mentions this in his *True Confession*, pp. 40v–40r (see note 86 below). For a summary of the correspondence, see WABr 10: 384–87.

39. WABr 10: 387.

40. See WABr 10: 384–87.

41. The full text is in Max Lenz, ed., *Briefwechsel des Landgrafen Philipps des Grossmüthigen von Hessen mit Bucer* (Leipzig, 1880–91; Osnabrück, 1965), 2: 223–25.

42. *Ibid.*, 2: 226; see also 2: 225–31.

43. For a thorough historical introduction, see WA 54: 119–40.

44. KK 2: 78–79; WABr 10: 420. Much of the material that follows is summarized in the introduction to Schwenckfeld's 12 December 1543 letter to Luther (WABr 10: 420).

45. C.Schw. 4: 832; 8: 33, 34; WABr 10: 421.

46. E.g. C.Schw. 7: 537, 566, 607–10, 710–12. Citations found in the index to C.Schw., vol. 7.

47. One section is entitled: "Was M. Luther, Philippus, und Brentz, von der Gottwerdung vnnd Göttlichen herrlichkeit des Menschens in Christo selbst ahnfengklich geleert vnd geschriben, aber nachmals solichs bey mir verdampt haben." C.Schw. 7: 865 lines 18–21.

48. WABr 10: 424 lines 119–31.

49. WA 54: 90 lines 37ff, 88 line 7.

50. WA 39/2: 93–121.

51. WABr 10: 421–26. The appendix from Luther's works can be found in C.Schw. 8: 704ff.

52. The citations from Vadian, Luther, and Bugenhagen are found in C.Schw. 8: 695–719. See also WABr 10: 423 lines 102–9, 424 lines 138–39.

53. WABr 10: 421.

54. WABr 10: 424–25. *On the Councils and the Church* can be found in WA 50: 509–653 (LW 41: 9–178), and the postil in WA 10/1/1: 180–247.

55. WABr 10: 425–26.
56. WA 54: 141 (LW 38: 287).
57. WA 54: 120.
58. WA 54: 141 (LW 38: 287).
59. *New English Bible* translation.
60. WA 54: 141 (LW 38: 288).
61. WA 54: 142. Cf. LW 38: 288, which reads, "... but I refused to believe it because none of them was willing to admit this publicly in writing." The German reads: "... welchs ich nicht hab wollen gleuben, weil es keiner öffentlich von sich hat wollen schreiben."
62. WA 54: 147 (LW 38: 293 n. 15).
63. WA 54: 142, 144, 153–54 (LW 38: 288–89, 300–301).
64. E.g. WA 54: 154 lines 17–18, 142–43 (LW 38: 302, 289).
65. WA 54: 143 (LW 38: 289–90).
66. WA 54: 143–44 (LW 38: 289–91).
67. E.g. WA 54: 141–42, 144, 155–56.
68. WA 54: 154 lines 3–16 (LW 38: 302).
69. E.g. WA 54: 152, 155–57 (LW 38: 299, 304).
70. WA 54: 154, 142–43 (LW 38: 302–3).
71. WA 54: 157 (LW 38: 305–6).
72. WA 54: 144–48 (LW 38: 291–96).
73. WA 54: 158, 161 (LW 38: 307–8, 312). Cf. WA 54: 158 lines 28ff (LW 38: 308).
74. WA 54: 158 (LW 38: 307–8).
75. WA 54: 160 lines 30ff, 162 lines 11ff (LW 38: 311, 312–13).
76. E.g. WA 54: 156 lines 23ff (LW 38: 305).
77. WA 54: 162 (LW 38: 313).
78. WABr 10: 85–88, esp. 86 lines 13–14.
79. WABr 10: 178 lines 6–8.
80. WABr 10: 237–38.
81. WA 54: 162–67 (LW 38: 313–19). Cf. WABr 10: 556 lines 31–32.
82. WA 54: 164–65 (LW 38: 316–17). Cf. WABr 10: 85–86, 171–72, 178, 556.
83. WA 54: 164 (LW 38: 315–17); WABr 10: 172 lines 6–9, 86 lines 25–27 and n. 7.
84. WABr 10: 556.
85. WA 54: 165 (LW 38: 316).
86. The full title is *Warhaffte Bekanntnuss der dieneren der kirchen zü Zürych, was sy vss Gottes wort, mit der heiligen allgemeinen Christlichen Kirchen gloubind vnd leerind, in sonderheit aber von dem Nachtmal vnsers Herren Jesu Christi: mit gebürlicher Antwort vff das unbegründt ergerlich schähen, verdammen vnnd schelten D. Martin Luthers, Besonders in sinem letsten Büchlin, Kurtze Bekenntniss von dem heiligen Sacrament, gennant, vssgangen.* It is located in the Simmlersche Sammlung and is on microfilm at the Foundation for Reformation Research (FRR 1022.174 [miscatalogued as 1022.17a]). All references are given as *True Confession*, then the page and an *r* for recto and a *v* for verso. A summary appears in WA 54: 126–33.
87. Lenz, *Bucer*, 2: 223–25.
88. *True Confession*, p. 41v.
89. *Ibid.*, pp. 32v–32r.
90. *Ibid.*, pp. 133v, 134r.
91. *Ibid.*, pp. 135r–136v.
92. *Ibid.*, pp. 136v–136r.
93. *Ibid.*, pp. 131v–131r.
94. WA 54: 425–30, 447–58.

CONCLUSION

1. Wilhelm Gussmann and Hans Preuss have gathered from a variety of sources an impressive collection of the special characterizations Luther's followers made of him. Inasmuch as Luther's age delighted in hyperbole, these characterizations must be evaluated with caution. It seems likely, however, that they reflect at least a fairly widespread feeling that Luther was a special man and that God was using him to His purpose. See Wilhelm Gussmann, "Elias, Daniel, Gottesmann. Zur Geschichte des Schlagwortes im Reformationszeitalter," in *Quellen und Forschungen zur Geschichte des Augsburgischen Glaubensbekenntnisses* (Kassel, 1930), 2: 233ff; and the previously cited work by Hans Preuss, *Martin Luther. Der Prophet*, pp. 36–71. See also Hans Volz, ed., *Die Lutherpredigten des J. Mathesius* (Leipzig, 1930), pp. 64–65, 82 (cited in WABr 1: 167 n. 4).

2. WA 51: 469–572 (LW 41: 185–256).

3. WA 53: 417–552 (LW 47: 137–306).

4. Max Lenz, ed., *Briefwechsel des Landgrafen Philipps des Grossmüthigen von Hessen mit Bucer*, 2: 223–25. I have cited only a few excerpts from Bullinger's critique.

5. CR 92: 815–18.   6. St.L 20: 582.
7. St.L 17: 1604.   8. WABr 3: 387.
9. St.L 17: 1593, 1595.   10. CR 92: 848–49.
11. See note 4 above.

12. See *True Confession*, pp. 136v–136r.

13. CR 11: 727–28 (Philipp Melanchthon, "Funeral Oration over Luther," in *The Protestant Reformation*, ed. Lewis W. Spitz [Englewood Cliffs, N.J., 1966], pp. 69–70).

14. CR 11: 729–30 (Spitz, p. 72). Cf. Bucer's letter to Bullinger in Chapter 8, note 42.

Index

Abraham, 115, 119, 181
Agricola, John: leaves Eisleben,
    156–57; wife of, 156n, 165; Luther
    on, 157, 162–70, 165n, 168n, 174,
    178, 182; his *Three Sermons*, 158f;
    and reconciliation with Luther,
    158–60, 162, 164–65, 167, 170; his
    A Short Summary of the Gospels,
    158–62, 158n, 160n, 173, 175ff; his
    teachings, 159, 161, 171–72; and
    the "Theses Circulated Among
    Brethren," 162–63, 175f, 176n,
    177; his "Complaint," 170–72, 177,
    228n76; on Luther, 171, 179; his
    "Defense," 172, 174f, 177, 228n76;
    Wendelin Faber on, 172–73, 175f,
    176n; and Melanchthon, 174–75,
    175n, 176, 176n, 178f; mentioned,
    132, 187
Alber, Matthew, 83f
All Saints Church, 8–9, 22, 40
All Saints Church, Chapter of, 7,
    13–14, 15f, 21, 34
Allstedt, 35–40, 52
Allstedt spirit. *See* Müntzer, Thomas
Amsdorf, Nicholas von, 8f, 11–12, 20,
    29, 70, 74f, 111, 140, 184
Anabaptists, 120, 168, 180, 209n4
Anhalt, Prince George of, 193
Arius, 87, 106
Augsburg, 38, 92, 139–40, 141, 144,
    147ff
Augsburg, Confession of, 132, 154, 164
Augsburg, Diet of (1530), 128f

Augustinians, 7f, 10
Austria, Archduke Ferdinand of, 121

Basel, 82, 107, 151, 183f, 183n
Bavaria, King of, 121
Berlin, 175
Beyer, Christian, 10, 11n
Biberach, 148
Bila, Dietrich of, 55
Black Bear Inn, meeting at, 39–41
Bohemia, 182
Bora, Kathrine von, 71n, 165
Bornkamm, Heinrich, 3
Brandenburg, Joachim II of, 175
Brandenburg, Margravate of, 127
Braunschweig, Duke Heinrich of, 69
Brenz, John, 86, 106, 187
Briessmann, John, 74, 80, 84, 136
Brück, Gregory, 146, 159, 172, 194,
    228n76
Brunfels, Otto, 82
Brunswick-Lüneburg, 147
Bucer, Martin: his translation of
    Bugenhagen's *Psalter* and Luther's
    Postil, 91–93, 98, 101; Luther on,
    92–93, 98, 109–10, 132–39 *passim*,
    150f; his *Preface by M. Bucer to the
    Fourth Volume of Luther's Postil*,
    93–94; on Luther, 93–94, 133,
    135–36, 185–86, 203f; and Marburg
    Colloquy, 106, 109–10; negotiates
    with Luther on Coburg, 132–36,
    137; on Lord's Supper, 133–34, 136,
    138–39, 152ff; and negotiations

following Coburg meeting (1530–31), 136–39, 142f, 143n, 225n35; anonymously composes Frankfurt clergy's reply to Luther, 143n; and Kassel Conference, 145–47; and Wittenberg Concord, 147–55; his *Statement . . . to Münster*, 150; and Bullinger, 194–95, 202
Bugenhagen, John: and the sacramentarians, 86, 150, 188, 193n, 220n37; his *Psalter*, 91–93, 98, 101; and Agricola, 158, 165, 170
Bullinger, Heinrich: publishes Zwingli's *A Short and Clear Exposition of the Christian Faith*, 149, 151; and the Zurich Bible, 185–86; on Luther, 186, 194–96, 202–3, 204; his *True Confession*, 194–96
Burer, Albert, 32–33

Camerarius, Joachim, 74
Capito, Wolfgang, 33, 103, 150, 154
Carlstadt, Andreas Bodenstein von. *See* Karlstadt, Andreas Bodenstein von
Casel, Gregory, 86–89
Cassiodorus, *Tripartite Ecclesiastical History* of, 168
Castle church of Wittenberg. *See* All Saints Church
Cellarius, Martin, 24–25
Charles V, Emperor, 128, 132
Coburg, 129, 134, 148
Coct, Anémond de, 83
Constance, 128, 147, 149
Cruciger, Kaspar, 149f, 164

Denmark, 158
Dietrich, Veit, 129, 134, 184
Drechsel, Thomas, 9, 25. *See also* Zwickau prophets

Eck, John, 107
Einsiedel, Haugold von, 9, 11, 14, 16, 212n47
Eisenach, 13, 148f
Eisermann, John, 11–12

Eisleben, 64, 156–57, 163, 170ff, 173
Electoral Saxony, Elector Frederick the Wise of (d. 1525): and Wittenberg Movement, 7–10, 11n, 12, 14–16, 15n, 30; and Karlstadt, 9, 15, 21, 35, 55, 76–77; and Luther's return to Wittenberg, 13–14, 17–18, 20f, 30, 32; mentioned, 6, 26, 28, 34, 69, 128
Electoral Saxony, Elector John of (1525–32; before 1525, Duke): and Karlstadt, 34f, 47, 79f; and Müntzer, 36f; and negotiations with the sacramentarians, 104–5, 127ff, 136, 138
Electoral Saxony, Elector John Frederick of (1532–47; before 1532, Duke): and Karlstadt, 36, 44–47, 52, 55; and Müntzer, 36f; and Luther's visitation (1524), 37, 39; and negotiations with the sacramentarians, 146, 148; and Agricola, 156n, 157n, 158–60, 158n, 160n, 165–74 *passim*, 228n76
Elevation of the host, 9f, 14, 56, 193–94
Erasmus, Desiderius, 48, 92, 99, 121–22, 205
Erfurt, 10
Esslingen, 147ff

Faber, Wendelin, 172–73, 175f, 176n, 230n80
False Brethren, characteristics of, 22–24, 26, 36, 37–38, 53, 89f, 120–21, 178
Forster, John, 147f, 150
Franciscan church of Wittenberg, 8, 10
Frankenhausen, battle of, 66–67, 68
Frankfurt am Main, 73, 93, 101, 142–44, 147, 149
Frosch, John, 139–40
Froschauer, Christoph, 185, 202

Gemmingen, Freiherr von, 149
Gerbel, Nicholas, 48–49, 51, 58, 83, 110–11, 129, 148

Gerichius, Cyriacus, 167n
Glatz, Kaspar, 46, 74–75, 77, 216n44
Gotha, 148
Grimma, 149
Güttel, Kaspar, 23, 170, 228n76, 230n80

Hausmann, Nicholas, 35, 47n, 128–29
Heldrungen, 68
Herwagen, John, 92–93
Hess, John, 84
Hesse, 148
Hesse, Landgraf Philipp of: and
  Marburg Colloquy, 104–7, 110; and
  negotiations leading to Wittenberg
  Concord, 129–31, 136, 144–47,
  225n11; mentioned, 69, 182, 193n
Huber, Kaspar, 141, 147
Hus, John, 116

Iconoclasm, 10f, 15–16, 21, 34ff, 40–41,
  43–44, 52–53
Infant baptism, 9, 25, 34–35, 74, 130,
  148
Isny, 148
Italy, 183

Jena, 34, 39–41, 42, 45–46, 50, 52, 55
Jonas, Justus: and Karlstadt, 9, 55,
  183–84; and Wittenberg Ordinance,
  11–12, 20; and the sacramentarians,
  127, 129, 132, 146, 150, 225n35;
  mentioned, 7, 165
Jud, Leo, 47n, 82–83, 92, 220n37

Kahla, 41n
Karlstadt, Andreas Bodenstein von:
  and the Wittenberg movement,
  6–9, 11–12, 12n, 14–17, 20–24, 23n,
  40–41; on the Lord's Supper, 7ff,
  23f, 34, 40, 48, 56–57, 79–80; his
  wife, 9, 21, 47, 77, 79, 183, 183n; and
  iconoclasm, 11, 21, 23f, 34, 52–53;
  and the Wittenberg Ordinance,
  11–12, 15–17, 20, 23, 40–41; Luther
  on, as fanatic or false prophet (to
  1530), 22–24, 26, 35, 44–58, 74ff,
  80, 89f, 97, 106, 213n101; Luther on,

as fanatic or false prophet (after
  1530), 115–23 *passim*, 142, 168,
  180–85 *passim*, 189, 191, 194; Luther
  on death of, 183–85, 194; other
  comments of Luther on, 12, 12n,
  20, 40–41, 42, 129ff, 140, 151; his
  preaching in the Parish church,
  22–23, 23n, 40; in Orlamünde,
  34–35, 36, 41–47, 52–55, 74–75; and
  infant baptism, 34–35; on Luther,
  39, 40–41, 45–46, 47n, 75, 77; in Jena,
  39–41, 45–46, 50, 52, 55; and Müntzer, 39f, 45, 77–78; his banishment,
  44–48, 47n, 50, 52, 54–55, 78n; in
  Strasbourg, 48–49, 129f; and the
  Peasants' War, 73–74, 77–78; his
  return to Electoral Saxony, 74,
  75–80; his *Apology of Dr. Andreas
  Karlstadt for the False Reputation
  of Insurrection Which Is Unjustly
  Attributed to Him*, 77–79; his
  *Explanation of How Karlstadt
  Regards and Wishes His Teaching
  on the Highly Revered Sacrament
  and Other Matters to be Regarded*,
  79–81, 84; and Zwingli, 79–80, 82,
  83–84; and Marburg Colloquy, 107;
  mentioned, 87, 142, 156
Kassel Conference, 144–47
Keller, Michael, 139
Kempten, 148
Kolb, Franz, 82–83
Königsberg, 74
Krautwald, Valentine, 103

Lake Constance Association, 63
Landau, 148
Lang, John, 25
Lauterbach, Anthony, 167n
Leipzig, 38, 40, 69
Lindau, 148
Link, Wenzel, 10, 26, 71, 75, 111, 141
Lochau, 167n
Lord's Supper. *See under individual
  theologian by name*
Luft, Hans, 158ff, 173
Lüneburg, 166n, 174f

Lüneburg, Duke Ernst of, 134, 138
Luther, Martin: and his return to
    Wittenberg, 6f, 12–14, 17–18, 19–20,
    20n, 30–31, 212n60; on the Wit-
    tenberg Ordinance, 7, 10–12, 19–21,
    23–24; his *A Sincere Admonition
    by Martin Luther to All Christians
    to Guard Against Insurrection or
    Rebellion*, 8, 11, 18–19; on rebellion,
    10–11, 17–19, 37–38, 44, 52–53,
    60–73, 79; on his responsibility for
    rebellious opponents, 17–22 *passim*,
    20n, 39, 58, 60–63, 106, 117; on
    the struggle between the true and
    false church, 22, 37, 49–53 *passim*,
    95, 99, 112–16, 164–69 *passim*, 178,
    180–83; defines characteristics of
    true prophet or apostle, 22, 27–28,
    116–20, 122–24, 125; and censorship,
    24, 34, 46, 158–60, 158n, 160n; meets
    with Zwickau prophets, 24–25; his
    "Invocavit Sermons," 26, 32; finds
    position for Zwilling, 26; on Luther
    (to 1522), 27–30; on Luther (1522–
    30), 17f, 26–32 *passim*, 38, 38n, 47n,
    49–50, 61f, 95, 99; on Luther (1531–
    46), 116–20, 125, 131, 162, 165n,
    166–69, 178, 224n81; on Melanch-
    thon, 29–31; as seen by supporters,
    32–33, 48, 174–75, 179, 185–86,
    204–5; and rumors of reforms in
    Orlamünde, 34–35; recommends
    Müntzer for position in Zwickau,
    35–36; letter from Müntzer to, 36;
    visitation by, 37, 39; his *Letter to
    the Princes of Saxony Concerning
    the Rebellious Spirit*, 37–38, 41; on
    his opponents' consciences, 38, 51,
    62–63, 65, 130, 191, 192–94; his
    A Letter to . . . Mühlhausen, 39; his
    encounter with Karlstadt in Jena,
    39–41, 45–46, 50, 55; in Orlamünde,
    41–44, 50, 55; and Karlstadt's
    banishment, 44–48, 50, 54–55; on
    his opponents' uncertainty of belief,
    46, 55–56, 80–81, 84, 88ff; his
    judgment on opponents confirmed,
    48–49, 50, 68, 110–11, 128, 140–42,
    155, 190–92; letter from Strasbourg
    preachers to, concerning Karlstadt,
    48; his *A Letter to the Christians
    at Strasbourg in Opposition to the
    Fanatic Spirit*, 49–51; his doctrine
    of the Lord's Supper, 50, 56f, 87–88,
    94–97, 108–9, 134–45 *passim*, 143n,
    192–94, 193n; his *Against the
    Heavenly Prophets*, 51–58, 74, 77,
    90, 101; on his responsibility for the
    sacramentarians, 58, 95–96, 103,
    106, 117, 131, 142–44, 180, 185–94
    passim; his *Admonition to Peace*,
    61–63, 64–65, 67; on signs of the
    coming judgment, 61, 63, 66, 181–83,
    231n6; sees Satan attacking him
    personally, 62, 70, 98, 143, 168–69,
    194; his foreword and afterword to
    the Weingarten Treaty, 63–64; in
    Eisleben during Peasants' War, 64;
    his *Against the Robbing and Mur-
    dering Hordes of Peasants*, 64–66,
    69–73; informed of Müntzer's cap-
    ture, 67, 68–69; his commentary on
    a collection of Müntzer's writings,
    67–68; on criticism of his attack on
    the peasants, 69, 70–73, 98; on Münt-
    zer's confession, 69–70; his Pente-
    cost sermon (1525), 70–71, 73; his
    *An Open Letter on the Harsh Book
    Against the Peasants*, 71–73; and
    Kathrine von Bora, 71n, 165; on
    his responsibility for the princes'
    excesses, 73; and Karlstadt's return
    to Electoral Saxony, 74, 75–80; his
    foreword to Karlstadt's *Apology . . .
    for the False Reputation of Insur-
    rection*, 77–79; his foreword to
    Karlstadt's *Explanation of How
    Karlstadt Regards . . . His Teaching
    on the Highly Revered Sacrament*,
    80–81, 84; meets with Casel, 86–89;
    on his opponents' disagreement
    with one another, 89f, 191; his
    *Letter to the Congregation at
    Reutlingen*, 89; his prefaces to the

translations of the *Swabian Syn-gramma*, 89–90; his foreword to Bugenhagen's *Psalter*, 91–92; his *Postil*, 91–93, 98, 101, 188; on Jud's pseudonymous treatise, 92; on his opponents' misuse of his name and authority, 92, 98, 109–10, 142–44, 167–68, 178f, 187, 189, 194; his concern for events after his death, 92, 98, 167ff, 178f, 180, 182; his *The Sacrament of the Body and Blood of Christ—Against the Fanatics*, 93; his *That These Words of Christ "This Is My Body," Etc., Still Stand Firm Against the Fanatics*, 93–98, 101–2; his *Confession Concerning Christ's Supper*, 101–4; and the Marburg Colloquy, 104–11, 130ff, 190–92; his lectures on Galatians (1531), 112–14, 116–25, 140, 157, 166; draws parallels between himself and St. Paul, 112–13, 116–20, 125, 162, 194, 224n81; his *Genesis Commentary*, 114–16, 119n, 124; on Anabaptists, 120, 168, 180, 209n4; draws parallels between his false brethren and St. Paul's, 120–21; uses St. Paul's example to justify his own actions, 122–24, 191–92; and the Schwabach articles, 127; on an alliance with the Upper German cities, 127–28; on the Strasbourgers' reception of Karlstadt, 129f; on the Coburg, 129, 134; letter to Philipp of Hesse from, during the Diet of Augsburg, 129–31, 225n11; letter from Bucer to, on Coburg, 132–34; and meeting with Bucer on Coburg, 134–36, 137; and negotiations with Bucer (1530–31), 136–39, 225n35; on intercommunion, 137–38, 143, 143n; and Augsburg, 139–40, 141, 144, 147f; his *Open Letter to Duke Albrecht of Prussia*, 141–42; his *Letter to Frankfurt am Main*, 142–44; and Kassel Conference, 145–47; and Wittenberg Concord, 147–55; on

the history of the sacramentarian controversy, 152–53, 190–92; and Agricola's *A Short Summary of the Gospels*, 158–62, 158n, 160n; and reconciliation with Agricola, 158–60, 162, 164–65, 167, 170; on law and gospel in the antinomian dispute, 161–62, 164; and the disputations against the antinomians, 162, 164f, 166–67, 167n, 169, 172; and "Theses Circulated Among Brethren," 162–63, 170; on his responsibility for the antinomians, 166, 167–68; his *Against the Antinomians*, 167–70, 172; his *On the Councils and the Church*, 169–71, 172, 188; and Agricola's "Complaint," 170–72, 177, 228n76; and Agricola's "Defense," 172, 174f, 177, 228n76; his *That Preachers Should Preach Against Usury*, 172; letter from Faber about Agricola to, 172–73, 175f, 176n; his "Response" to Agricola, 172, 173–74, 228n76; his *A Simple Way to Pray, Written for a Friend*, 173; on the Council of Trent, 181–82; and Philipp of Hesse's bigamous marriage, 182; and the Zurich Bible, 185–86; his *Short Confession on the Lord's Supper*, 186–94; his *Concerning the Last Words of David*, 187–88; his *Against the Asses of Paris and Louvaine*, 196; his *Thirty-Nine Articles*, 196; his *Against Hanswurst*, 202; his *Against the Jews and Their Lies*, 202; opponents, *see under individual opponent by name. See also* False brethren, characteristics of

Mainz, Archbishop Albrecht of, 12, 28, 33
Mallerbach, Virgin at, 35–36
Mansfeld, 170f
Mansfeld, Count Albrecht of, 67f, 71, 156–57, 157n, 175
Mansfeld, Count Ernst of, 67f

Marburg Colloquy, 104–11, 130ff, 135, 190–92, 195
Meissen, Bishop of, 14
Melanchthon, Philipp: and the Wittenberg Movement, 7–9, 11–12, 16f, 20, 20n, 22, 30–31, 55, 212n47; and Karlstadt, 9, 11, 17, 30–31, 55; Luther on, 29–31; on Luther, 30, 174–75, 179, 204–5; his *Loci Communes*, 30; his foreword to Bugenhagen's *Psalter*, 91–92; and the Marburg Colloquy, 104ff, 107f, 111; and the Schwabach articles, 127; and the Diet of Augsburg, 129, 132–34, 225n11; and Kassel Conference, 145–47; and Wittenberg Concord, 149–50, 154; and Agricola, 157, 162–63, 167, 170, 174–75, 175n, 176ff, 176n; and the Zurich Bible, 185; and Schwenckfeld, 187; mentioned, 91n, 139, 183n, 193n, 225n35
Memmingen, 147–48, 149
Memmingen Agreement, 61
Menius, Justus, 139, 149f
Mochau, Anna von, 9, 21, 47, 77, 79, 183, 183n
Mochau, Christoph von, 183n
Mühlhausen, 39, 60
Müller, Karl, 12n
Müller, Kaspar, 71
Müntzer, Thomas: in Zwickau, 35–36; in Allstedt, 35–39, 216n12; in Prague, 36; Luther on, as fanatic or false prophet, 36–39, 52, 58, 65, 67–70, 97, 106, 115–19 *passim*, 168; Luther on capture and death of, 67–70, 140–42; his "Princes' Sermon," 37; in Mühlhausen, 39, 60; Karlstadt denies agreement with, 39f, 45, 77–78; his capture and execution, 66–69; his name used as a label, 128, 157, 157n; mentioned, 156, 197n, 198n, 209n2
Myconius, Frederick, 149f
Myconius, Oswald, 183–84

Neuheller, Jodocus, 147

Noah, 113, 119, 119n, 124, 181
Nuremberg, 128f

Ochsenfart (Catholic theologian), 24
Oecolampadius, John: Luther on, as fanatic or false prophet, 82ff, 89–90, 97, 102, 120–21, 123, 130ff, 180, 189–93; Luther on death of, 140–41, 190–91; his *Genuine Exposition of the Words of the Lord, "This Is My Body," According to the Most Ancient Authors*, 84; on the Lord's Supper, 84–86, 108–9; on Luther, 90–91, 109, 203; his *Reasonable Answer to Dr. Martin Luther's Instruction Concerning the Sacrament*, 90–91; his *That Dr. Martin Luther's Misunderstanding of the Everlasting Words, "This Is My Body," Is Untenable. The Second Reasonable Answer of John Oecolampadius*, 101; his *Concerning Dr. Martin Luther's Book Entitled "Confession": Two Answers, by John Oecolampadius and Ulrich Zwingli*, 103–4; and the Marburg Colloquy, 104, 106–11; his *Dialogue*, 132–33; and negotiations following the Marburg Colloquy, 136ff, 151f; his letters published posthumously, 149; mentioned, 86, 88
Orlamünde, 34–35, 39, 41–47, 50, 52, 54f, 74–75
Orlamünde, City Council of, 34f, 47, 54
Orlamünde, congregation of, 40f, 47n, 78
Osiander, Andrew, 106, 111
Oswald, John, 13

Parish church of Wittenberg, 8, 10f, 26, 40, 193
Pellican, Konrad, 82f, 99
Philipp of Hesse. *See* Hesse, Landgraf Philipp of
Pomerania, 174
Prague, 36

Preus, James S., 12n, 15n, 20n
Probst, Jacob, 131–32, 184
Prussia, Duke Albrecht of, 141–42

Reichsregiment, 14, 18
Reinhard, Martin, 39–44
Reuchlin, John, 99
Reutlingen, 83, 89, 149
Rhegius, Urbanus, 147
Rhenanus, Beatus, 32
Rörer, George, 118, 164
Rothenberg ob der Tauber, 75
Rühel, John, 67, 68–69, 218n31

Sagrena, 9
Sailer, Gereon, 147–48, 150
St. Anthony brother, 11
St. Augustine, 145, 205
St. Francis, 116–17, 195
St. Jerome, 122, 125
St. Paul, 37f, 112, 116–25, 162, 191–92, 224n81
St. Peter, 119, 122
Saxony, Duke George of, 36, 69
Schmalkalden, 127f, 156n, 167, 187
Schmalkaldic Articles, 156n
Schmalkaldic League, 140, 156n
Schnepf, Erhard, 129
Schurf, Jerome, 8, 18, 32
Schwabach, 127
Schwabach articles, 105, 105n, 110, 127f
Schwenckfeld, Kaspar: on Luther, 187–88; Luther on, 103, 180, 182–83, 187–89, 191; mentioned, 106
Spalatin, George: Luther on Wittenberg Movement to, 8, 10f, 12–13, 24–25, 26; Luther on Karlstadt to, 35, 45, 55, 75, 76–77; mentioned, 12, 30, 194
Speyer, Second Diet of, 104, 127
Staupitz, John von, 29
Stein, Wolfgang, 42, 45f, 55
Stifel, Michael, 89
Storch, Nicholas, 9, 25, 35f. *See also* Zwickau prophets
Strasbourg: and Karlstadt, 34, 48–51,

129f; its clergy on Luther, 48, 204; Luther's *A Letter to the Christians at Strasbourg in Opposition to the Fanatic Spirit* to, 49–51; mentioned, 33, 82, 86–89, 107, 128, 147f
Stübner, Marcus, 9, 24–25, 36. *See also* Zwickau prophets
Sturm, Jacob, 109
Swabian League, 63
Swabian Syngramma, 86, 89–90

Tetrapolitana, 132, 140
Torgau, 129, 165
Trent, Council of, 181–82
Turks, 180, 182, 189
Twelve Articles, 60, 61–63, 65

Ulm, 147ff
Ulscenius, Dietrich, 212n47

Vadian, Joachim, 187f
Valla, Lorenzo, 99
Vienna, 174

Wartburg, 6, 55
Weimar, 39, 45, 148
Weingarten Treaty, 63–64
Weissenburg, 148
Westerburg, Gerhard, 73
Wittenberg, 8, 181, 185, 212n60
Wittenberg, All Saints Church of. *See* All Saints Church
Wittenberg, City Council of, 8, 10f, 11n, 20f, 40–41, 212n60
Wittenberg, Franciscan church of, 8, 10
Wittenberg, Parish church of, 8, 10f, 26, 40, 193
Wittenberg, University of: and the Wittenberg Ordinance, 10f, 15f, 20; and censorship, 24, 34, 41, 46; and Karlstadt in Orlamünde, 34ff, 42, 54; and Agricola, 165, 170; mentioned, 7, 13–14, 29
Wittenberg Concord, 147–55, 183
Wittenberg Ordinance, 6f, 10–24 *passim*

Witzel, George, 173, 175
Worms, Diet of (1521), 6, 38
Württemberg, Concord of, 144
Württemberg, Duke Ulrich of, 144
Wycliffe, John, 103

Zasius, Ulrich, 27
Zeitz, 157
Zurich, 48, 82, 107, 128, 140–42, 180–90 *passim*, 194f, 202
Zwickau, 9, 35–36, 47n
Zwickau prophets: Luther on, 9, 13, 22–26, 30–31, 35, 38, 52, 54; and Müntzer, 36
Zwilling, Gabriel: and Wittenberg Movement, 6f, 10f, 14f, 16n, 17, 20–23, 26; Luther on, 20, 22–23, 26
Zwingli, Ulrich: and Karlstadt, 47n, 48, 79–80, 82–84; Luther on, as fanatic or false prophet, 82ff, 88ff, 97, 102–3, 120–21, 130ff, 180, 189–93; Luther on death of, 140–42, 185, 190–91; other comments of Luther on, 47n, 81, 110–11, 151f, 165n; his *Letter to Matthew Alber*, 83f; his *Commentary on True and False Religion*, 83–84, 85; on the Lord's Supper, 83–86, 108–9; his *Rearguard or Supplement Concerning the Eucharist*, 84; and original sin, 86n, 88, 130, 152; his *Friendly Exposition of the Eucharist Affair, to Martin Luther*, 93; his *A Friendly Rejoinder and Rebuttal to the Sermon of the Eminent Martin Luther Against the Fanatics*, 93; Luther's understanding of the doctrine on the Lord's Supper of, 96, 130f, 136–37, 152–53; his *That These Words of Jesus Christ, "This Is My Body Which Is Given For You," Will Forever Retain Their Ancient, Single Meaning*, 99–101; on Luther, 99–101, 203f; his *Concerning Dr. Martin Luther's Book Entitled "Confession": Two Answers, by John Oecolampadius and Ulrich Zwingli*, 103–4; and the Marburg Colloquy, 104, 107–11; his *Fidei ratio*, 132; his letters published posthumously, 149, 151; his *A Short and Clear Exposition of the Christian Faith*, 149, 151, 182, 190–91; his works reissued by the Zurichers, 185; mentioned, 92, 136, 138

TE DUE